Business Writing in the Digit@l Age

This book is dedicated to
Greg, my personal gold standard,
and
Victoria, at once inspiration and reality check.

Business Writing in the Digit@l Age

Natalie Canavor

Los Angeles | London | New Delhi
Singapore | Washington DC

Los Angeles | London | New Delhi
Singapore | Washington DC

FOR INFORMATION:

SAGE Publications, Inc.
2455 Teller Road
Thousand Oaks, California 91320
E-mail: order@sagepub.com

SAGE Publications Ltd.
1 Oliver's Yard
55 City Road
London EC1Y 1SP
United Kingdom

SAGE Publications India Pvt. Ltd.
B 1/I 1 Mohan Cooperative Industrial Area
Mathura Road, New Delhi 110 044
India

SAGE Publications Asia-Pacific Pte. Ltd.
33 Pekin Street #02-01
Far East Square
Singapore 048763

Acquisitions Editor: Lisa Cuevas Shaw
Assistant Editor: MaryAnn Vail
Editorial Assistant: Mayan White
Production Editor: Eric Garner
Copy Editor: Taryn Bigelow
Typesetter: C&M Digitals (P) Ltd.
Proofreader: Susan Schon
Indexer: Sheila Bodell
Cover Designer: Anupama Krishnan
Marketing Manager: Helen Salmon
Permissions Editor: Karen Ehrmann

Copyright © 2012 by SAGE Publications, Inc.

Printed in the United States of America

Library of Congress Cataloging-in-Publication Data

Canavor, Natalie

Business writing in the digital age / Natalie Canavor.

p. cm.
Includes bibliographical references and index.

ISBN 978-1-4129-9250-3 (pbk.: acid-free paper)

1. Business writing. 2. Business communication. I. Title.

HF5718.3.C365 2012
651.7′4—dc23   2011031260

This book is printed on acid-free paper.

11 12 13 14 15 10 9 8 7 6 5 4 3 2 1

CONTENTS

PREFACE

Before you choose to read this book, you may wonder: Can I actually improve my own writing? And will this book help me do that?

The answer to both questions is "definitely." If you are already a pretty good writer, you're prepared to learn techniques that take most professional writers decades of trial and error to work out. If you don't consider writing your strong point, you'll benefit immediately from seeing what works, and why.

Business Writing in the Digital Age aims to give you greater confidence as a writer wherever you now fall along the spectrum of skills. The strategies it shows you depend neither on grammatical knowledge nor formulas. Instead, the content is grounded in practical experience—what accomplishes goals in today's digital world.

That experience comes from my own practice of journalism, editing, public relations and organizational communications, *PLUS* the distilled insights of three dozen specialists from the corporate, nonprofit and government arenas who use their writing to succeed. These professionals work in a broad range of fields—marketing, journalism, strategic communications, government administration, business counseling and graphic design, to name a few.

In addition to building your personal foundation for writing well, this book focuses on the kinds of writing you'll probably need to do, wherever you are: everyday communication like e-mail and letters; business documents like proposals and business plans; e-media from websites to blogging, social media and PowerPoint; and materials that help you access opportunity, such as résumés, cover letters and networking messages.

While this book demonstrates every idea with examples, their purpose is more than modeling the various message formats. They guide you through a thinking process that equips you for any writing challenge ahead of you. You'll know what to say and how to say it in every medium—and new channels yet to be invented.

For many people, writing for career success looks very different from the academic style they learned in school. See this difference as an advantage: You'll find that the criteria for practical writing make instant sense and are thus easy to absorb and meet, even if previous teaching methods didn't work for you.

If you're a business or communications student, you'll find that this book's strategic view of writing as a tool for accomplishing goals is natural and comfortable. The concepts should meld neatly with all your course work and not incidentally, help you perform better in your program.

Will you become a faster writer? Perhaps not, but you'll learn to invest your time much better, knowing how to plan your message and revise it. Almost no one writes well spontaneously. We all need to improve the first version of whatever we write. So beyond showing you how to make good decisions on content and delivery, this book gives you a practical resource of fix-it techniques to hone messages that accomplish goals.

How important to you is writing better?

In today's world—whether you want to be a business leader, nonprofit manager, consultant or government decision maker—you are what you write. Your everyday message flow establishes your credibility, authority, reliability and much more. Your business documents often represent make-or-break opportunities you can't afford to miss. Entrée to employers, clients, investors and collaborators depends on writing. Building and maintaining relationships relies on writing both in formal business venues and the less formal ones of social media.

Write well, and you possess a fundamental competitive edge now and throughout your career—or the many careers today's futurists predict for you.

Read this book, practice your skills through the opportunities and projects in each chapter, and you'll gain a jumpstart on a major leadership and management asset. *Business Writing in the Digital Age* aims not only to improve your communication abilities quickly. It also offers you the tools and mind-set to write ever better over the long range, on your own.

Invest yourself in good writing: It will empower you.

❖ ❖ ❖

I welcome comments and questions about business writing and this book. Find me at businesswritingnow.com.

ACKNOWLEDGMENTS

This book would not exist without the enthusiasm, thoughtful support and input of the Sage team. My editor, Lisa Cuevas Shaw, understood what was possible before I did, and her gentle, responsive, open-minded guidance shaped this book. As the book grew and more people stepped in to supply their expertise, I've appreciated the high level of professionalism and caring shown by all, including assistant editor MaryAnn Vail, production editor Eric Garner, and marketing manager Helen Salmon.

I owe special thanks to copy editor Taryn Bigelow, who made what can be a stressful process fun and generously contributed her good ideas for making this book better (and more consistent!) than it would have been.

Finally, thank you Neil J. Salkind of Studio B, my favorite "connector"—many of my best opportunities start with you. I feel especially inspired by your confidence in bringing me to SAGE. Just as you predicted, it's been a wonderful experience.

ABOUT THE AUTHOR

Natalie Canavor is a business writer, author and communications consultant whose background includes journalism, magazine publishing and public relations. Throughout her career, she has originated programs to share the benefits of good writing. Today she conducts workshops on writing-for-results for business audiences and teaches at New York University. She presents courses on corporate communications writing and message strategizing, and also gives an advanced writing seminar for the M.S. program in Public Relations and Corporate Communications.

She continues to develop print and online projects for a wide range of corporate and nonprofit clients. Her byline has appeared on hundreds of features and columns in the *New York Times, Newsday, Long Island Business News, Communication World* and a host of business and technical publications. She also wrote a six-year column on better writing for the International Association of Business Communicators' *CW Bulletin*, read online by 16,000 professionals worldwide.

As a national magazine editor, she created four successful start-ups, including *Today's Filmmaker, Videography,* and *Technical Photography.* As a corporate communicator, she directed a 14-person department for New York State's largest educational agency. She counseled agency management and local school leaders on communication strategy, oversaw all print and e-media and developed communications-skills training programs.

She is coauthor of a popular book for businesspeople, *The Truth About the New Rules of Business Writing;* and earlier, wrote the best-selling *How to Market Your Photographs.* Her work has earned dozens of national and international awards for articles, video scripts, websites and publications. She is former president of the International Association of Business Communicators/Long Island, which recognized her as Communicator of the Year, and served as a founding officer of IABC's Heritage Region.

Chapter 1

BUSINESS WRITING IN THE DIGITAL AGE—AND YOU

➤ Why is good writing important in today's business world?

➤ Why is it important to you?

➤ How has the digital age redefined business writing?

➤ How will this book help you?

Congratulations on choosing to read this book. Absorb the ideas presented here, practice with the activities, and you'll develop one of the most important tools for succeeding in today's business world. This is true whether you plan on a corporate, nonprofit, government, entrepreneurial or consulting career. It's even true if you're a creative individual who wants to earn a living with your work.

WHY GOOD WRITING IS IMPORTANT IN TODAY'S BUSINESS WORLD

Once upon a time few people needed to write. They did business in person, or worked in places where professional specialists were responsible for most communication. Managers typically depended on support staff to correct and improve their documents.

Come the digital revolution, and all this changed. Soon after computers replaced typewriters, people found themselves writing everyday messages on their own. And as communication channels grew from e-mail to websites and most recently, blogs and social media, more and more people were called on to write. Plus, there seems to be an ever-increasing mountain of material that needs writing. Today's media offer organizations and individuals infinite ways to be heard and known—but all require writing.

It's taken the business world a while to catch up to this reality. But the realization is dawning.

Good business writing saves time and money. It prevents mistakes and helps solve problems. It bridges time zones and culture gaps, connecting people. It empowers individuals and helps organizations succeed.

Unfortunately, the general quality of writing in the business, government and not-for-profit worlds is dismal. The evidence for this is not just anecdotal. Recent research studies demonstrate that bad writing is a significant challenge to American industry. Writing that comes from government agencies, for its part, is considered so bad that a federal law was passed in 2010: The Plain Language Act, which mandates that all documents aimed at the public be clearly written.

In business circles, far more attention has been given to face-to-face communication than writing. In-person skills are of course critical. But there's no way around the fact that writing is the key communication tool of the 21st century. Everything we do from planning to marketing to interacting with other people depends at critical stages on what we write. From everyday e-mails and social media posts to websites, proposals and business plans, the written word makes or breaks us.

Why do so many people seem oblivious to the new importance of writing? It can be hard to view the big picture when we're living in it. The last 10 years have seen major shifts in how we work and behave. Technology empowers us to communicate quickly and globally. By enabling us to reach people anywhere, bring them to us and directly interact, it's reversing centuries of one-way, top-down communication.

We haven't even begun to realize how this shift affects us. To begin with, we now live in an opt-in world. Possibly excepting political despots or rulers of multibillion-dollar empires, no one any longer owns a captive audience. People are not obliged to read what you write—they must choose to. Readers' attention must be earned.

I tell subordinates, don't give me your mediocre material to try out. We need you to produce your best work before you give it to us so we know we can trust you. Otherwise we can't let you deal with the client directly.

—Arik Ben-Zvi, managing director, The Glover Park Group

Further, the digital revolution affects how we relate to one another in basic ways. It enables a growing number of people to work at home or in remote locations and rely on virtual teaming. Through online media, we can collaborate with people we may never see across national boundaries—and across the corridor. You can even work in an office where people come to work each day and text each other instead of talking.

Across the generations we're using the telephone less, too, and moving steadily toward written, voice-free exchanges.

The bottom line: The new range of communication options doesn't just supplement the traditional varieties or speed up delivery. It is transforming how we relate. We talk less, telephone less, meet less. The channels we rely on all demand one thing—writing. But just as this huge need to write well becomes understood, the skill proves hard to come by.

SIDELIGHT: BAD WRITERS LOSE OPPORTUNITIES

The most significant report on the importance of writing in business is *Writing: A Ticket to Work . . . or a Ticket Out,* issued in 2004 by the National Commission on Writing for America's Families, Schools and Colleges. A year earlier, the same group issued *The Neglected "R": The Need for a Writing Revolution,* a benchmark study. Both reports were hard on the schools for failing to teach adequate writing skills. A few findings:

- People who cannot write and communicate clearly will not be hired and are unlikely to be employed long enough to be considered for promotion.
- Half of all companies take writing ability into account when making promotion decisions.
- Eighty percent or more of companies in the finance and service, insurance and real estate (FIRE) sectors—the corporations with the greatest employment growth potential—assess writing during hiring.

About one third of respondents said that one third or fewer of their current and new employees possess writing skills that companies value. As far back as 2004, companies were spending more than $3 billion annually on writing remediation.

WHY WRITING IS SO IMPORTANT TO YOU

This is where the value of writing to you comes in. Writing well gives you unprecedented opportunity to succeed, whatever your career path.

For starters, it's the price of admission. Good opportunities today are intensely competitive. You'll rarely set a foot in the door without first presenting yourself in written form. This is true for management positions in business, industry, nonprofit and government arenas, and also if you aim to be an entrepreneur or consultant or adviser.

Moreover, a growing number of employers realize that writing skills are critical to their own success and consider them when hiring and promoting.

Many have noticed that badly written proposals don't win the project. Ill-prepared reports don't persuade. Dull PowerPoint presentations, websites full of stale copy and off-target social media campaigns fail to motivate—or contribute to the bottom line.

Employers are finding that fuzzy communication undercuts the most expensive efforts to keep customers, stockholders and donors happy. It also makes it impossible for an organization to demonstrate transparency and build trust. Even the art of selling, traditionally a face-to-face endeavor, depends on producing the right written message somewhere along the way.

WHO CARES ABOUT GOOD WRITING?

Among others, the people who run businesses, nonprofits, government agencies, and nongovernmental organizations—and do the hiring. Here's a sampling of opinion.

Communicating clearly and effectively has NEVER been more important than it is today. Whether it's fair or not, life-changing critical judgments about you are being made based solely upon your writing ability. Therefore, having excellent command of your online digital persona will enable you to quickly surpass those who present themselves weakly in the new competitive arena. Since you probably won't get a second chance, what kind of digital first impression will you choose to make?

—Victor Urbach, president, Altegent LLC; Publisher, *The Urbach Letter*

For a long time writing has been devalued in the private sector—it was the redheaded stepchild in the communications food chain. But the shift to a knowledge based economy meant it was only a matter of time before people recognized that writing matters a lot, that strong clear compelling content affects the bottom line. Now they do. The realization is dawning at a time when even in communication firms, the number of people who can write is actually dwindling.

—Dan Gerstein, president/founder of Gotham Ghostwriters, and political consultant, analyst and commentator

We've made writing a much bigger part of our focus and our screening process, because if people can't learn to write they're relegated to a lesser role. We give a writing test asking candidates to distill down the ideas from a batch of documents as if they were writing a quick policy brief with a limited number of words. We assess the clarity of their communication and also how they were able to take in, understand and express various ideas.

—Erin Mathews, director of Iraq Programs, National Democratic Institute (an international development agency)

When someone is interviewing for a job, representing another organization or coming from a consulting firm, I judge them on their writing because it will affect me. It's one of the biggest things—I care less about people's interpersonal skills, I don't need to be friends with them. But if they can't write well I'm stuck. In my job and others I work with, writing is so much of what you do that if you can't do it well you can't do your job well.

—Alicia Phillips Mandaville, director of development policy, Millennium Challenge Corporation (a U.S. foreign aid agency)

A nonprofit's messaging is critical to success. You need support from the community, donors, funders—and the only way you can get that word out is through writing: websites, brochures, appeal letters, reports to funders. Writing is even more important today because everyone is seeking the same amount of money from a more limited pool. Someone who can communicate powerfully and effectively will always go straight to the top. When we do executive searches we won't even pass a letter with an error on to the next level.

—Ann Marie Thigpen, director, The Center for Nonprofit Leadership at Adelphi University

There's also a growing sense that poor communication affects us on a daily basis. The flow of e-mail, letters, tweets and online posts is how we connect with everyone, from coworkers to clients, collaborators and the general public. If anyone ever totals the time we spend interpreting badly written e-mails and fixing the confusion, the figure will stagger us.

Yes, a dizzying array of new communication channels confronts us with new ways to market, establish expertise, reach specific audiences, and create communities. But how to take advantage of so much opportunity without good writing? The online highway is so crowded that poorly written materials don't even get you to the gate.

Employers who are painfully aware of the writing deficit generally blame the schools. In response, many state systems and school districts are introducing new strategies to teach writing. This will eventually reverse the tide, or at least that's the hope—but it will take time.

SIDELIGHT: PROOF THAT THE WORLD NEEDS BETTER WRITERS

A few recent studies have underscored the need for writing skills and their importance to employers.

The Job Outlook 2010 Survey by the National Association of Colleges and Employers placed strong communication skills at the top of the list of what employers seek in potential employees. While the report notes that GPA remains an important gauge of ability, good communication can tip the scales toward one candidate over another. The most-wanted skills after communication were analytic, teamwork and technical skills, followed by strong work ethic.

In 2009, a research study called **The Ill-prepared U.S. Workforce: Exploring the Challenges of Employer-provided Workforce Readiness Training** reported a "workforce readiness training gap" in response to what the surveyed employers identified as high-need areas. Written Communication and Oral Communication were two of the top four needs identified. Most important of all was Creativity/Innovation—"the need to demonstrate originality and inventiveness in work; communicate new ideas to others; and integrate knowledge across disciplines." (Those sound like writing jobs to me.)

Towers Watson, a human capital consulting firm, issues yearly reports tying good communication to the bottom line. While acknowledging that it's hard for many companies to quantify the connection between communication practice and ROI figures, they cite numbers. The 2009/2010 report stated,

> Effective employee communication is a leading indicator of financial performance and a driver of employee engagement. Companies that are highly effective communicators had 47% higher total returns to shareholders over the last five years compared with firms that are the least effective communicators.

So, right now you have an unusual opportunity. Develop your writing skills and you will stand out. You are more likely to be hired, better able to build the positive image you want and better prepared to prove your value. You will, in fact, be more valuable. If you question this premise, think about people you've worked with who were identified early as rising stars; often good writing is one of the abilities that distinguishes them. Consider also all the people hired off the Internet because they write good tweets, blogs or comments.

Writing well on the job makes you more efficient because people who get your messages understand them. You succeed more often because you're more likely to get the response you want.

Moreover, in an environment of shifting leadership style, better writing strengthens your chance to move up the ladder. Traditional top-down management is on the wane and collaborative approaches are on the rise. By producing effective everyday messages, you can showcase your competence, capabilities, professionalism and resourcefulness.

Producing first-rate business documents provides another way to prove yourself. Online media open up opportunities that didn't exist before—amazing access to people you want to reach. You can't show up in a CEO's office, but you can send a well-thought-out comment or idea through an in-house channel or online medium.

Another incentive to develop your writing: It is an indispensable—if generally unheralded—leadership asset. Good communication skills are always named as an essential tool of good leaders. But we often ignore the writing component, despite the fact that it is one of only two basic ways human beings can communicate and think. And, as opposed to oral communication, writing is our memory—the foundation upon which civilization and knowledge have been built. It is no accident that many of the best leaders write well.

WHAT'S THE REAL MESSAGE?

Writing often holds subliminal messages that undermine the writer's intent. It's important to think about what you're really saying and how it may be interpreted. Here are some examples to bring the point home.

Website statement:

Our consulting service empowers you to optimize your talent resource allocation by providing an array of value-added, cost-effective, cutting-edge planning tools.

Takeaway: *This firm will produce a wordy pretentious report that costs a lot but won't help us.*

Grocery chain mission statement:

We are a market-focused, process-centered organization that develops and delivers innovative solutions to our customers, consistently outperforms our peers, produces predictable earnings for our shareholders, and provides a dynamic and challenging environment for our employees.

Takeaway: *Yes, but what does the company do?*

Medicaid application information for the public:

Apply if you are aged (65 years old or older), blind, or disabled and have low income and few resources. Apply if you are terminally ill and want to receive hospice services.

(Continued)

(Continued)

Apply if you are aged, blind, or disabled; live in a nursing home; and have low income and limited resources. Apply if you are aged, blind, or disabled and need nursing home care, but can stay at home with special community care services. Apply if you are eligible for Medicare and have low income and limited resources.

Takeaway: *We don't really want you to understand this.*

U.S. Post Office wall plaque:

OUR GOALS
We stand for continuous improvement, positive change and making breakthroughs in what we do and how we work. Each of us will bring our finest effort to bear on each task and endeavor while looking for better, easier, faster and simpler ways to serve our customers, and achieve our goals and improve performance.

Takeaway: *Given our tendency to repeat ourselves, don't expect us to identify redundancies in how we operate.*

A bank message on late payments:

Acceptance by the bank of payments in arrears shall not constitute a waiver of or otherwise affect any acceleration payment hereunder or other right or remedy exercisable hereunder. No failure or delay on the part of the bank in exercising, and no failure to file or otherwise perfect or enforce the Bank's security in or with respect to any collateral, shall operate as a waiver of any right or remedy hereunder or release any of the undersigned, and the obligations of the undersigned may be extended or waived . . .

Takeaway: *Don't expect any human considerations to interfere with how we do our work.*

From the Environmental Protection Agency:

This program promotes efficient water use in homes and businesses throughout the country by offering a simple way to make purchasing decisions that conserve water without sacrificing quality or product performance.

Takeaway: *Clarity doesn't count enough for us to write well.*

Job application cover letter A, opening line:

I hereby respectfully submit my résumé for your kind consideration.

Takeaway: *This person will handle writing assignments in the best 19th-century traditions.*

Job application cover letter B, opening line:

Writing in response to Ur job post you will like my qualifications.

Takeaway: *This candidate will embarrass any employer who hires him.*

Best of show:

One take on passage of the Plain Language Act, which appeared in the February 24, 2011, issue of *FEDweek* (which describes itself as the most widely circulated free information resource in the federal government):

President Obama has signed into law (P.L. 111–274) legislation requiring agencies to use plain language in documents directed toward the public and to train employees in clear writing—for example, writing that does not utilize abstruse verbiage rather than use plain words, nor is redundant by making a point more than once (that is, twice or more), nor contains sentences that keep going even when the point at which they should have stopped arrived far before the period, with period in this case referring to a punctuation mark, rather than a measure of time, such as the time it takes to read writing full of unnecessary dependent clauses, sometimes known as subordinate clauses, that make it difficult for the reader to recall the subject by the end of the predicate, and that would not pass the law's standards.

Takeaway: *This is*

    (a) *a joke*

    (b) *an excellent demonstration of why better writing should be legislated.*

Q&A: IS WRITING LEARNABLE?
CAN ANYONE LEARN TO WRITE BETTER?

Yes and yes. Many people never develop their writing skills and may even feel an aversion to writing. If this applies to you, it just means that the teaching methods you encountered in school didn't work for you. Some people are lucky and at some point find a teacher who's equipped to teach writing rather than reading and literature.

(Continued)

(Continued)

A few more luck out and find a good mentor while on the job. But most people don't have this experience.

Also, what most of us learned in school reflects an academic style suited to the 20th century at best. Practical business writing is different, and once you understand your target, and equip yourself with some useful techniques, you can definitely improve your skills. That doesn't mean that every single person can become a great writer. But it does mean that knowledge and practice will enable you to express yourself more clearly and successfully, and you'll know how to keep improving over time.

If you are already a capable writer, this book will help you become an even better one. You'll also learn to more readily recognize good writing, an important skill for your work as part of a team or as a leader.

And, of course, good writing will help you succeed if you are currently a student.

GOOD WRITING REDEFINED FOR THE DIGITAL AGE

All this doesn't mean that traditional writing skills must be revived. While many principles of good writing hold steady, and are very helpful to know, the academic, literary style most of us are exposed to in school doesn't work in business.

Here are some of the essentials of good writing for the digital age:

- ✓ Write clearly, simply, conversationally and engagingly, with specific adaptations for each medium.
- ✓ Write strategically, using every piece of writing as a tool for accomplishing immediate and long-range goals, both our own and our organizations'.
- ✓ Frame every message and document in terms of "you," not "I," and make it instantly clear why the reader should care.
- ✓ Plan messages to take better account of our opt-in world by understanding how they are perceived, what people want, and how what we write affects our readers.
- ✓ Employ good techniques of persuasion and advocacy to state our case and represent our interests.
- ✓ Use writing to make all our enterprises more transparent and trusted.
- ✓ Write for an overscheduled, information-loaded, low attention span, impatient and skeptical audience—which is all of them.
- ✓ Write in ways that foster dialogue and interaction.

✓ Write for a globalized world with many non-native English speakers and many who don't speak English at all and will read translations.
✓ Write, consciously, in ways that build and maintain relationships.

The last point deserves more depth. An environment that leads us to interact through writing rather than face-to-face is depersonalizing, even dehumanizing. It starves us for warmth and authenticity. We need to purposely counter this drift by writing more caringly. The curt, abrupt style that texting and instant messaging foster does not contribute to relationship building.

Especially with ever-faster delivery speed, we've become careless of how our messages make other people feel. The fact that we communicate without hearing tone of voice, or seeing visual cues, leads us to chilly exchanges where we not only lack the in-person advantage, but also miss the cues that a written message can contain.

Digital media benefit from personalization in a different way. Even though we're writing for unknown and unseen audiences when we blog or contribute to an online conversation, individual voice is an asset. Readers respond to the sense of warmth, spontaneity and authenticity that the best bloggers are able to generate.

In sum: If you want to inspire trust, build teams, motivate subordinates, cultivate relationships with colleagues or clients, influence people, keep customers, be someone other people want to know better or just want to get things done—then use the tools of thoughtful writing. Aim not just to be clear, but also warm and empathetic. You'll be repaid hundreds of times over for this investment of energy.

This book will help you with all these needs—they are all a part of better writing.

The goal is to make you a more confident, capable and resourceful writer able to approach any writing need methodically. You'll find, too, that building this skill will help you clarify your thinking process—something that always comes in handy.

SIDELIGHT: THE PLAIN LANGUAGE MOVEMENT ADVANCES

Two Washington, D.C.–based groups are advocates for clarity in all government communications. Both work to promote awareness of clear writing and provide training. The government group Plain Language Action and Information Network (www.plainlanguage.gov) was founded in the mid-1900s. The private-sector, non-profit Center for Plain Language (www.centerforplainlanguage.org) was established

(Continued)

(Continued)

in 2003. The movement's biggest achievement to date is passage of the Plain Writing Act signed by the President in October 2010 (P.L. 111–274). The act requires government agencies to use plain language in documents directed to the public and to train their employees to apply guidelines such as simplicity, brevity, plain words and clear organization. How compliance will be enforced is not yet clear. The full Plain Writing Act is posted at www.plainlanguage.gov.

The Plain Language movement is also international—check out the Plain Language Association International at plainlanguagenetwork.org and www.clarity-international.net.

VIEW FROM THE FIELD: GOVERNMENT-SPEAK MEETS PLAIN LANGUAGE

We define plain language as something your intended readers can understand and use the first time they read it. Given that, I don't believe there's any material that cannot be put in plain language. In fact, if it's very technical there's an even greater responsibility to put it into plain language.

We understand the Plain Language Act is not a silver bullet, but its passage has brought the writing problem more to the forefront and hopefully agencies will really start to take notice. It's important that Congress made a statement that this is important. It will affect what the government produces that goes out to the public, and we believe that if government writes better, it will leak into the business world.

We believe that communicating clearly improves an organization's bottom line and helps it give better customer service. A lot of people think that using all those big words leads people to respect them more—but studies show this is just not true. People who write clearly are thought to be better educated or smarter.

Why don't people complain more? I think they take it for granted that the government puts out stuff they can't understand and that's the way the world is. It's very frustrating.

—Annetta Cheek, board chair, Center for Plain Language
(check out the annual awards program for the best and
worst writing at www.centerforplainlanguage.org/awards)

HOW TO USE THIS BOOK

Preferably, work with this book in the sequence presented. The chapters lead you through a natural learning progression. After considering the strategic nature of writing, you'll develop the practical skills of clear expression. Subsequent chapters cover the various major areas of writing with a focus on how to apply the basic process you're mastering, and the differences involved in producing each kind of document.

The premise is that you can build the capacity to handle more complex documents by starting with everyday messages. When you know how to write an e-mail that achieves its goal, you're a long way toward writing a powerful proposal. The strategies are essentially the same.

Along the way, various features give you a range of ideas and resources. **Sidelights** offer insights that may not always directly relate to writing, but will enrich your perspective. **View From the Field** insets offer practical tips and guidance from a wide range of specialists: professional communicators, psychologists, negotiators, businesspeople, graphic designers and experts on specific kinds of writing.

Think Global features will orient you to the new, growing need to write for international and diverse audiences. **Going Deeper** sidebars will give you more detailed guidance on important areas, ranging from graphics to résumé writing. **We're All Screenwriters** will remind you that you're often writing to be read online, perhaps in miniature format. And **Success Tips** offer practical, useful ideas to help you stand out from the crowd in the workplace.

You'll find that sometimes one contributor's insights somewhat contradict another's, or don't completely align with my viewpoint. Writing is not a science. There are many ways to successfully write the same message, and there are many different legitimate ideas of what works. Plus, we differ from one another. A technique that's successful for one person may not help someone else.

So, read with an open mind and absorb all the ideas and strategies. Adopt those that resonate for you. Engage in the **Action Time** activities within each chapter, as well as the more substantial **Practice Opportunities** at each chapter's end.

I hope that in addition to assembling your own repertoire of concepts, techniques and tricks-of-the-trade to make you a better writer, you will emerge from reading this book with a new energy for writing and more enjoyment of the process. And that beyond improving your ability to express yourself more clearly and forcefully, you'll absorb the central idea this book is built on—that writing is a strategic tool and that everything you write matters.

Business writing is part craft, part psychology, part negotiation, part management strategy, and part detective work. Build your practical skills but also exercise your imagination. You'll find yourself well rewarded.

PRACTICE OPPORTUNITIES

I. Write a Memo to Yourself

Think about the career path you're preparing for. What written materials can you anticipate being called on to write? List them, including both the everyday kinds of communication (perhaps e-mail, tweets, social media posts) and formal business documents such as various kinds of reports, proposals, website material and so on. For each entry on your list, write down what a well-written message might gain you.

II. Start a Personal Reference Resource of Strong Writing

This week, collect at least three examples of writing you like from any arena such as newspapers, magazines, online articles, blogs, book excerpts. For each one, write a paragraph explaining why you chose it. Start a file, organized however you like, to keep the examples in. Plan to add at least one example per week on an ongoing basis.

III. Group Discussion

In a group of four or five, share one or more of the examples you collected for Activity II. Discuss: Does everyone agree on the quality of each example? If not, what are the reasons for disagreement? What generalizations can you make as a group about the characteristics of good writing? Does this give you any ideas about the ways you'd like to improve your own writing, and what you want to learn from this book?

Chapter 2

WRITING STRATEGICALLY

LEARN HOW TO . . .

Build the foundation for every document:

- ➢ Plan your messages
- ➢ Identify your immediate and long-range goals
- ➢ Understand your audience
- ➢ Maneuver generation gaps
- ➢ Write to groups, gatekeepers and the universe

The limits of my language are the limits of my mind. All I know is what I have words for.

—Ludwig Wittgenstein, Austrian Philosopher

View writing as a strategic tool for accomplishing your goals.

Yes, it's how to get things done, open doors and connect with people and immediate opportunities. But effective writing does far more than accomplish the goal-of-the-moment: It's a powerful tool for achieving your long-range ambitions, a tool to use consciously.

From letters to e-mail to proposals, blogs and business plans, every message offers a chance to build toward your future. The better your writing, the more you'll succeed.

This chapter gives you a framework for planning all your documents and making the right decisions about content, structure, tone and style.

🌐 SUCCESS TIP

Don't depend on "merit" alone to succeed. No matter how good you are, you have to look it and prove it. Whatever your field, writing gives you one of the best ways to do this.

15

WHY PLANNING IS ESSENTIAL

Effective writers don't just plunge into any written communication—first they plan. And always, they begin with two questions that guide them through every necessary decision.

Question 1: What's my goal? What do I want?

Question 2: Who—exactly—is the audience, the person I'm writing to?

Of course, these questions are not new to business management students: They structure all thinking about strategy, marketing and other subject areas. We'll look at how the questions apply to writing.

When you define your goal and consider audience characteristics, it becomes much easier to figure out the content, your key messages—the facts, ideas or arguments that will make your document work. And once you've systematically determined content, organizing it becomes a more natural process. You'll also be able to decide what tone the message should take.

Whether writing a proposal, a report, an e-mail or a blog post, professional writers base everything on how the factors of goal and audience intersect. Thinking this through may mean spending more time up front than you're used to. But having a plan saves time on the writing itself, and your results will be so much better—immediately—that you'll feel well rewarded.

But why does even a "simple" e-mail merit such thought?

Perhaps you've clicked "send" for one or more of the following:

- A carelessly written message to a superior or colleague that ends up forwarded right up the company hierarchy
- An embarrassing e-mail to a friend that you assumed was private, but instead was widely circulated
- A badly executed cover letter for a job application that showed up on the Internet as a laughable example
- A message meant for one person that instead went to a whole group, or someone who in particular should not have seen it, like a competitor

Remember the long run, too. E-mails never go away. As we see in scandal after scandal in the corporate and political worlds, they can always be retrieved to embarrass or, in a worst-case scenario, indict you. All these possible mistakes apply to social media and other digital channels, too.

Building a great reputation in any setting is a step-by-step, long-range process. *Use every message to present yourself in the way you want to be seen.* In fact, because e-mail is so important to the everyday business flow in nearly every organization, it's a stellar chance to continuously showcase yourself and impress others.

Let's look at our two basic questions in more depth.

Q&A: IF YOU WERE WONDERING . . .

Q: Everywhere I look I see badly thought out, badly written material: If that's the norm, why should I bother to do better?

A: Absolutely true, poor writing in the corporate world and beyond surrounds us: on the Web, in many publications (which are cutting staff), and certainly in our in-boxes. That means that in a competitive world, good writing gives you a genuine competitive edge. Well-done e-mails, letters, proposals, presentations, posts and résumés have a far better chance to win, whatever is at stake. Not to mention that you'll simply get more done every day.

Additionally, many organizations review writing skills in hiring and promotion decisions.

PLANNING STEP 1: IDENTIFY YOUR GOALS

First, Look Past the Obvious

In our early education, most of us had the same goal when assigned to write something, whether a term paper, book review, report or essay: Please the teacher and get a good grade. But in the workplace and practical environment of business school, you need to know your goal for every piece of writing. What do you want to accomplish with the document? What's the desired outcome? What do you want the person to do as a result of your message?

This can be trickier than it looks at first glance. Suppose, for example, you're inviting a group of people to a meeting. Your immediate, or primary, purpose is to get people together at the right time and place. If that's all you want, you just need to say,

Attend a meeting to plan the White Proposal, Thursday 2 p.m., Room 123.

But if you're running the meeting, you're responsible for making it productive. This may mean motivating attendees to feel enthusiastic; and you may want them to think about the subject beforehand and come prepared with thoughtful contributions. You may need to deliver an agenda so they know what to expect, and invest time in planning.

So your message might better say,

> This Thursday at 2, we'll hold the kickoff meeting to plan the White Proposal. This is a terrific opportunity to land a project that will stretch our capabilities and establish our niche. Please think about the role your unit can play in developing the proposal and come with ideas for our brainstorming. The agenda is attached. . . .

This version frames the meeting enthusiastically—enthusiasm is contagious—and also energizes the readers: You've told them that the opportunity is big, and their role might be significant. You've also promoted a team feeling, always more engaging than a directive.

But if you're addressing people on distinctly different levels, rather than a group consisting more or less of peers, there's more to consider. Whether you're writing to project teammates or office colleagues, every message is a tool for building relationships—or damaging them. So it must take account of how you relate to the recipients—their status in the organization, stake in the subject, expected contribution to the meeting and so on.

A message to your subordinate might begin,

> Jerry: Please plan on attending Thursday's meeting on the White Proposal.

While if you're inviting your supervisor, you'd do well to say something like

> Dear Joan: I've set up the meeting on the White Proposal for Thursday at 2, in line with your schedule. Every unit will be represented and I've put your intro first on the agenda, which is attached.

Certainly when you're on the job, even a simple message must reinforce your professional image with superiors, colleagues, collaborators, suppliers and everyone else you're writing to. It should contribute to your relationships in a positive way. And in addition to representing your organization's multilevel interests effectively, it should ideally contribute to your own long-range goals.

If that sounds like a lot of weight for a simple e-mail to carry, then how much thought should go into a complex document like a proposal or report?

Often, quite a lot. But fortunately, the process we're outlining applies to every kind of document, both digital and print, and after a while can be applied intuitively. At heart, good writing is good thinking, so developing your writing skills also helps you in general. You'll be better able to define and solve problems, engage others, manage their perceptions and influence their actions.

Define Goals to Shift Your Vision

Closely identifying a document's purpose—or its role in accomplishing a purpose—can be surprisingly helpful. The cover letter you write for a proposal, for example, need not bear the burden of selling your product or service. It just needs to set the reader up to read the proposal itself in a favorable light, and demonstrate that you've read the specs very carefully and your firm is a good prospect for solving the problem.

Cover letters for résumés similarly need not summarize your credentials. They should promote interest in reading the résumé by highlighting what a good match you are with the job (and by showing that you write well). The résumé's job, in turn, is to get you an interview.

Being clear on goals gives you important guidelines, whatever the medium. And it can save you from falling into a lot of common traps and making unnecessary mistakes.

How to Use Your Goals Analysis

Here's how to begin your new systematic writing strategy: Practice writing down and defining as closely as you can the "goal" of every message you send on as many levels as apply.

These may include

1. The immediate action or response you want (like showing up at the meeting)

2. The below-surface response you want to achieve (like feeling enthusiastic and being prepared)

3. Your organization's goals in the specific instance (e.g., a productive meeting that produces useful input and can be referred to in a progress report)

4. Your personal long-range goals

When you're conscious of your personal goals, you automatically act in line with them.

You'll recognize opportunities you might otherwise overlook for a productive contact or an extra assignment. And you'll see ways to build toward your goals in almost every message you write, whether an e-mail or a report or a presentation.

For example:

Bill has been elected a board member of his professional association. No one ran against him, so he doesn't take it seriously at first.

He dashes off a memo to his boss:

> Mark, guess what, I'm now on the WBEL board. LOL?

Then, he thinks some more, and realizes he has an opportunity to

1. Raise his profile in the department
2. Strengthen his relationship with the person he reports to
3. Perhaps bring his existence as an asset to the attention of higher-ups

He rewrites,

> Mark, I'm happy to report that I am now a WBEL board member. I was elected last night. As of June, I'll be involved in all the decision making about programs and venues, and, of course, look forward to contributing our company perspective and making new contacts for us.
>
> The inauguration lunch is on May 1 and I'd like to invite you as my personal guest. Can you come?

This message is likely to accomplish all three of his goals.

Note, of course, that the goals you make evident in a piece of writing should never be at odds with those of your employer—unless you're aiming to lose your job. Let's assume for now that your goals and those of your employer are basically aligned (though the more aware you are of your own long-term goals, the more selective you'll feel about where you want to work).

ACTION TIME: PART 1

Select a substantial e-mail or letter you wrote recently and review it from the perspective just outlined. If you have one that yielded disappointing results, use that. Did you fully articulate your goals? Did you take account of your personal sub-agenda? Is what you wanted to accomplish made clear to the reader? Think about whether you'd write the document differently now—and hold onto it for further development.

So far, it's been all about "you." Now let's move on to "the other"—the person or group you're writing to.

PLANNING STEP 2: UNDERSTAND YOUR AUDIENCE

Why Audience Analysis Is the Key

When it comes down to it, most messages ask for something. The request may be basic:

> Please send me price points for your new product line.

A request may be implicit rather than stated:

> Please read this message and absorb the information in it.

And requests can be more overt:

> Can we get together next Tuesday to talk about your budget?

or

> Can we agree to move the project ahead on this basis?

If you're asking anyone for something, even if it's only to pay attention to the content, your message must be properly received. What you want must be expressed to the receiver in terms he or she can hear, understand and relate to. Moreover, you must usually give the reader something she wants, or considers desirable, for your request to succeed.

If, for example, you want your supervisor to buy you a new computer, you need to match your message to who she is and what argument will make sense to her. Is she a technology buff? Efficiency freak? A must-keep-up-with-other-departments type? Does she have a new computer herself, or is she making do with an outdated one? How does she make decisions—based on data, or impulse? Does she show concern with staff members' well-being and desires? You need to take account of such factors and a whole lot more.

People are different—in how they perceive, what they value, what they care about and how they make decisions. But there is one universal to count on: self-interest. We react to things and make decisions based on "what's in it for me." This doesn't mean people are selfish and ungenerous—they may be motivated by a charitable cause, an ideal or belief or a commitment to what's good for other people above everything else.

We don't see things as they are; we see them as we are.

—Anais Nin

But in the business world, if your department head cares about the quarterly profit/loss statement, you can't suggest a workplace improvement because it would make people happy, and expect to succeed (unless you could prove that happy people are more productive). If you want to persuade employees that a new benefit is better than one it replaced, telling them how much the company is saving will get you nowhere. They want to know how their lives will improve, in real-world terms.

The bottom line is that at the same time you're defining "what I want to achieve" for the message you're writing, you need to systematically analyze "who is the person I want it from"—your audience. It's the only way to determine your best content: what will achieve your goal with the individual or group you're addressing, what to emphasize and what language, structure and tone will make this message succeed.

Understanding your audience also tells you what communication channel to use. If your boss doesn't like texting, obviously you wouldn't make a request that way. But you probably would if you wanted advice on the best computer from your 16-year-old cousin.

While we instinctively make such decisions all the time, you'll succeed more often in the work environment when you approach a writing challenge methodically.

SUCCESS TIP: GET OUT THERE AND GET REAL

Especially if you're starting a new job or playing a new role in the organization, build a person-to-person pattern of interacting with people. Send fewer e-mails and digital messages. Instead, walk down the hall, introduce yourself and look for chances to hold one-on-one conversations. You'll gain a reputation as a "people" person and not only will colleagues react more positively to your ideas and requests, but you'll find it easier to write good materials and documents. You'll know your readers better and can draw on this knowledge to frame your written messages.

GOING DEEPER: SOME FACTORS THAT DETERMINE WHO WE ARE

Here are factors that can influence how individuals receive and react to messages. Only some will be relevant to each situation, but take the trouble to develop your awareness of what can matter. It will always help you.

- Age and generation
- Economic status

- Cultural/ethnic/religious background
- Gender
- Educational level (high school, college or more)
- Where they grew up and now live
- Role/status in organization
- Political views
- What they care about
- What they're interested in
- Their relationship to you

If the person is above you in the organization's hierarchy, it can also be important to know or figure out

- Leadership style: Top-down, collaborative or somewhere in between?
- Management style: Fair, consistent?
- How he or she makes decisions: Slowly or quickly? Based on what?
- Open to new ideas? Willing to take risks?
- What kind of explanations does he prefer: Big-picture? Detailed? Logical?
- Likes confrontation or avoids it?
- Sensitive to people's concerns?
- What makes him happy? Angry?
- Does he have a sense of humor?
- Is he comfortable with emotions? (assume not)
- Any apparent pro or con feelings toward people your age? Either gender?
- Communication style? This can suggest many clues (see the "Sidelight: A Psychologist on Communication").
- How does the person prefer to receive information: e-mail, in person, letter, telephone, texting, social media channel? PowerPoint? Formal or informal reports?

Depending on the subject of your message, you may also need to know things like

- What does the supervisor already know about the subject? What more might he need to know? Any prior experience with the subject?
- How he feels about the subject
- His comfort level with technology
- Attitude toward innovation and change

Communicating Through Personal Filters

If audience analysis sounds like a lot of trouble, consider that a primary purpose of every message is to maintain or establish good relationships. You can't do that without taking account of the individual you're writing to. Further, to achieve your goal, you must choose the right strategy for your document. Putting yourself in someone's mind empowers you to answer that all-important question, "What's in it for me?" You can't give people what they need if you don't know who they are.

Everyone sees the world through an individual "filter" that evolves through a combination of genetics and life history—factors such as family background and interaction patterns, temperament, physical appearance, culture, school and work experience—everything we were born with and that we've experienced. We interpret everything we encounter and that happens to us through this filter, which also determines our expectations, reactions, assumptions and fears.

Don't ever doubt that you see the world through your own filter. The more conscious you become of your filter's characteristics, as well as those of people with whom you need to communicate, the better you'll succeed. *See communication as a bridge between different worldviews and you'll be way ahead in your personal life, as well as business life.*

The good news is that once you start thinking about your audience analytically, it becomes second nature. Of course, the higher the stakes, the more thought it's worth. An e-mail or text message asking a friend to meet for lunch won't require a review of his comfort level with new ideas. But if you want to get project approvals from your supervisor, or convince a client prospect that you're worth 20 minutes of her time, use audience analysis.

You need to know different things about people according to the nature of your request. If you want the recipient to understand and follow your instructions on how to file for reimbursement, then education level is important. If you need to know how formal to make your message to a client, then her position, age and management style are relevant.

There's another very important reason why knowing your audience pays off: Written communication lacks all the cues we depend on in face-to-face interaction. When we can see other people, we unconsciously adapt what we say, and how we say it, based on their reaction. If we're moving the conversation in the wrong direction, their facial expression or body language alone can signal a need to switch focus. Or else they may stop listening or interrupt us.

With written communication, we can't gauge the reader's response. Therefore, provided you want more than a random hit-or-miss success ratio, you need to target the message properly and anticipate response. In a way, you need to hold the conversation in your head and write on that basis.

ACTION TIME: PART 2

Take another look at the message you reconsidered in terms of goals and think now about the person you were writing to, your audience. Did you pitch the message well? Take account of his or her personality, communication preferences and other factors? Did you make "what's in it" for the other person, or why he or she should be interested, clear?

Draft a new version of the message based on goal and audience.

Psyching Out People You've Never Met

As a trial attorney will tell you, the clues about who someone "is" are everywhere: in what the person says and does, his voice, what he wears and how he wears it, what he reads, how he walks, what he laughs at, how he shakes hands, what his office looks like. If you spend time with people or have access to their work environments, observe. And, always, listen. True listening with your whole attention is the best way to understand someone else.

But in a great many instances, you're writing to people you haven't met yet and may never meet. How do you analyze them?

A phone conversation can tell you a lot if you have that opportunity. Listen for the individual's conversational pace—what provokes enthusiasm, any repeated words or phrases that indicate a focus or concern or a way of thinking. One individual may cite numbers often, another, an interest in people. And, of course, ask intelligent questions if the context allows, such as "What kind of data would you like to see and at what level of detail?"

SIDELIGHT: A PSYCHOLOGIST ON COMMUNICATION

To build rapport and communicate effectively, look past your own perspective and try to understand how someone else sees things. Remember, people are more open to your viewpoint when you make the effort to understand theirs. People have genuinely different ways of looking at things and interacting and you need to respect this right.

(Continued)

(Continued)

Read their cues. Pay attention to how they talk about things and talk in frames of reference they will understand. This helps them make sense of what you're saying and opens up your own capacity for real rapport.

When you write, draw on what you know about the person. See them in your mind's eye and use your intuition to reverse roles with them. This will help you better understand how they see things and, if they are not getting your point, can show you in what way you are not attuned to how they see things and what they need.

If you're writing to someone you haven't met, do some research: Talk to colleagues, gather information. The more you understand a person's frames of reference, language, values and priorities, the more you can develop the rapport for a working relationship. Review their written communications. Look for clues in how they respond to written messages, too. Notice whether the person uses personal language, technical terms, generalizations. Consider what kind of data they need to make decisions, and whether they decide fast or slowly. Take serious account of that in deciding how to proceed next.

—Susan H. Dowell, psychotherapist

Practice Reading Between the Lines

It's amazing how much "attitude" may be revealed in even a short, simple e-mail or post. In a large communications department I worked in, a rule required that at least one other person review every significant piece of writing that went out of the office, even e-mailed memos. The feedback rarely concerned technical issues like grammar. What did emerge often were comments such as "I see you don't like this person," or "You're recommending this course of action but it doesn't sound like you believe in it."

It can be extremely hard to keep your own feelings out of your writing, so be aware of that challenge (and have a friend check out your message when it matters). On the other hand, keep your antennae up for clues when you're on the receiving end.

Reading between the lines is a particularly useful technique when you're applying for a job or responding to an RFP (request for proposals). Read the ad, posting or RFP a dozen times or more and pick up its language, hot buttons and rhythm.

You can also pick up the subtext of a message by close attention to what is *not* said, as well as what's included and general "atmosphere." A good way to do this is to ask questions and imagine the answers. For example: Why did this job ad specify "attention to detail," "detail oriented" and "meticulous follow-through" so many times? Perhaps the last person in the job fell through in this area, so I need to marshal my evidence that I'm strong here.

How to Invent an Audience

Another useful strategy when you're writing to someone you don't know is to invent a construct of what that person is most probably like. If it's a human resources (HR) director, for example, visualize others you've known who held that job and consider what would interest and impress them. Or just take a few minutes to see through their eyes and figure out what—if your positions were reversed—the HR director would care about and want to know. Ask yourself, what's in the other person's self-interest in this situation? Assume the other person's role for a few minutes and you'll have helpful answers.

It's always easier to write to an individual than to an anonymous abstract person. But if you can't conjure one up appropriate to the situation, then write to a Standard Modern Businessperson (SMB). You can safely assume your SMB wants your written message to be

- Respectful but friendly
- Clear in its goals (your reason for writing)
- Well planned and written
- Logical in its progression of facts or ideas
- Targeted to his/her self-interest, the "what's-in-it-for-me" factor
- Self-contained—no need to look up other documents or do research to understand it
- As brief as possible to get the message across
- Objective
- Nonemotional
- Positive in spirit
- Oriented to solving a problem rather than posing one
- Good for the bottom line (you score lots of points when you can show this, even in a very minor way)

You can also assume that your SMB is a human being and put the old Golden Rule to work on your behalf. All (or nearly all) of us want to feel

- Liked
- Valued
- Treated with courtesy and respect
- Part of the team

When a message doesn't convey these things implicitly, we react negatively, whether the message itself has merit or not. And we especially do not like anything that actively makes us feel

- Overlooked or left out
- Disrespected
- Disliked
- Uncomfortable
- Depressed
- Inadequate
- Laughable
- Held up to ridicule or contempt
- A sense of failure

Try never to criticize anyone in writing, whatever his or her relationship to you. This applies to informal situations and most formal ones, with the exception of performance reviews and documentation. A careless written remark can easily torpedo a relationship and create an enemy. Similarly, irony and sarcasm are dangerous ingredients in business writing. When you criticize someone in person, you can establish a supportive atmosphere and be a responsive listener; and when you say something sarcastically or ironically, your tone of voice conveys, "I don't really mean it."

But the critical or sarcastic memo is delivered without face-to-face cues and can devastate your audience—and boomerang badly.

On the other hand, it is a rare individual who doesn't want to look good to superiors, colleagues and staff—particularly superiors. And we relish good news, including any about a staff member or the department. So make the most of every opportunity to bring good tidings and craft those messages well. These are the documents most likely to ascend the corporate ladder and help pave your own way.

CROSSING THE GENERATIONAL DIVIDE

If you're reading this book and review the generational characteristics outlined next, you probably identify most closely with Gen Y. What does this differentiation mean to how you communicate?

To begin with, it may explain a lot of the experiences you've already had, both good and bad, in dealing with bosses and colleagues. When you grew up and what was happening is a big factor in shaping our personal filters. Plus, people care about different things at different times in their lives. These facts give you some strong suggestions for how to communicate more successfully.

Right off, paying attention to generational sensitivities can save you a lot of pain. It's a fact that while Baby Boomers are retiring in droves, they still maintain seats of power in almost every industry. Many will stay there indefinitely, because they're workaholics and because economic conditions make it necessary.

So even if your immediate supervisor and the person she reports to are Gen X or maybe even Gen Y, ultimately, Boomers are running the show. The higher you go up the chain of command, the truer this is—it's an unusual board of directors that isn't composed mostly of Boomers.

KNOW YOUR GENERATIONS

Different age groups have different characteristics, and understanding the differences can be remarkably useful. Here are the broad outlines of the basic groups you'll encounter in the workplace, starting with the youngest.

Generation Y (Millennial Generation or Net Generation)

Born 1980 on

Brought up with devoted support from Baby Boomers, these young people are strong "natives" of digital technologies and instant communication media—Facebook, YouTube and online gaming are natural environments. Culturally tolerant and liberal in views; civic minded. Come to the workplace with high expectations and desire to shape their jobs to fit their lives. Dislike following orders blindly and do not automatically grant respect to the more experienced. Like to know "why" and want to work on their own without being micromanaged. Short attention span, like challenge and change, hate repetitive work, want workplace to be fun. Creative, optimistic, but not company loyal. Like to participate rather than watch. Prefer text messaging and social media networking to face-to-face communication.

Generation X

Born 1965 to 1980

Relatively small generation. Many now occupy middle-management jobs. Brought up in the first period of two-income households, rising divorce rate, latchkey environment.

(Continued)

(Continued)

Value independence, self-sufficiency, freedom and responsibility, resourcefulness. Adapted to and comfortable with computers and technology. Ambitious and hardworking but want work/life balance. Possess entrepreneurial spirit, like flexible hours, and chance to work at home. Favor diversity, challenge, creative input, autonomy, working alone rather than in teams.

Baby Boomers

Born 1946 to 1964

A very large group. Often the power holders in corporations, law firms, consultancies and most other organizations (except dot-coms). Loyal, work centric, cynical. Value office face time. Motivated by perks, prestige, position, high levels of responsibility, praise and challenges. Define themselves by professional accomplishment and tend to be workaholics. They are very competitive and believe in hierarchical structure, do not like change but will challenge established practice. Confident and comfortable with confrontation. Many are of retirement age but holding on and believe that Gen X and Y should "pay their dues"—like they did.

To learn more about this illuminating subject, enter "generation gaps" or "generational differences" in your search engine and thousands of references will come up written from various angles: general business management, human resources, marketing and more, plus numerous major articles in established publications.

Note that Boomers tend to like face-to-face meetings. They've adjusted to e-mail and smart phones, but it's usually not smart to text important messages to them or use texting abbreviations in your e-mails. And don't friend them! Even if they're simpatico with social networking, Boomers tend to prefer keeping their personal and business lives separate. And they much prefer that you do too: If you post an unduly revealing page, comment, photo or video, prepare to face negative consequences from your company executives, and those at other companies where you want to work.

Keep in mind that people in this generation are more formal in their business relationships and this affects what they expect, and like, in written materials. Well-written, well-thought-out and proofread messages work with this audience. Careless, sloppy, spontaneous messages are apt to insult them and instantly undermine your credibility and professional image.

Most important of all is what the differences suggest about the harder-to-define quality called "tone," the voice built into a message. When business executives are asked to identify the biggest problem with employee writing, "wrong tone" is usually complaint #1 when they talk about younger staff members.

We can see on the generation chart why this happens. People born after 1980 or so tend to be antihierarchical and skeptical of authority. In their view, age does not automatically make someone worthy of respect. But Boomers, who probably worked their tails off to get where they are, demand respect with a capital R.

The intergenerational writing problem is further complicated by Gen Yers' immersion in a digital world where communication is telegraphic. Thus, a careless 25-year-old might e-mail a client this way:

> Jack—here's the info you wanted. Still waiting for the new numbers—let me know when you'll send ASAP.—Mel

When he should have written something more like

> Dear Jack:
>
> To follow up on our phone conversation, I'm attaching a report on the Black acquisition. I've marked the relevant areas. If this doesn't provide all the information you need, please let me know and I'll dig further.
>
> As soon as we have the new numbers, we'll move ahead on preparing the agreement. Thanks.
>
> Best regards, Mel

If you think the second version is a bootlicking waste of time, think again. Mel's credibility and professional image are very much at stake here. Jack may not react to (in his perception) the rudeness, which Mel saw as efficiency, if he thought about it at all. But Jack is likely to register it, remember it and even talk to Mel's higher-up about it.

Look at it as necessary business protocol to write in a respectful—no, not obsequious—tone. And do so whenever you're in doubt about the relative status of your audience or where your e-mail might end up.

The guidelines equally apply when you report to a young boss or client. He or she may in fact be especially sensitive to signs of respect, and disrespect. And so are clients and customers, by definition. They do not want to be addressed as a peer or feel ordered around by a junior associate.

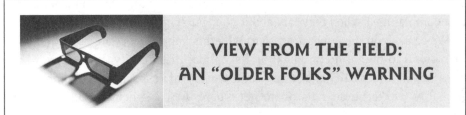

VIEW FROM THE FIELD: AN "OLDER FOLKS" WARNING

One of my gripes with younger people is that with e-mail and all the other business communication tools we have today, they don't get back to you in a timely manner. That's a subliminal message and makes you think, wasn't my message important? Aren't I important? It's so appalling that anyone who does respond within 24 hours, or a business that does so, has a real point of differentiation. And be aware of generational nuances. People who text shouldn't use that jargon in e-mail—us older folks don't understand it.

—Paul Facella, president, Inside Management Ltd.;
former Corporate Vice President, McDonald's

If you're a Gen-Yer, take comfort in knowing that adapting to the intergenerational gap isn't a one-way business. The Boomers who run law firms, accounting practices, corporations and all the rest try a bit desperately to understand the younger generation, because they know very well that the future (and maybe their retirement incomes) depends on it. They need to attract the best talent and retain it—a real challenge because younger people don't have the long-term loyalty of their own age group. Also, few companies are structured to meet Gen-Y priorities. Perks like flexible hours, lots of time off and a fun workplace are hard to graft onto an old organizational stalk.

Marketing people spend a huge amount of time analyzing generational characteristics to better calculate how to sell to each group, especially Gen X on down. And not-for-profits are very stressed about finding ways to appeal to younger donors, and how to use venues that reach them. If they fail, their revenue streams will literally age out.

So you need to take this divide seriously, too.

HOW TO WRITE TO GROUPS

Writing to groups is harder and more complicated than writing to individuals, depending on the group's size and diversity. Professionals who design communications for really big groups, like mass markets, customarily "segment" the audience and tailor different messages because the same one will not succeed with all. Similarly, a large company must send different information to employee groups about subjects like a change in benefits, because their concerns are different.

There are times when you should do this too—if you're sending a résumé or inquiry to prospective employers, for example, you'll need to take a different tack for consulting firms and marketing departments.

Often, however, one message must be effective for a wide range of people with different educational levels and interests. Good presenters often pick one person at a time to focus on while speaking. Similarly, many good writers think about one individual, or imagine one, and write to that person.

SIDELIGHT: THE WORD FROM SUPER PRO WARREN BUFFETT

Here's how the financier, known for his remarkably clear writing on complex financial subjects, pulls it off:

Write with a specific person in mind. When writing Berkshire Hathaway's annual report, I pretend that I'm talking to my sisters. I have no trouble picturing them: Though highly intelligent, they are not experts in accounting or finance. They will understand plain English, but jargon may puzzle them. My goal is simply to give them the information I would wish them to supply me if our positions were reversed. To succeed, I don't need to be Shakespeare; I must, though, have a sincere desire to inform.

No siblings to write to? Borrow mine: Just begin with "Dear Doris and Bertie."

—From *A Plain English Handbook: How to Create Clear SEC Disclosure Documents*

Rather than writing to a faceless group, then, try picking a "typical" representative of the audience to think about, and assemble a list of characteristics from our audience analysis outlined earlier in this chapter. Different factors count depending on your subject and goal. If you're presenting a new companywide data entry program, for example, it's important to consider education, probable degree of knowledge, possible resistance and the audience's view of "what's in it for me" (which encompasses "how much trouble will this cause me").

Addressing Gatekeepers and "Serial Audiences"

Often a document needs to be read by different people or groups in succession. There may be a "gatekeeper"—for example, a manager's assistant—who vets incoming messages and may choose not to pass some of them on to the boss. And with nearly every job application you send, there's probably a whole staff of people with the power to short-circuit you.

In other situations, you can anticipate that a message is likely to ascend the company ladder. You deliver a project report to your boss, for example, and see a good possibility that she'll send it to her boss, and the chain might continue to some unknown point. Or you submit your consulting proposal to the HR executive who invited it, and you count on his passing it on to the relevant department head.

Here are ways to handle this:

1. Be very conscious that you're writing to a serial audience when preparing the message.

2. Avoid anything that could annoy the immediate recipient, and anything not suitable to the audience that may lie beyond.

3. Use all the principles of good writing and proof carefully.

4. Err on the side of formality when unsure of the tone to take.

5. Keep your eye on the ultimate target—what communicators call the "primary audience"—the person or group that will ultimately make the decision to hire you, or deliver whatever you're asking for.

6. When opportunity allows, make friends with gatekeepers. It's best to have your supervisor's personal assistant regard you favorably, for example. Public relations people and politicians court editors and reporters for the same reason: They're gatekeepers, or mediators, whose approval is essential if they are to reach their audiences.

Sending Messages to the Universe With Digital Media

Digital media give us something that never existed before: A way for just about anyone to reach millions, probably billions, of people across the country and around the world, with a click, every day, every hour. All the rules of marketing and advertising are morphing into new "truths" as a result.

Anyone can now get his message out via a website or blog or social media post, for example. But when an audience is so vast and indefinable, how can you understand it to shape a better message?

The premise of goal and audience now works in reverse: Instead of knowing to whom you're writing and tailoring the message, you can create a message that your ideal audience will want to find. Through search engine optimization and global networking, this potential audience has the means to find you, rather than the other way around. And if you give it something it wants or needs, and leverage that interest intelligently, your audience will come.

So it's just as relevant to think about your goals and intended recipients in depth and figure out their age range, education, interests, values, hot buttons and all the rest.

Once again the lesson is, don't throw out the basics of good communication because the technology is new and the media channels behave differently. The principles are as important as ever, but apply in new ways.

In the next chapter, we'll explore how the groundwork of goals and audiences pays off and shows you what to say, how to say it, what *not* to say and options for organizing your message or document.

PRACTICE OPPORTUNITIES

I. Chart Your Own "Goals"

Based on this chapter's discussion of goals and the idea of the personal agenda, write down your own essential goals for

1. This year of study

2. The entire degree program you'll be completing

3. The first year of the job you hope to get after completing your program

Consider whether this exercise gives you a different perspective on what you want to achieve—and what difference that might make in what you do, how you spend your time and how you prioritize.

II. Group Project: Define Your Generation

In class or as an assignment:

Working with others in your general age group (preferably in a group of three to five), review the description of the "generation" you belong to by virtue of when you were born.

A. Discuss:

Which described qualities do you agree with?
Which do you disagree with?
What else should have been included?

If you come from different countries and cultures, can you find differences? Similarities?

B. Write:

Collaborate on writing a better description of your generation, in 300 to 500 words. Include cultural comparisons. Share with class and talk about results.

III. Read Between the Lines

Identify a job posting in your field that you'd like to apply for someday, if not now. Clip it or print it out. Analyze in writing:

1. How would you describe the person they're looking for? Be as specific as you can.

2. What are the most important qualifications? Personal qualities?

3. What kind of problems do you think the hired person is likely to face?

4. What can you tell about the company—is it formal and highly structured? Does it value innovation and new thinking? What kind of "personality" does it have?

5. What clues does this give you about how to present yourself in a résumé in terms of

   - Qualifications and experience
   - Personal qualities
   - Any less obvious factors you can cite to suggest you're a great match

6. Any qualifications or qualities you don't have? Can you think of ways to cover for these lacks, or bridge to proven capabilities you do have?

7. Can you figure out who will read your application initially . . .

8. And who will probably make the actual hiring decision?

9. How can you accommodate the need to address at least two different audiences?

10. What key words and terms should you build into your response?

IV. Analyze Your Supervisor

If you're currently working, your supervisor is your best candidate for this. If not, choose someone you've reported to in the past, at any kind of job.

1. Build a written profile of the person, considering the various factors described in this chapter. Take into account age and generation, communication style, personality, status in the organization, office appearance and as many of the other factors as possible. (If this sounds challenging, think about what you'd tell your younger sister who would take over the job when you leave or are promoted.) Write up the profile (should be at least 500 words).

2. Review the profile and write down everything your analysis tells you about how to best communicate with this individual and get what you want. Include clues and intuitions, as well as clear indicators.

3. Write an e-mail to the person requesting approval to attend a conference relevant to the job and industry.

Chapter 3

PUTTING STRATEGIC IDEAS TO WORK

LEARN HOW TO . . .

- ➢ Use "goal" and "audience" to determine content
- ➢ Organize your documents
- ➢ Adopt the right tone
- ➢ Strategize challenging messages

No matter what you do in life, you will have a huge advantage if you can read a paragraph and discern its meaning. . . . You will have enormous power if you are the person in the office who can write a clear and concise memo.

—David Brooks in "History for Dollars" in the *New York Times*

Recently, a colleague and I presented a business writing workshop to a group of successful accounting professionals in their 30s. We talked about how to apply goal and audience concepts to everyday documents like e-mail, and began discussing "tone"—the emotional feel that messages convey. A participant interrupted. We'll call her "Amy."

"Wait a minute," Amy said. "I'm a very direct person and a very busy one. If I want something from a subordinate, I write, 'I need you to have the Green report on my desk tomorrow by 2.' You're telling me I have to take the time to personalize what I write and care about their feelings? You're saying I have to . . . sugarcoat it?"

Our answer: "Well, we wouldn't call it sugarcoating—we'd call it being courteous and considerate—but basically, yes."

We found that Amy was far from the only person in the group who felt this way. But Amy and others should know this: Many executives have shared with us that "tone" is the biggest problem they face with employee writing. One CEO, head of an investment firm serving multimillionaires in their 50s and up, relayed that a number of clients had complained that the company's messages were often abrupt and even rude.

Amy, of course, was writing to people who report to her, not a client. That actually makes no difference. In both cases, relationship building is an important underlying goal, though an unstated one. As observed in Chapter 1, we depend on writing to build bridges between people in a business environment that steadily grows more impersonal. How your subordinates feel about you, and your messages, can be just as critical to success as how your clients feel.

Keep this context in mind as we explore techniques for planning effective messages.

Let's use some examples to practice putting the ideas of goal and audience to work. In the process, we'll establish some "universal principles" to guide business writing. The examples assume an e-mail format, but the principles apply equally when you communicate via social media or other online tools, and to long-form documents such as proposals and reports.

Suppose you are incoming president of an Entrepreneur Group and responsible for planning 10 guest appearances by prominent local businesspeople.

DEFINE YOUR GOALS

1. Immediate: Draw good speakers to the program.

2. Longer range: Establish contact with business leaders who could prove valuable in job hunting.

3. Accomplish these things without killing yourself. This means recruiting enough people to share the burden.

Clearly the start point is to get help. The folder you received from the outgoing president includes this recruitment e-mail from last year:

To: All Entrepreneur Group Members

Subject: Need help—important!

As incoming president, I'm taking on responsibility for assembling the next 10-month roster of speakers. Please help! Participate in the planning, organizing the logistics,

> taking care of speaker needs and general follow-up. This is the most important aspect of our club's work and we should all want to get good results. ***If enough people volunteer, the shared workload will be a lot easier.***
>
> Our first meeting will be on April 10 at 7 p.m. in Room A.—Jane

Does this make participating sound like much fun? Satisfying? No. Nor does it help to know that the writer will probably take all the credit for good outcomes. But the worst is that volunteering sounds like a risky business that could sop up an open-ended amount of time. The message is unlikely to succeed.

APPLY THE AUDIENCE CONCEPT

Let's see how considering "audience" can help. What do you know about the people to whom you're writing?

That's easy—despite differences in gender, background, national and ethnic origins and so on, they're much like you. They want to

- Look good, get a good résumé credit, be recognized and appreciated
- Establish good contacts for finding jobs
- Achieve all this by doing as little as possible
- Contribute within a collegial atmosphere (which doesn't characterize many initiatives run by inexperienced managers)

Universal Principle 1: Always look through your readers' eyes and ask, "What's in it for me?" Determine what you need to accomplish your goals within that perspective.

In this case, it means figuring out what to offer that will appeal to the audience and overcome resistance to a time commitment. Some simple, private brainstorming, or conversation with a friend, can provide a set of sales points in line with the list of audience needs or characteristics.

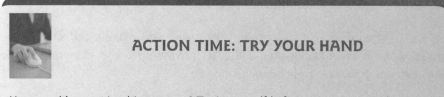

ACTION TIME: TRY YOUR HAND

How would you write this message? Try it yourself before going on to read one way to handle it. Start by thinking of all the ways you can meet the needs listed above.

Here's a version that capitalizes on the factors I've spelled out.

To: Entrepreneur Group

Subject: Meet successful area businesspeople

Dear Colleague:

I invite you to join this year's Speaker's Program Task Force.

As this year's president, I plan to appoint up to 10 members who are able to make the most of a chance to become personally acquainted with the region's leading business-people in a range of industries.

If you become part of the team, your commitment will involve

- A brainstorming session to come up with a shortlist of the people we'd most like to meet and hear speak
- Telephone and e-mail contact as needed and a checkpoint meeting or two
- Direct contact with one or more people on the A-list to recruit them and plan logistics (we'll match you up insofar as possible with people you'd like to meet)
- Welcoming "your" speaker to campus and introducing him or her

This year, all members of the task force will be listed in every program.

If you're interested in being part of the best-ever Speaker's Program, drop me a return e-mail telling me about yourself in a paragraph. I'll pick the best candidates by the end of next week.

Will this message succeed? The opportunity seems more tempting and the responsibilities less onerous. There's more incentive to participate. This version uses a little reverse psychology, too, by presenting the work as a privilege rather than a burden—and a chance to be part of a winning team, which everyone likes.

You might have thought that Jane's original e-mail basically delivered the same message and that recipients would work out the reasons to participate on their own. This is a mistake and it leads us to consider . . .

Universal Principle 2: Never assume your reader will make a deductive leap—especially one that would help your cause. It's always up to you, the writer, to spell things out and draw the "right" conclusions.

It's the writer's job to do the reasoning. It pays off.

Observe also that when the writer made the effort to see the invitation from her audience's perspective, the message's general spirit—its tone—shifted. It conveys more positive energy, frames the work as a team effort and suggests that the person in charge is nice and will be easy to work with. This is not trivial: It entices people to join the team and sets a good atmosphere for the project.

When you thoroughly consider what you want from your reader's viewpoint, it not only guides you to choose the right content, but leads you to naturally adopt the right tone. This contributes to achieving your immediate goal and to building relationships for the long term.

USE AN ORGANIZING STRATEGY THAT WORKS FOR YOU

Many people find it challenging to organize their writing even for brief messages.

Here are a few options with which to experiment.

"Organic" Organization

Let's look at the sample message. It's simple, logical and effective. The "lead," in journalistic terms (the first sentence or paragraph), focuses on the most compelling argument for volunteering. Many writers find that spending a lot of time crystallizing the lead enables them to organize the rest of the message in a natural, organic way.

Since this is an e-mail, the lead is incorporated into the subject line. This suggests another useful generalization.

Universal Principle 3: Always lead with your strong point. Once you figure out what your reader cares about and how you can relate to that, flaunt it immediately.

Aim to accomplish several critical things:

- Tell readers why they should care, instantly, to draw them in.
- Capsulize the message's content.
- Set the audience up to read the message with the "right attitude."
- Ask clearly for what you want—generally, this is your "call to action."

The lead of a business message should function pretty much like a reporter's lead does for a newspaper, magazine or online article (excepting the call to action, generally not applicable to articles).

Every year, it becomes harder to attract and keep readers' attention. This is especially true with online reading and anything you read off a screen, big or small. You often have only a few seconds to engage your audience: Don't waste them.

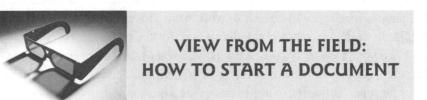

VIEW FROM THE FIELD: HOW TO START A DOCUMENT

The most important thing in a letter or business document is to get to the point right away so the reader knows who you are and what you want. For example, "I'm writing at the recommendation of A who thought you might be helpful in giving me a reference to XYZ company." Or you might need to get across a client's key message points.

It's also very important that in the first paragraph you put yourself in the readers' shoes. What are they worried about? Why do they need the product or service? You have to engage people immediately by appealing to their self-interest. And you must understand what the appeal is before writing—the "what's-in-it-for-me" factor.

How do I start? Sometimes I sit and stare at the screen and think, if I were the recipient of this letter, what's going on in my life that I would respond to? It can help to get a little background on the industry if it's one that's unfamiliar to you. You might read about trends, or talk to someone in the business and ask, what are the big things these people are dealing with? Doing some market research can help put you in the readers' mind-set and tell you what they're concerned about.

—Leila Zogby, president, Leila Zogby Business Writer, Inc.

For most professional writers, once the lead is determined, the rest of a message tends to flow organically, with some tweaking. The content of the Entrepreneur Group memo was basically determined by our simple brainstorming list. But leading with strength meant starting with the "contact with important people" carrot, so the rest of the list needed juggling.

Journalists were traditionally trained to write in "inverted pyramid style," meaning to start with the most important story element and then successively work down to the least important facts or ideas. There was a reason for this: Editors prefer to trim articles to fit by cutting as much as necessary from the end, rather than reading every story through to find the most expendable bits.

News articles are still generally written this way, and the method applies nicely to most business writing purposes.

Universal Principle 4: Craft your lead thoughtfully, then use your ideas, arguments and facts in the simplest, most straightforward way that works.

In the case of an e-mail, letter or online communication, this means sequencing your brainstormed list. In the case of a lengthy document, it means staying clear on the major subtopics or sections and putting them in a logical order.

It's useful to think about everything you write as three parts:

1. The lead

2. The end

3. The middle: everything that goes between the first two elements

The "middle" may consist of a paragraph, or 50 pages; either way, it typically contains the informational content. For example, a memo explaining how to fill out a form would lead with a statement about why an employee is getting these instructions ("On March 3 you must begin using a new system for purchase orders") and end with a statement about what is expected ("I count on your office switching to the new system on March 3. Of course, let me know any questions about it ASAP.")

In between would come the details about how to implement the system.

Organize With a Formal Outline

If the classic outline many of us practiced in school works for you, with major categories identified by numbers and subsections identified by letters, by all means use it. For an alternative that's specifically geared for business writing, see the Sidelight on "An Easy Organization Technique." This approach is useful for many people and adapts to a wide range of purposes.

SIDELIGHT: AN EASY ORGANIZATION TECHNIQUE

Most people plunge into writing without planning—which is fine for a two-sentence e-mail, but not for writing that is longer than a paragraph or two. They write one sentence at a time without being sure where they're going, and probably will cut and paste throughout their writing. This "plunging-in approach" will get the work done, but it's a long and painful experience.

It's better to do an outline. Come up with your main point, one that describes what your piece of writing is about. It should contain a key word that is generally a plural noun that relates to how the piece will be broken up. For example, if you're writing to

(Continued)

(Continued)

communicate the reasons for something, the key word is "reasons." Or, depending on your main point, the key word might be "benefits" or "steps" or "procedures" or "advantages." Determining your main point and the key word within it helps you construct an outline, and the writing becomes easier.

Generally, your main point should appear as the last sentence of the first paragraph. Preceding your main point is a first sentence or two that explains why you're writing this e-mail or letter. Often it is in response to a person writing to you. At other times, you may be asked to do a piece of writing, or you may see a need to put something in writing.

Based on the above suggestions, here is an example of an introductory paragraph:

Two years ago, our firm instituted a certain procedure for cashing checks. Unfortunately, serious problems have arisen with that procedure, and we have been forced to change the process. Below are the three **steps** that you should now follow to cash checks.

Now you know what the next three sections, usually paragraphs, need to be. That is, each paragraph will deal with a new "step," which is the key word.

The key word approach can help you create a good flow if you make sure to use transition words between sentences and paragraphs so people see how one statement relates to the next. Numbers can help: You can begin the second paragraph with *The primary advantage is* . . . The third paragraph can begin with *Secondly* . . . And so on.

—Dr. Mel Haber, president,
Writing Development Associates

Organize by Telling Your Message to Someone

This technique apparently helps the brain bypass the part of the brain we use for writing and go straight to the part we use when talking. Whether the reason this succeeds is psychological or physical, the idea makes sense. Oral communication probably preceded writing by a few million years, so we're better at it. Most people create first drafts that are complicated, wordy and confusing. But if we tell our story to someone else we can typically be clear and to the point.

So talk it through with someone. If the person is not steeped in your subject, all the better. Start specifically, like "I want a new office and to convince my boss I need to tell him . . . ," or "The process to follow for filing the form is . . ." or whatever is appropriate. You're likely to find that you can relay the reasoning or procedure fine, and that the process shows you your main point and how things fit together. It also reveals what is extraneous and what is missing.

This is not, by the way, an unsophisticated technique. Journalists use it all the time to figure out what's most interesting about a story they're developing, or to understand where the story's heart lies. Then they know how to develop a piece they are happiest to write and that has the best chance of reaching the audience.

Organize Through Graphic Techniques

Whether your document is short (like an e-mail or letter) or lengthy (like a report or proposal), you'll find it helpful to stay organized by building in graphic options. This has a big payoff; it makes everything, regardless of length, more easily understood by readers. In fact, if you don't build in graphics while you're writing, you may have to add them later anyway.

Graphic tools are even more important to online writing because people tend to scan and their attention must be captured and managed. Website designers use graphics very deliberately to attract the readers' eye and move it from point to point, taking account of typical viewing habits, which are studied. Online articles, blogs, profiles and other materials also benefit from graphic choices.

To structure a document, whatever the medium, many writers create a series of subheads before writing anything. This lets them build a logical sequence of facts or ideas and presto! A ready-made outline to follow.

Universal Principle 5: Use formatting techniques in all media to clarify your message and make it more accessible.

"Going Deeper: Graphic Options for All Writing" gives you a primer on using graphics to your advantage.

GOING DEEPER: GRAPHIC OPTIONS FOR ALL WRITING

Your visual repertoire can be used to make your messages look and feel organized—and, in fact, they'll usually be more organized. Here are some options.

Use subheads to introduce a new thought or section. Choose the format you prefer:

A larger font
A different font
Boldface
Italic

(Continued)

(Continued)

<u>Underlining</u>

YOU CAN USE UPPERCASE FOR YOUR SUBHEADS

or

Write them sentence-style, with just an initial cap

or

Use Upper/Lowercase (u/lc)

or

SMALL CAPS

You can combine some effects—bold with a different font, for example—but you must be consistent.

Use lead-ins for the beginning of a paragraph or section. Boldface, with or without italic, can also be used to **highlight a fact, figure, idea or conclusion in the body of your copy.** There are also times when <u>underlining is a good way to highlight,</u> but this can look outdated or falsely suggest that the phrase is a hyperlink. And of course color works, if the medium accommodates it.

Use bullet points, but remember that they have their pro's and cons. They are good for

- Listing ideas or facts telegraphically
- Summarizing
- Saving space
- Presenting at-a-glance facts or ideas

But do not depend on bullet points too much. While bulleting is a good way to present information for an audience with a short attention span—which, admittedly, is most of them—bullets need narrative context to have meaning. Further, readers can't really absorb more than perhaps four to seven at a time, depending on the material. Check out how you respond to bulleted lists yourself. Recall tends to be poor, too, because as stand-alone items without context or detail, bullet points give the mind little to hold onto.

This applies to all media, including résumés. Listing responsibilities or accomplishments in bullet form doesn't work if you don't also use narrative-style paragraphs to interpret the big picture. As Principle 2 says, never expect readers to draw conclusions for you. They may draw the wrong ones.

Number your points. This can work well to pull a reader through your information or argument. Some reasons for this:

1. People like to know how much is ahead of them.

2. It's satisfying to feel a beginning and an end to a message.

3. A clear sequence can be easy to absorb and remember.

So, in print or speech, statements like "We can expect three basic results from this action" or "Here are the seven steps to filing the new form," are quite effective. Followed of course by steps one, two, three and so on in logical order.

Graphic techniques also include the use of boxes, sidebars and pullout quotes—all demonstrated throughout the book you're reading right now. These give you good ways to incorporate relevant information without breaking the flow of a narrative.

Always, **extensive and strategic use of white space** is critical to accessibility and eye appeal of EVERY message. This is particularly true of long documents but should be taken into account even with brief ones. Short paragraphs contribute to this cause. And, of course, whenever you have options for making your point visually, through a chart, graph or image, consider that. But keep the document consistent and keep visuals relevant.

A word on font, or typeface: Be sure you're using a very readable font and refrain from using capitals, italics or bold face for entire e-mails or large portions of text. Don't mix more than two fonts as a general rule. (For a designer's advice on fonts and other graphic basics, see p. 182.)

WE'RE ALL SCREENWRITERS: READING HAS CHANGED

Writers today must take account of how on-screen reading has transformed reader expectations for print as well as electronic media.

Virtual media—particularly websites—have made us a nation of scanners. In everything we read, we look for what's relevant or interesting to us individually. We "dive" for information rather than systematically reading almost anything. We demand choices. We bring this new attitude to all media and messaging.

In response, few magazines or newspapers present us with dense, unbroken copy any more. They draw on the full range of graphic techniques as well as photographs, illustrations, pre-article summaries, charts, graphs, captions—deploying all the access points they can devise to pull impatient people in and feed them at least a piece of the story.

A growing number of books (like this one) do the same. And note how the most effective sales letters and charitable solicitations are brimful of headlines, subheads, underlining, pullouts, "handwritten" notes and more.

Creating websites has been described as "packaging information" as opposed to writing. This is a helpful way to think about most of what you write. You can't focus only on the words. You should also consider the graphic presentation, your audience's predilections and every technique you can draw on to deliver your message in a clear, attractive and compelling manner.

SUCCESS TIP: FOCUS ON GOOD CONTENT

If you've wondered why this book spends so much time talking about content rather than the technicalities of writing, here's the answer.

Good business writing is rooted in good substance. Once you practice looking at things through your audience's eyes, and using the demonstrated structure, you'll quickly know whether you have the right material to make your case—whatever you're writing. When you discover a gap in information or logic, don't try to cover it up: Dig up the facts you need, or think your message through further. You'll find that your projects, as well as your messages, succeed much more often.

Good writing is not "a way with words." It's a tool for accomplishing your strategic goals. It's essential to know your goal, analyze your audience and figure out how to make your best case.

Finally, End Well

Note that in our Entrepreneur Group memo, the final sentences circled back to the lead, and told readers how to follow up. The generalization is

Universal Principle 6: End every document in a way that reflects and reinforces your goal.

For example, "Please let me know if you are available to meet on March 2" or "Contact Jane if this new process isn't clear" or "I look forward to receiving the application." When possible, end with a "call to action"—a clear statement of what you want the reader to do. But be sure this suits the task: Telling a prospective employer to "call as soon as you receive this résumé" isn't a good idea.

BE SURE TO ADOPT THE RIGHT TONE

As we've seen with some of the examples, a document can look well planned and written but still fail if the tone, or "voice," hits the wrong note for readers. Just as with "live" interaction, the general feeling you project in a written message strongly affects how your words are received.

In a person-to-person situation, tone clearly results from, well, tone of voice. The same words can mean many different things according to our voice's pitch, rhythm, speed and so on, factors that reflect our state of mind and attitude. Moreover, in communicating face-to-face, we read facial expression, body language, conversational pauses and a whole host of cues that convey interest, astonishment, disagreement or dozens of other feelings.

With writing, none of these elements exist. A message's effect may be subliminal; it can be hard to pin down exactly what creates a message's emotional content. But controlling tone is critical. *When you're asking for something, obviously it's counterproductive to show disrespect for the other person—or anything that he or she might interpret as disrespect.*

Nevertheless, many people make this mistake routinely, unaware that they're undercutting themselves. Often this happens because of generational differences.

If your messages are influenced by texting and casual social media exchanges, for example, you may write letters and e-mails in a style that strikes people over 30 as abrupt, discourteous and rude. (In business settings, it usually doesn't serve you well with younger people, either.) If you're part of a generation that doesn't grant automatic respect to authority, as we saw in Chapter 2's generational analysis, you may compound the problem further—and never realize why you're not getting where you want to go.

ACTION TIME: FIND WHAT'S WRONG AND FIX IT!

Here are some sample e-mails. Can you identify what's inappropriate? Where the tone goes wrong?

Rewrite each of these so they have a better chance at succeeding.

1. To a supervisor:

   Dana—I have a great idea for solving the problem we talked about last week. Let's meet on Thursday at 3 p.m. to talk about it.—Robin

2. To a professor:

   Dear Prof: I looked online again for the syllabus you were supposed to post and couldn't find it. I need it by tomorrow—so last chance.—Mike White

3. To a client:

   Dear Mr. Black—I sent you the Kittredge draft last week but have heard nothing. Did I miss something? The deadline is close, please advise.—Mark

4. To a prospective employer:

   I'm sure you'll agree that my qualifications more than meet your criteria as described in the job posting. I look forward to meeting you. I'll call on Tuesday morning to find out when it's convenient for you. Sincerely, Ann Green

5. To a subordinate:

   Jerry, attached is a research project I need you to get done by Friday. Plan on working late if necessary. Thnx—Amelia

And the takeaway is . . .

Universal Principal 7: Choose your tone carefully and keep it in line with your goal and audience. Everything you write should reinforce and build positive relationships.

How can you sharpen your writing ear to achieve the tone you want?

1. **First, recognize that just as with face-to-face interaction, your tone usually conveys your actual feelings.** So if you're writing to a boss or client you don't much like or respect, but they're in a position to do you harm or good, take particular care with what you say and how you say it.

2. **Anticipate that people older than you and/or higher on the totem pole expect "good manners" in person and in writing.** Take extra pains to show courtesy and respect. This alone will make you stand out because many who've preceded you in the workplace find the new generation rude; if you adopt their framework, they'll be impressed. And since, in general, the "older" generation means people 30 and above, respect is an important card to play.

3. **Remember that tone is contagious.** Projecting a negative attitude will provoke the same from your reader. That never helps, so try to communicate with a positive spirit. If you want an enthusiastic response, show your own enthusiasm. Friendly and respectful are generally good hallmarks to strive for.

4. **Take pains to use the full trappings of courtesy.** Even in an e-mail.

Some do's:

- Write "Dear" in the salutation, or Hi, or something similar.
- Use first names only if suitable; if in doubt, use Mr. or Ms., or the person's full name.
- Use full sentences, not telegraphic texting-style statements.
- Edit and proof scrupulously (even if the More Important Person sends careless e-mails full of errors).
- End with a conservative sign-off, for example, Sincerely, Best regards, Thanks (though it should be noted that e-mail lacks a repertoire of good sign-offs).

Some don'ts:

- Don't make assumptions not appropriate to the relationship (like setting the time for a meeting with your supervisor).
- Don't issue peremptory orders or express impatience (even with a subordinate).

5. Don't antagonize your readers, whatever your relationship to them. This is as true for peers, and people who report to you, as it is for people who you report to. So avoid being judgmental, critical, sharp or unnecessarily abrupt.

6. Practice feeling genuine consideration for the person or group you're writing to. Take a moment to say something that feels like you have a personal relationship with the person, even if it's banal:

> I hope this finds you well.
>
> Did you have a good holiday season?
>
> Hope your weather is good—it's terrible here!

Better yet, when possible, make a personal connection or relate directly to the reason you're writing:

> It was great seeing you at the regional meeting last week. I'd like to follow up on . . .
>
> Thanks for the note. I'm happy to answer your question about upcoming deadlines.

Referring back to Amy, if you questioned why she should bother with seemingly empty sentiments when asking her subordinate for something, here's why. Everyday messages are often the only way we connect with other people. A relationship, and the trust that goes with it, builds gradually over time. If you take the initiative to humanize your messages—carefully, and when appropriate—you contribute toward creating that relationship.

Especially when you're dealing with a client or other significant person, acting just a little bit like you already have a relationship can help that building process. But never take liberties or become personal in a way that might offend.

7. Adapt to the corporate culture. E-mail sent by Citibank staff may differ in tone quite a lot from messages written by employees at Facebook or a nonprofit, or it might not. An organization can be formal or informal based more on its own history and the nature of its leadership, rather than the industry it's part of. In a new work environment, it's a good idea to spend some time analyzing the degree of formality, general style and appropriate subject matter of the written communication you see.

8. Adapt to the medium. Generally, a letter needs to be more formal than an e-mail. A report or proposal is typically more formal yet. Online writing, such as for websites or blogs, generally works best when it feels more casual, friendly and individual than print marketing materials. A good website looks very accessible and spontaneous—though in fact, these qualities are always achieved through the most arduous planning and rewriting.

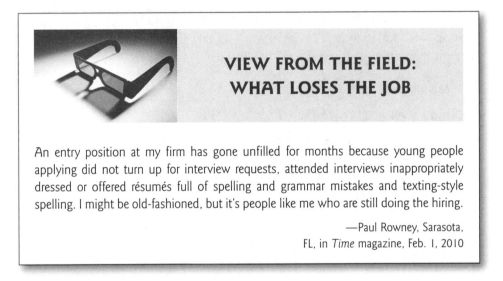

**VIEW FROM THE FIELD:
WHAT LOSES THE JOB**

An entry position at my firm has gone unfilled for months because young people applying did not turn up for interview requests, attended interviews inappropriately dressed or offered résumés full of spelling and grammar mistakes and texting-style spelling. I might be old-fashioned, but it's people like me who are still doing the hiring.

—Paul Rowney, Sarasota,
FL, in *Time* magazine, Feb. 1, 2010

TESTING THE IDEAS

A Workplace Recruitment Challenge

Let's check out how the principles translate to a workplace memo. Ellen's consulting firm has asked her to head up an internal research project to revamp the summer associate program. This involves some tedious research and writing, so she needs to recruit a team.

The challenge: Ellen's colleagues are already pretty overwhelmed with client work, which makes the money. What can she give this audience in order to achieve her goal, recruiting help so she can turn out a good report?

She brainstorms a list of factors:

1. Consultant evaluation and prospects are partly based on participating in internal "volunteer" projects.

2. This project is relatively high profile.

3. The work could shape and improve a program that many staff members experienced themselves.

To lead with strength, Ellen opens with the most emotionally appealing element.

Lead *Subject line:*

Project opportunity: Revamp summer associate program

Colleagues:

I'm looking for three people to work on a new internal project that might recast the entire summer associate program

Middle   The team, which I'll head, is charged with reviewing hiring strategies, salaries, the learning experience the program provides and the impression made on associates. Top management will review our report and I expect our recommendations to be seriously considered.

If you had reservations about your own experience as a summer associate, or observed shortcomings in how the program is run, this is a chance to make a real contribution. We can come up with a plan the firm will use as a blueprint—a great addition to your portfolio.

Close   Please call with any questions. Let me know if you're interested by February 7.

Convincing? Ellen isn't so sure. So she considers what could make her project more attractive than competing opportunities. Reconsidering the #1 problem for her audience—time pressure—she opts for a larger committee and to hit the time problem head on. She adds to the middle:

I've planned the work to give team members maximum flexibility in allocating their time. Only two face-to-face meetings will be scheduled— to launch the project, and review results at the end. It should prove possible to do your share independently on your own schedule, and I expect that to take about four hours per week for two months. We'll teleconference weekly to be sure we're all on track.

Knowing that many firm projects require an open-ended commitment, Ellen gains an important competitive advantage with this tack.

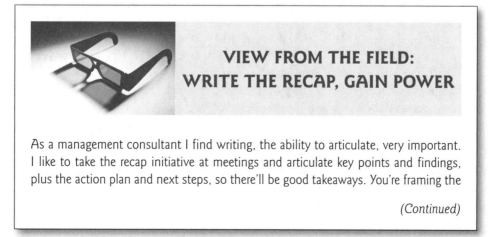

VIEW FROM THE FIELD: WRITE THE RECAP, GAIN POWER

As a management consultant I find writing, the ability to articulate, very important. I like to take the recap initiative at meetings and articulate key points and findings, plus the action plan and next steps, so there'll be good takeaways. You're framing the

(Continued)

(Continued)

issue for people and yourself too. People are very grateful, and give you feedback, let you know if there's been further conversation. Information is power. The more of it you are able to accumulate and get your arms around, the more power you have.

—Paul Facella, CEO of Inside Management Ltd.,
former McDonald's corporate vice president;
author of *Everything I Know About Business
I Learned at McDonald's*

Drawing Important People to Campus

Let's try another exercise, to see how the principles can be used to write speaker invitations.

The Entrepreneur Group is ready to write to the selected business leaders. What could entice these people to accept a speaking invitation?

Start with brainstorming what they have in common. Most probably, they

- Are busy people with extremely crowded schedules
- Like to be recognized as leaders
- See community connection as important
- Share an interest in supporting the region and the schools that contribute to growth and make it a good place to live
- May be interested in hiring future graduates, connecting with faculty and/or interacting with young people

Here's one way to write a "generic" version of the letter.

Dear _____:

The Green University Martin School of Business is inviting the region's most prominent business leaders to address our students and faculty this coming year. Recognizing how important Premiere Industries is both to our area's economy and the community we share, and your own contributions as a leader, we hope you will accept our invitation to be part of the Executive Speaker Program.

We ask for just an evening of your time. In addition to an address of approximately one hour, we'd like you to be our guest for dinner and meet leading members of our business school community. We hope to schedule your appearance for March and can offer you a choice of dates during the month.

> The Executive Speaker Program will give our aspiring business managers the chance to become acquainted with the Quadruple Cities' most inspiring leaders. The Martin School of Business has worked hard to earn an impressive ranking internationally, and I believe you'll also find the evening stimulating.
>
> With your permission, we plan to publicize your appearance with the local media and videotape your presentation for our heavily used archive. If helpful, committee members will be happy to work closely with you to support you in what you choose to present.
>
> I'll plan to call you next week to ask if you are able to accept our invitation and answer any questions. Or if more convenient, please call me at any time before then.

The letter takes account of the recipients' busy schedules and makes their commitment as convenient and pain free as possible; reminds them of the community and give-back context of a university; flatters their importance and suggests some tangible benefit in the way of positive press and contact with faculty and select students.

It could work. But is it good enough?

Universal Principle 8: Writing is more powerful when you personalize your message to the individual. When the stakes are high, take the trouble to know the person.

How can you do this if it's someone you've never met? Start with questions. In the case of our theoretical guest speakers, for example, you could ask

Is he or she

- A graduate of the school, or parent of kids who have been or might be?
- A former business major? MBA?
- A donor to the university or school?
- Connected with any particular community cause?
- Proud of something in particular? Known for something in business circles?
- Passionate about his or her work?

Does the company

- Hire your university's graduates, or those from your school?
- Send employees to any university program for training?
- Sponsor any campus programs?

You can research the answers—online and/or by finding people to talk to who know the person or the company. You can try to identify a professor, board member or school supporter who knows the individual personally or can connect you with someone who does.

This thinking applies to every occasion when you're requesting something important. Look for ways to successfully relate to your audience. Obviously, it helps if your potential speaker has direct ties to your school, a relationship with a professor or a strong community spirit. In each case, you'll use this information prominently, probably in the lead. For example:

> I'm taking the liberty of writing to you as a Green U. alumnus because we'd very much like to include you as a Martin School of Business Guest Speaker.

A basic letter can be adapted to each recipient's characteristics. Here are "Three Ways to Personalize Messages" to add to your tool kit. They work well for many documents, including job-hunting letters.

THREE WAYS TO PERSONALIZE MESSAGES

1. Name-drop in any available way. In business, people respect connections and references because it's far more comfortable and trust inducing than dealing with total strangers. If you have (or can find) a mutual connection, use it and use it early. For example:

> At John Black's suggestion I am writing to ask . . .

> Professor Blue, whose class on Corporate Culture I am currently enjoying and with whom you also studied at White, believes I would be an excellent candidate for the internship your company is offering . . .

2. Do your homework and be sure it shows. People like to know they're recognized, or that you took the time to find out about them or their organization—especially when you can identify something they're proud of. For example:

> Our selection committee was particularly impressed with how you've established Brown Industries as one of the top in its field nationally in only 10 years.

> Your support of the community through the scholarship program and hospital building fund makes you an excellent model for future corporate leaders, beyond your business leadership, so we will especially value your participation.

3. Use compliments; they may work magic. Even VIPs like to feel good about themselves and know that other people recognize how special they are. This is not to suggest twisting the truth but rather, that you find something nice you can say with sincerity. (Try this technique sometime with a hostile boss or colleague and you'll be amazed at the turnaround.) For example:

> Several classmates have told me that you are an exceptionally interesting and inspiring speaker, so I'm very pleased to extend this invitation.

> I'd like to share that when we canvassed the committee members for their top speaker picks, your name came up in every instance.

A Bad News Message

Let's test these various principles out in a different context, communicating news that's unwelcome or outright bad.

Let's say it's your unhappy lot to develop a memo announcing that the company will cancel its tuition reimbursement benefit. Your boss gives you the draft she began:

> To: All Staff
>
> Subject: Cancellation of tuition reimbursement
>
> Please be advised that economic conditions dictate some employee benefit cutbacks. As of June 30, Rose Co. will no longer provide tuition reimbursement. It is regrettable if this causes inconvenience but as you'll understand, the decision is in the company's best interest.
>
> —Talent Management Dept.

ACTION TIME: FIND WHAT'S WRONG AND FIX IT!

What's wrong with this message? Stop and think about it before reading the analysis. Consider how you'd feel as a recipient. Plan a better message.

Here's why the message fails both in tone and content. The writer should have considered two basic audiences—those directly affected and those who are not. A program beneficiary is bound to be upset when an entitlement is taken away arbitrarily. Worse, it sounds like more benefits may be on the chopping block. Maybe even jobs. If you're someone not directly affected by this cut, you'd have the same uncertainties.

Further, because the bad news is delivered so impersonally—no one is even taking responsibility for the decision—you're likely to think bad thoughts about your employer. Not to mention that it sounds like the company is on the downslide, and more than one member of the audience might come to the same conclusion: time to update the résumé.

Studies show that the manner in which bad news is delivered, even in worst-case scenarios like layoffs, strongly affects how employees perceive a company and feel about their jobs. This is no small matter because when times are tough, management needs to build an everyone-must-pull-together spirit.

Good managers therefore put a lot of thought into anticipating reaction to bad news, figuring out how best to frame it and determining whether anything can be done to offset the negative impact. And, plenty of consultants find their bread and butter in telling executives how to handle these situations.

In the example we're using, then, the goals are

- Deliver the bad news in the most acceptable manner possible
- Be honest and realistic (anything else will backfire)
- Express empathy in a businesslike way
- Reassure employees that there are no current plans for more cuts
- Assure everyone the company has a good future

Because you're not speaking for yourself in this case, which is often the situation, you'll need to gather information.

You might want to find out

- Who made the decision?
- Exactly why was it made?
- Might the benefit be reinstated someday?
- Are other benefit cuts being effected or contemplated?
- Might layoffs follow?
- Is the firm's situation precarious? To what degree?
- What can be said about the company's communication history and treatment of staff?
- What are the options for the message's authorship?

Did your plan for a better message take account of some or all of these ideas? Here's one way to reframe the message.

To: All Rose Company Staff

Subject: Suspension of tuition-reimbursement program

Dear Colleagues:

I'm sorry to tell you that as of June 30, the company will not offer tuition reimbursement.

As the Management Team has communicated over the past year, the Rose Co. has lost several important clients because of the overall poor economic climate. Additionally, a few clients have had to temporarily reduce their service level.

We're working hard to broaden our client base and diversify services, as you know, and are seeing a promising business uptick. But right now we must effect some economies. We don't want to reduce staff beyond natural attrition. And we don't want to trim benefits like health insurance that are critical to our corporate family's well-being.

Accordingly, we have decided to reduce new equipment spending, cut conference travel and suspend the tuition program. We realize that losing the program will disappoint many of you and we continue to value our staff's commitment to continued learning. We'll be happy to reinstate this perk when it becomes practical to do so.

Meanwhile, I trust you'll agree with our priorities and our commitment to sharing the news with you openly and honestly. I know that with your help, Rose Co. will weather the current nationwide downturn and provide a supportive employment climate for all of us.

I'll keep you closely informed of our progress.

Sincerely,
Ed White, CEO

This memo puts the cut in context, establishes a team feeling, reassures readers about the company's future and makes them feel valued. It's hard to disagree with the expressed priorities. It sounds like management is handling the economic challenge well and staying with the ship is a good bet. And, employees can trust company leaders to communicate straightforwardly.

Note that there are various strategies for communicating bad news, such as "sandwiching" it between positive statements. (For example, "Bob, it's been terrific to have you as a vendor all these years. But the company has grown and we're moving on. Let's remember the good times.")

But this cushioning approach ill suits today's skeptical, impatient, even cynical audience. It's much more successful to impart the bad stuff immediately. Show caring and give reasons when you can. Try to find something truly useful to offer rather than just empty rhetoric. "I can suggest a contact who may have a job lead for you" or "We're bringing in some job-search experts for you to consult with" is a lot better message than, "With all your talents, I'm sure a great future awaits you."

These principles should help you avoid a bad-news messenger's worst fate in most situations where you have that role. As you move up the ladder, remember that up-front honesty and compassion for others should guide your response to crisis. Introduce mitigating factors when possible. Where an apology is in order, make it. Unfortunately, this lesson seems never to get learned in the corporate and political arenas.

The experimental memo from "Ed White" claimed a good communication history for the company only because I chose to assume that was true. Just as in personal life, good relationships must be built over time. This is true for external communication as well as internal. An institution needs to foster employee, public and media trust over the long run through good communication to successfully weather a crisis.

Universal Principle 9: Be as honest, straightforward and authentic as you can in every message you send and every document you create.

SIDELIGHT: NEED TO APOLOGIZE? HERE'S HOW

Visiting hundreds of companies and writing about their *crisis du jour*, I noticed that organizations that apologize have better outcomes. And individuals who do it well rise higher and have better relationships. Clearly accountability—taking responsibility and rejecting defensiveness—is an important skill. So I started to put it together into a systematic approach, the 5Rs model:

- Recognition—acknowledge the specific offense
- Responsibility—accept personal responsibility, no excuses
- Remorse—there's no substitute for "I apologize" or "I am sorry"
- Restitution—here's what I'll do about it, concretely
- Repeating—I promise it won't happen again

You never know when the need to apologize will come upon us, but if you're not prepared, instinct kicks in—we want to defend ourselves, hide, deny responsibility.

But the cover-up is always worse than the crime. Train yourself in small things and it will be easier to apply to big things.

Written apologies are more formal than spoken but work about the same.

These days, apologizing is a leadership skill. We see our decision makers dodging and weaving instead of accepting responsibility, and that disappoints us. We don't expect them to be perfect, just willing to learn. In the long run apology leads to better outcomes and more durable relationships.

—John Kador, author of *Effective Apology*
(see his blog, *www.effectiveapology.com*, for
interesting comments on the public apology scene)

In the next chapter, we'll start to look at concrete ways to improve what you write. The ideas that guide good writing are essential, but you also need to craft good sentences, choose the right words and produce cohesive documents.

PRACTICE OPPORTUNITIES

I. Write a Better Note for Amy to Send to Her Subordinate

It should ask "Susan" to deliver a report by a specific time in a way that will make her feel appreciated, part of a team and happy to work hard on Amy's behalf.

II. Group Work: Plan and Pitch an On-Site Visit

As a group, brainstorm to identify an interesting company in your area to visit. Come up with as many reasons as you can to justify the time required to plan, organize and make the visit.

1. Collaborate on a letter making your case to the professor.

2. Write a letter to the appropriate person at the company asking that the firm host the class.

III. Write a "Stop Order"

Write a convincing e-mail to the class telling everyone to stop texting, tweeting, Facebook viewing and so on during class time or business meetings.

IV. Draft a "Please Rescind"

Write an e-mail to a supervisor asking that the rule against texting, tweeting and Facebook monitoring during work hours be rescinded, explaining why.

V. Create a "How To"

Write a detailed document telling someone exactly how to do something practical, step by step. Make it as clear as you possibly can by the way you write it, and the use of graphic techniques. Examples of possible subjects: explaining to a relative how to use the newest smart phone; fixing a computer, car or plumbing problem; making oatmeal cookies or a paper airplane; purchasing a new computer, building an aquarium, training a dog to sit or whatever interests you. Your subject can be one you already know about or one that you'd like to research.

VI. Sum Up This Chapter's Content

Draft a 300- to 500-word summary describing the most important things you learned from this chapter, using at least three of the organizing techniques covered. Exchange your draft with another student and talk about the similarities and differences in content, and how each of you handled this task.

Chapter 4

GOOD SENTENCES, THE RIGHT WORDS

THE HEART OF GOOD WRITING

LEARN HOW TO . . .

- ➤ Assemble strong sentences
- ➤ Adopt practical guidelines for readability
- ➤ Choose the right words
- ➤ Use vigorous verbs

> *But it ain't watcha write, it's the way atcha write it.*
>
> —Jack Kerouac

The sentence is the building block of written communication. I won't try to define the sentence, which is a lot more slippery a job than your early grammar lessons led you to believe. Nevertheless, if you write better sentences, combine them effectively and use the structured thinking principles covered in the last two chapters, you're en route to becoming a powerful, flexible writer.

This book does not focus on grammar; if you think you'll benefit from mastering rules and a more formal foundation, check out the resources listed in Chapter 5. All are excellent and you can find an approach to supplement the practical strategy we'll pursue here.

Let's look first at your choices for how to build a sentence.

ASSEMBLING THE SENTENCE

Structure Without Grammar

In the beginning, there is the simple declarative sentence: Someone is doing something, or something is happening.

Examples:

> Ellen hit Mark.
> The dog was frightened.
> The dog ran away.
>
> The leaves are turning red.
> Autumn is coming.
> The air is getting chilly.
>
> The auditors found a mistake.
> Jerry denied responsibility for the mistake.
> Jerry was caught.
> Jerry apologized.

Then there are sentences with more than one part, or clause, often separated by commas. Here are some two-part sentences:

> Ellen hit Mark, and the frightened dog ran away.
>
> The leaves are turning red and the air is chilly, sure signs that autumn is coming.
>
> The auditors found a mistake, but Jerry denied he was responsible.

A more complex, longer sentence can have three or more parts or sections:

> Ellen hit Mark, frightening the dog, who ran away.
>
> When the leaves turn color and we start pulling sweaters out of the drawer, it's time to face the fact: Autumn is on the way.
>
> After the auditors found a mistake, Jerry denied responsibility, but eventually had to confess his error and apologize.

Or

> Jerry apologized for the accounting error, although earlier, when it was discovered, he had tried to evade responsibility.

Which sentences are correct? All, of course. It depends on the information you're delivering, the tone of what you're writing and so on. But note that the longer sentences give the writer the ability to make connections between events more clearly. And if you read the sentences aloud, their rhythms are quite different.

When simple declarative sentences dominate your writing, it sounds childish—exactly like a first-grade reader or many sixth-grade social studies textbooks. Yes, there are great writers who use the simplest language and structures (like the novelist Ernest Hemingway and the poet Emily Dickinson), but you have to be seriously good—an artist—for that to work.

On the other hand, when writing consists entirely of long complicated sentences, it becomes hard to follow and, pretty quickly, boring. It picks up a rhythm that, well, puts the reader to sleep. For example:

> Wanting to express subtle thoughts and ideas, Jane often used lengthy, complicated sentences in her business correspondence. When this problem was brought to her attention, she responded that she preferred not to insult her readers' intelligence. She was told that people found her messages confusing, and might not read them to the end. After thinking about the issue further, she decided to rethink her premise.

In fact, more of us share Jane's writing problem than the "first-grade" approach: We tend to begin writing a message or document in a complicated, even convoluted way, disregarding how it "sounds," and need to work our way to simplicity and good rhythm. That's one of the main reasons you need to see every message as a first draft and plan to edit it.

How could the paragraph about Jane read better? Here's one way.

> Jane often used long complicated sentences in her business writing. Told that this was a problem, she explained that she wanted to express subtle ideas, and not insult her readers' intelligence. But her messages confused people. Often they didn't read them to the end. Confronting these facts, Jane decided to change her writing style and use sentences of varying length. She finds this technique much more successful.

Note that the two versions are almost exactly the same length, so the changes in this case don't save space. And the same information is delivered. But do you agree that the second version is more engaging? The reason is simple but important: Version 1 repeats the same sentence structure, sentence after sentence—each is perfectly correct, but together, make it tough for the reader. Version 2 deliberately breaks the pattern by combining sentences with different structures.

If you don't want to think about structure at all, just consciously try to begin each sentence differently. In the second "Jane" version, for example, the simple sentences like the first one usually alternate with more complicated ones that require commas.

Absorb this basic idea and your writing may improve dramatically. It's easier to keep your reader's attention and sound interesting just by alternating the length and structure of your sentences. This pulls people along. The faster they can read what you write, the more successful your message will usually be.

The best thing is, you don't need to think about grammar to do this. But you do need to reexamine what you want to get across and see if you can recombine the ideas, wording and sentences so the sum of the parts makes a better whole. You may also need to cut sentences up to make some short and punchy.

In your own writing and everything you read, make it a point to train your ear. Be aware of rhythms: when they work, and when they don't.

PRACTICE TIME: SENTENCE RHYTHM 1

Rewrite this paragraph. First read it aloud to identify the problems. When you've written a new version, read that aloud as well and see if you're satisfied.

Carol is working on an MBA. She finds the pressures very demanding. She has almost no time to spend with friends. She doesn't even have time for phone calls. She doesn't have much time for e-mail or keeping up with Facebook either. The only time she sees other people is in class or team projects or study groups. She recently decided to change this pattern. She'll begin by brainstorming ideas for how to set aside some personal time each week. She also needs to think about whom she can spend that time with. Everyone she knows is constantly working.

PRACTICE TIME: SENTENCE RHYTHM 2

Rewrite this letter asking for a recommendation. Again, read the before and after versions aloud.

Dear X:

Not only are you an exceptional business adviser whose unique vision adds significant value to the company, but your constructive management style helps the entire team to develop new skills each day. Because you are a leader in your field, I was wondering if you'd write a letter of recommendation supporting my application to the Green University International MBA program.

While this job affords me constant learning and I continue to enjoy my experience here, I hope that gaining an MBA will enhance my management skills at the international level. It should also prepare me for a future in management, since I hope to become a great manager, like you, one day.

I realize that my acceptance would mean my departure from the firm, but there should be ample time to train a replacement. If permitted, I would love to help secure a replacement and provide thorough training, as well as feedback to ensure that the new role maximizes efficiencies and focuses on future growth. And after I've completed my schooling, I hope I have the opportunity to work with you in the future.

If you do decide to grant me this request, I have prepared a folder that includes a letter outlining specifics and a pre-paid envelope for mailing. If for any reason you don't feel comfortable writing a letter on my behalf, I completely understand.

PRACTICAL GUIDELINES FOR READABILITY

How Long Should Sentences Be?

There is actually a semi-scientific answer to this question. It comes from readability research on what makes writing most understandable. As the Sidelight feature on "The Shrinking English Sentence" shows, the average number of words per sentence in written materials has radically fallen over the centuries, and today there is more or less agreement that **sentences should average between 14 and 22 words to be most comprehensible.**

And speech? Linguists have determined that the spoken sentence typically consists of 7 to 10 words.

How about online material? Somewhere between what works for print documents and what's typical for speech.

SIDELIGHT: THE SHRINKING ENGLISH SENTENCE

People began studying readability and its relation to sentence length in the late 19th century. An English literature professor named Lucius Adelno Sherman analyzed sentence length historically and found (in his 1893 book, *Analytics of Literature*) the following averages:

Pre-Elizabethan times	50 words per sentence
Elizabethan times	45 words per sentence

(Continued)

(Continued)

Victorian times   29 words per sentence
Late 19th century   23 words per sentence

Sherman observed that over time, sentences had become simpler and more concrete as well as shorter. He noted that this was because spoken language was affecting written language—as it should: "The oral sentence is clearest because it is the product of millions of daily efforts to be clear and strong. It represents the work of the race for thousands of years in perfecting an effective instrument of communication."

Today, journalism experts believe sentences should be as short as 14 words on average for maximum readability. But not all written documents need to be understood by everyone.

Since the research agrees that sentence length is one of the two key ingredients of readability (word length is the other), it's important to consider these guidelines seriously.

A few takeaways for the business writer:

1. Academia remains partly immersed in pre-20th-century writing, especially for English majors. So the writing style encouraged by some professors reflects an earlier time and may be at odds with this book's guidelines, which are grounded in practical writing for today's high-speed digital world.

2. The "rule" doesn't mean that every sentence should be at least 14 words and no more than 22 words long. It means the average length should fall within those limits. For example, the last few paragraphs here—from the "How Long Should Sentences Be?" head through the end of this sentence—is 17.9 words. But one sentence is 41 words long and a few are less than 10 words. Using "average" length in this way supports the alternating rhythm recommended earlier.

3. Variation is fine based on individual writing style and the nature of your audience. Obviously, a highly educated audience will understand more difficult material more easily than a less educated one. If you're writing to an audience that ranges, say, from factory workers to managers, or you'd define the readers as "average," keep in mind that the "average American" is estimated to read at a seventh-grade level. And that just because people with a lot of education can understand something difficult doesn't mean they want to read it, or will stick with it.

After all, we're not talking about producing required textbooks. Virtually nothing you'll write is mandated reading. There are no captive audiences in the business world: You have to earn your audience with just about every single document you create by writing it well.

4. To check how you're doing, you don't need to count the words of every sentence. Your Microsoft Word program, and others, gives you a marvelous tool that does this for you. It's the Readability Statistics Index and you can ask your computer to bring it up every time you use spell check. The box materializes immediately after the spelling/grammar check and tells you the average sentence length of the document or highlighted piece, along with additional useful information.

Using the Readability Statistics—sometimes called the Flesch Index—is a great stress-free way to monitor and improve your own writing.

GOING DEEPER: HOW TO USE
THE READABILITY INDEX

The Readability Index gives you an instant way to check how readable your writing is, along with helpful clues about how to fix it.

To access it in Microsoft Word, bring up Preferences, and under Spelling and Grammar, make sure the "Show readability statistics" box has a check mark. Then it will automatically come up after you've checked spelling and grammar. You can also highlight a section of a document and get this information. As you see in the examples shown, the statistics include number of words, and number of characters, paragraphs and sentences. More useful is the "averages" section. These figures tell you whether your writing reflects the guidelines recommended here:

14 to 22 words per sentence

Short words, short paragraphs (more on this in Chapter 5)

Better yet, "readability" tells you percentage of passive sentences (the lower the better; try for under 10%), Flesch Reading Ease—that is, the percentage of people who will understand the piece—and Flesch-Kincaid Grade Level: how much education someone needs to comprehend your document. You may find it hard to write for less than an 11th-grade reading level, depending on your subject. Don't worry about this particular statistic unless you're writing for a relatively uneducated audience. However, the *Wall Street Journal* has claimed to be written at an 8th-grade level—check this out to see if it's true.

Following is a demonstration of how the Readability Index can help you. First, a not-very-well-written piece of prose along with the index stats. Then there's a rewritten version, with a new set of stats to match. It shows the difference achieved by editing/rewriting.

(Continued)

(Continued)

When you write, try checking the readability stats. If you're not satisfied with the outcome, experiment with fixing your sentences and word length—the major elements the system measures—and check again. If the document is important, you may want to go through another round of stats and look at the index again.

The good news: The guidelines eventually become built into your writing process and you instinctively write better.

Example

Text Version 1—Original

There have been a diminishing number of young people in the region, according to a variety of studies that have been issued on the subject by organizations ranging from smart growth groups to the offices of the county executives. Universally, it is agreed that a brain drain is untenable. The impact of losing our best and brightest would be that the region could become less vital and would offer fewer opportunities, which can only increase the problem. If this happens, Green Island is going to become a place that is dominated by an aging population, a situation that would have dire economic and social consequences. To solve this challenge, we need to be able to understand the perspectives of a variety of stakeholders and determine what program we can put into place in order to move forward.

Readability Statistics

Counts	
Words	137
Characters	660
Paragraphs	1
Sentences	5

Averages	
Sentences per Paragraph	5.0
Words per Sentence	27.4
Characters per Word	4.8

Readability	
Passive Sentences	60%
Flesch Reading Ease	44.4
Flesch-Kincaid Grade Level	12.0

OK

Text Version 2—Rewrite

Young people are moving away from the region, a number of studies show. We all agree that preventing a brain drain is essential. If we lose our best and brightest, Green Island loses its vitality.

As young adults find fewer opportunities, more and more will look elsewhere, leaving us with an aging population. The results will be economically and socially dire. To address this challenge, we need to understand the different stakeholders' perspectives and decide on a program so we can move forward.

Readability Statistics	
Counts	
Words	80
Characters	409
Paragraphs	2
Sentences	6
Averages	
Sentences per Paragraph	3.0
Words per Sentence	13.3
Characters per Word	5.0
Readability	
Passive Sentences	0%
Flesch Reading Ease	54.7
Flesch–Kincaid Grade Level	8.9

OK

IT'S ALL IN THE WORDS

What's in a Word? Count the Syllables

The second factor in calculating readability is word length. Research on this tells us that the short words are most understandable to the most people. That's no surprise. But how short? One or two syllables.

I am a bear of very little brain, and long words bother me.

—Winnie the Pooh (by A. A. Milne)

In business writing, unlike parts of the academic world, you don't get rewarded for using long, "sophisticated" words. Instead you lose readers.

Does this mean you need to simplify your thoughts? Absolutely not. It means that while you have a wealth of choices with which to express your precise meaning, you must work to be as clear as possible through words that really communicate this meaning to other people.

The English language was built on short words (see the Sidelight on "Why English Has So Many Words"), and, to this day, we seem to trust those words most and find the "fancy" words suspicious or even pretentious. **To succeed, use the one- and two-syllable words as much as you can and consciously use the longer words when you need them because a shorter word won't work, or you want the effect.** Just as sentence variety makes writing more interesting, a peppering of longer words can spark things up.

SIDELIGHT: WHY ENGLISH HAS SO MANY WORDS, AND HOW THAT AFFECTS YOUR WRITING

The English vocabulary is unusually rich and there are often abundant word choices for expressing the same thought. By way of comparison, English has about 200,000 words while French, for example, has half as many.

The short words mostly come from our Anglo-Saxon legacy, the original base of English. These include words like man, bad, good, work, dog, big, eat, love, in, out. Some Scandinavian additions arrived with the Viking invasions (leg, crawl, trust, take).

But many of the language's longer words derive from French—via the Norman invasions—and because the Normans occupied England as ruling aristocrats, they introduced words relating to government, the military and sophisticated living. For example, justice, felony, fraternity, sovereign, royalty, interior, elegant.

It's estimated that while the Anglo-Saxon words compose only 1% of today's English, they remain the fundamental words and half of what we typically write consists of those words. As Bill Bryson says in his interesting book, *The Mother Tongue: English and How It Got That Way*, "To this day we have an almost instinctive preference for the older Anglo-Saxon phrases."

Find the Words You Need

A big element in editing your own work—as well as other's people's writing—is to review the document and substitute short plain words for the long complicated ones. This is a basic way to achieve the rhythm you want: the word movement that sounds smooth when read aloud and pulls people through your message at warp speed.

ACTION TIME

Think of one- and two-syllable substitutes for these words.

Approximately	Demonstrate	Requirement
Utilize	Facilitate	Experiment
Substantial	Subsequent	Indication
Aggregate	Culmination	Disseminate
Genuine	Subsequent	Possibility
Terminate	Eliminate	Construct
Remediate	Convoluted	Imminently
Prevalent	Verbose	Fundamental
Opportunity	Materialize	Additionally
Fraudulent	Initiate	Optimum
Competencies	Optimize	Curriculum
Assistance	Substantiate	

Note that you don't necessarily need to always use the shorter versions. I've chosen to use the long way round a number of times in this chapter, and throughout the book. But your choices should be conscious.

How can you find the right words? Build a repertoire of useful short words that are often needed in everyday business writing and make a habit of using them. For example, "use" is often better than "utilize." "Hard" generally works better than "difficult." Instead of "investigate," you may want to say "study" or "track" or "look into" or "follow up."

Notice, too—as is the case with "investigate"—a simpler way of saying something may mean using a phrase instead of a single word.

And, use a thesaurus—nothing could be easier to do online. Just Google the word and a choice of free resources pops up with enough choices to overwhelm.

As you write or after you've finished a draft, check the Readability Statistics box. If it shows that your piece is 12th-grade level and will only be understood by 20% of readers, note the stat for word length—how many average characters per word your sample contains. To improve your readability, substitute shorter words and shorten your sentences.

Employing Colorful Words

Let's agree at the outset that colorful language is rarely needed for most business writing. You want to use concrete, familiar words and not come across as pretentious. This helps ensure that a range of people will understand your messages, including those whose native language is not English.

However, graphic wording can be useful in marketing copy and other writing where you want to stimulate readers' imagination. It's helpful to be aware of some techniques that creative writers use, even though you may not often draw on them. Also, developing your awareness of how language is used to influence you is worthwhile.

Choosing more specific words with more "atmosphere" is one way to make material more colorful. Since English offers so many options, you can check for similes as you write or when you have the first draft down.

Another way to enliven your writing is to use interesting modifiers—descriptive words. In general, business writers are told to minimize use of these adjectives and adverbs. This is valid: They slow reading down and often create a sense of overkill.

Mark Twain's statement—"If you find an adjective, kill it"—is often quoted by writing instructors. But he didn't mean that all such words should be cut, just the unproductive ones. In business writing, too, if used well, modifiers help bring copy alive. A good way to go about this is to choose words that engage the senses and lead the reader to taste, see, hear, feel and even smell what you're writing about. This is a staple technique for fiction writers.

For example, you don't need a context to form mental images for words like the following:

- glittering
- squeamish
- sluggish
- tangy
- salty
- heroic
- gaunt
- grungy
- sneakily
- slimy
- razor-thin
- twitchy
- squishy
- cranky

Your thesaurus is your friend here. Look up "big," for example, and you'll have a choice of enormous, huge, colossal, astronomical, titanic, mountainous, or ample, broad and stout.

Notice that some of these words are "prejudicial"; they incline readers to see what you're describing in negative or positive ways. To say that a report's documentation is "razor-thin"; that the market is "twitchy"; or that a new company venture is "heroic" carries more meaning than if the documentation is simply "light," the market "uneven" or the venture is merely worthwhile. Be careful not to use such words if you don't want the connotations.

A third way to make language more colorful is to use interesting or slightly surprising phrases. Examples: Aggressively selfish; risky collision; redemptive ignorance; expedient delay; blindingly oblivious; ironclad indifference; reptilian charm; spaghetti thin thinking; deliberately deaf.

Fourth, you can actively create extended graphic images. Think of a helpful comparison. A newspaper article about a fossil discovery, for example, does this simply: " . . . the dinosaur, the size of a gigantic turkey, was a meat-eating creature that lived more than 65 million years ago." Giving people graphic images can make concepts easier to grasp and more memorable.

Here's a sentence I wrote recently:

> Long Island established the American suburban pattern, characterized by numerous small communities, each absorbed in its own local affairs.

The revision:

> Long Island set the pattern for America's suburbs: an enormous patchwork of small communities, looking inward.

For some people, using graphic language, whether in print or speech, is a natural talent. The best storytellers flaunt this skill and we love them for it. But for most of us it's work: going an extra step or two beyond the clear and simple. It takes extra time to plumb the depth of your meaning, connect disparate ideas imaginatively and, probably, research the wording options.

And yes, when you aim for more specific words, you often end up using the long French or Latinate words that I cautioned against. But there is a loophole— *sprinkle your writing with the more complex, specific words when that serves your goal and suits your audience.*

And keep in mind that the true masters of writing can stick to the simplest language and yet paint unforgettable mental images.

SIMPLE CAN BE PROFOUND: AN EXAMPLE

Hope is the thing with feathers that perches in the soul / and sings the tunes without the words / and never stops at all.

—Emily Dickinson

THE VERB: CHOOSE VIGOROUS ONES

Using strong, active verbs is another way to inject life into all your writing and by far the best way to spark it up. Unless it creates an effect that doesn't support your goal, when you can deploy a strong verb, just do it.

ACTION VERBS

Consider "grumble," "squash," "enflame," "twitch," "droop," "slither," "tantalize" and "mope"—they create mental images and a feeling of action or "being there." But you may not find many occasions to employ such verbs. How does the active verb idea apply to your everyday business writing?

You have a mountain of choices. For example:

Instead of move, you could say galvanize, rush, accelerate, lunge, streak, scramble

Instead of tell . . . expose, instruct, enlighten, narrate, recount, lecture

Instead of introduce . . . unmask, reveal, uncover, divulge, bring into play

Instead of make . . . originate, invent, compose, build, fabricate

Instead of stop . . . halt, pause, conclude, block, stonewall, drop, shut off

Instead of hesitate . . . dither, hedge, vacillate, teeter, waver, wobble, pussyfoot

Instead of decide . . . , map, settle on, mull, figure, ponder, weigh

---

Improving the way you use verbs gives you one of the best tools for improving all your writing. Here are some techniques to know about.

Use verbs to carry the weight of every sentence, and use the simplest, most active form of the verb.

Which sentence is better in each of the following pairs?

1. Jane walked quickly to the exit.
2. Jane darted to the exit.

1. We managed to figure out how much the new computer system will cost.
2. We figured out what the new computer system will cost.

1. Many people are resistant to reading on-screen.
2. Many people resist on-screen reading.

1. A subject line should really be focused on letting people know what the message is about.
2. Focus subject lines on what the message is about.

In each case, the second sentence is more direct and compact. By simplifying the verb and focusing on the action, you can eliminate unnecessary wordiness and pick up a sentence rhythm that carries readers along.

Here's a more complicated example:

> This mistake has put us in the position of having to explain why business in the last quarter went down radically.

Notice the clues that tell you this sentence needs help. If you read it aloud, it dictates the singsong rhythm of poor writing. When you look at it analytically, you see that some parts are obviously awkward and wordy:

> This mistake has put us in the position of having to explain why business in the last quarter went down radically.

Spending a few seconds thinking about the sentence's meaning might suggest other alternatives, such as

> This mistake **forces us to explain** why business in the last quarter **plummeted.**

Simply substituting these stronger verbs for the roundabout versions cuts the word count from 21 to 13, produces a fast read with a natural rhythm and gets the idea across more vividly. Notice that many sentences with weak verbs can be fixed by using the present tense. "Resist" works better than "are resistant to"; "forces us to explain" is much better than "has put us in the position of having to explain."

Here are some more clues that your verbs need to be strengthened and that you're cluttering your sentences:

Too many words ending in *-ion.* For example:

> The function of the communication department is the production of newsletters.

This can better read:

> The communications department's job is to produce newsletters.

Generally, try to use only one *-ion* word per sentence.

Too many words ending in *-ing* (gerunds), such as

> We're implementing a system for tracking how well we're measuring performance.

Why not:

> The new system will track how well we're measuring performance.

Restricting yourself to one *-ing* word per sentence can help readability a lot. Often you can eliminate gerunds altogether, which is even better. The present tense may work well. Try to substitute it for *-ing* words whenever you can. For example, the above sentence could be improved this way:

The new system will track how well we measure performance.

Too many words ending in *-ed:*

> The subject line should really be focused on telling readers what they might be interested in knowing.

Better:

> Focus subject lines on what might interest readers.

The wordy, passive-sounding phrases "should really be" and "what they may be interested in" also tell you this sentence is poor, and so does the whole sentence's rhythm when read aloud. The nice thing about improving your sentences in the grammar-free way is that you can arrive at a conclusion from many avenues. Follow the clues that work best for you.

Too many words like "of" and "to" (prepositions):

> Our office is ready to advise staff members on how to use the benefit program to the maximum degree.

Better:

> We advise staff members on best use of the benefit program.

> To measure the progress of the project, a system of documentation will be implemented.

Better:

> To measure the project's progress, we'll document it.

In cases where you're repeating "to" and "of" constructions, you can often improve your writing by cutting what isn't needed or substituting words that make reading easier. You can often eliminate the "of" phrases by using *'s,* as in the last example—"progress of the project" became "project's progress." "The crown of the king" works better as "the king's crown."

Too many "ands" interfere with understanding:

> We're ready to communicate to all stakeholders and interested parties, and will ensure that good information and current thinking are available to the media and the public.

The solution here is often to break sentences up. Substituting words such as "also" and "as well as" can help, but don't depend on them too much. And as in all the examples, think about another way to say the same thing more clearly. For example:

> We're ready to communicate to stakeholders and interested parties. We'll deliver good information and current thinking to the media, plus update the public.

Too many sentences built on "to be" verbs—"is," "were," "will be," "should be," "has been." And too many built on "to have" verbs.

Without struggling to understand the passive tense, another slippery road to follow, you can develop an awareness of the traps these constructions drive you into. Usually, when you see more than one "to be" or "to have" verb in a sentence, change it. (Once may even be unnecessary.) Consider:

> There are strong indications that this is not the best time to ask for a raise.

vs.

> Clearly, this is not the best time to ask for a raise.

> It's hard to measure how much the community was pained by the decision.

vs.

> The decision pained the community immeasurably.

> To have edited your work after having written it is always advised. Upon review, you'll find that mistakes have been made.

vs.

> Always edit your work after writing it. You'll find that you've made mistakes.

> But editing is not a subject many of us were ever taught in our lives.

vs.

> But few of us ever learned to edit.

Also develop your inner ear for sounds that repeat. Too many words ending in *-ly* or *-y* can make sentences awkward and indicate adjectives or adverbs that should be cut. Repeating the word "by" also sounds bad and suggests a need to rework. An extreme example:

> The report by the committee was fortunately generally positive and gave us a blueprint to revamp policy by rethinking the guidelines.

How would you rewrite that?

EDITING: MANY WAYS CAN WORK

Keep in mind that there are nearly always more ways than one to solve a problem, in writing as in life. Editing is nowhere near a science, though you may want to argue whether it's an art. Certainly it rates as a craft.

Here's a sentence that I asked a group of professional writers to rewrite:

> A performance system will allow the development of innovative training techniques and methodologies and allow companies flexibility in tailoring their training to the specific job duties of their employees.

Here are three different results. All are workable.

> A performance system will allow companies to develop innovative and job-specific training techniques for employees.

> A performance system gives companies access to new and innovative training techniques and enables them to tailor training to specific responsibilities.

> A performance system allows companies to develop new training techniques. Companies also have more room to create customized training for each job.

Notice that each interprets the original sentence somewhat differently. Editing other people's work is often a challenge. If it's poorly written, the meaning can be hard to pin down and a rewrite might slant it wrong. When you revise your own work, it's a relative snap—you usually know what you meant.

In the next chapter, we'll move on to the bigger picture and turn sentences into paragraphs, and paragraphs into whole documents.

PRACTICE OPPORTUNITIES

I. Edit This Paragraph

Aim to make this letter clearer, improve wording, cut repetition and make it move faster. Also, figure out the core message and recast the paragraph to express it better. Then compare your version with your classmates'.

Dear Parent:

We have established a special phone communication system to provide additional opportunities for parent input. During this year, we will give added emphasis to the goal of communication and utilize a variety of means to accomplish this goal. Your inputs, from the unique position as a parent, will help us to plan and implement an educational plan that meets the needs of your child and enables him or her to reach their full potential. An open dialogue, feedback and sharing of information between parents and teachers will enable us to work with your child in the most effective manner.

II. Play with the Readability Index

A. Use the Readability Index to determine what grade level your favorite magazine is written for. Then check out the *Wall Street Journal,* your city's daily newspaper and online publications and blogs that you like.

B. Discuss results in class: What surprises you? Were the publications consistent in their grade-level appeal, or did different parts of them vary?

III. Rewrite Exercise

Select one page from a recent piece of your own writing; class work is fine. Edit it according to your best judgment based on the principles covered in this book, especially this chapter. Try to improve your use of words, create better sentences and use verbs more effectively.

Then use the Readability Index to check out the stats on your original piece, and the newer version. Is there a difference in the word length, words per sentence, total number of words, percentage of passive verbs and the readability indicators?

If you do not yet have an average of 22 or fewer words per sentence, and/or the percentage of passive verbs is more than 10%, rewrite the selection again and see if you can hit these targets.

IV: Write a Memo to Yourself

We all have our own individual writing problems. Self-editing is much easier once we recognize those problems and notice how we repeat the same mistakes. So review this chapter against your own writing patterns and think about which specific ideas can help you improve. Then write a memo to yourself describing how you plan to make your writing work better in terms of sentence structure, rhythm, word choice, use of verbs, unnecessary use of gerunds, and so on.

V. Sentence Fixer-Uppers

Try your hand at improving these sentences—many of which I wrote in first-draft form. Focus on improving the verbs, but also cut unnecessary words, use shorter words where possible and simplify each sentence.

Watch for the clues described above, including intrusive use of *-ing, -ed, -ion,* and the constructions involving "has" and "is" words.

1. There isn't an exact number yet of how many people we will need to hire, but we are going to try to keep the number as minimal as possible.

2. It has become a rather difficult time for our industry.

3. We're very appreciative of your interest in the products our company produces.

4. The subject line of an e-mail is the biggest factor in determining whether the message gets read or not.

5. Want to put your expertise in the spotlight?

6. Please note that the central speech you will present should focus on the new style of leadership.

7. This experience demonstrates that it's dangerous to ignore the competition.

8. We gave them warning that it would be necessary to develop additional funding sources to establish the new service.

9. You might have hobbies that lead you to an in-depth understanding of a subject.

10. When writing to a prospective employer, ask yourself, do they have a need that they may not have perceived yet that I could fill?

11. Our assumption was that better writing results from having practiced more.

12. The amount of interaction in contemporary office contexts is continually diminishing, because of technology.

13. This method will demonstrate the need for clarity.

14. In addition to their financial contributions to the candidate, the support group had the intention of increasing her public profile.

15. His presentation on the skills of negotiation has been scheduled to be delivered in March.

16. We need to be able to understand the perspective of a variety of stakeholders and what needs to happen in order to move forward.

17. New development is making our suburban sprawl become even worse.

18. Few things affect the quality of our life as much as the removal of intrusive sound in our environment.

19. People who do not have the support of a partner accord more value to their friends.

20. The work of the lab is to develop nano-engineered particles that can be much more powerful in catalyzing combustion.

21. Our greatest awareness of the complexity of movement is a by-product of watching babies' development.

22. The realtors also facilitated the legislation that enabled the work to be completed.

23. Jones needed to do something to revitalize the association.

24. We review your publications and websites and advise you on how to improve them.

25. The supervisor did an investigation of the accident and came to the conclusion that the agency had been in violation of safety regulations.

Chapter 5

THE WHOLE PICTURE

PULLING YOUR BEST MESSAGE TOGETHER

LEARN HOW TO . . .

- ➤ Create short paragraphs
- ➤ Build in good transitions
- ➤ Avoid word and tone traps
- ➤ Edit your own writing

> *When I see a paragraph shrinking under my eyes like a strip of bacon in a skillet, I know I'm on the right track.*
>
> —Peter DeVries, comic novelist

THE SHORT PARAGRAPH

Now that you've developed your sentence awareness, it's time to move on to the larger unit.

You may have been told to develop a "topic" or "thesis" sentence for each paragraph, build a single idea on it and end with a conclusion. That works, if you understand what a thesis statement is, but it's not an easy concept.

Alternatively, start with the readability premise. Research tells us that the best length for a paragraph is three to five sentences. In many cases, even fewer sentences are best for the first paragraph—the lead. When you keep your paragraphs short, it's easier to stay on track and recognize when you stray off your defined path.

Knowing when to break your paragraphs, or "grafs," becomes more commonsensical when they're brief. Basically, start a new graf when it feels logical to do so.

Typically, this is when you're beginning a new thought or subthought, or moving to a detail or clarification.

If you're the kind of writer who tends to spill it all out in a few long, breathless gasps, no problem: Consistently review your draft with an eye toward the white space. Have you produced a dense document with long paragraphs that break only a few times per page? Then splinter the material into shorter paragraphs of three to five sentences. Next, look at each paragraph to see if it makes sense or needs to be clarified.

Every document gains from short paragraphing in a number of ways:

1. It more readily engages the eye, and therefore the interest of readers. A packed document with scant white space is challenging, even forbidding to the modern sensibility. Your reader might choose not to read the message at all.

2. It heightens the chance of keeping your reader with you, because the message seems to move so much faster.

3. A "spacey" document is far easier to follow and grasp than an unbroken dense one, and therefore more likely to succeed, whatever the goal.

In addition to checking that each graf works, check whether the grafs lead one to the next, and relate neatly. Brief paragraphs are easy to move around so you can experiment with making your message read more logically. You'll often find that the last sentence of one paragraph works better when you move it to begin the paragraph that follows.

And there's a magic tool for melding all those paragraphs into a convincing, flowing, logical message that makes what you write seem persuasive and even inevitable: the transition.

TRANSITIONS: WORDS, PHRASES AND DEVICES

Transitions are an important part of the infrastructure that connects your ideas, examples and overall argument. Take care with them, because successful writing requires that all connections are clear to your audience. You never want your readers to wonder, "Why is she telling me that?" or substituting their own reasoning for your own, even unconsciously. Ambiguous connections generate misinterpretation, or indifference.

Good transitions, on the other hand, instantly improve all your writing because they smooth it out and eliminate the choppy, disconnected effect that signals poor writing (and thinking).

Transitions are critical at the sentence, paragraph and full-document levels. For example, you could write,

> John doesn't like classical music. He went to the concert his friends chose.

The two thoughts don't connect. Instead they could read,

> John went to the concert his friends chose, **even though** he doesn't like classical music.

or

> John doesn't like classical music. **Nevertheless**, he went to the concert his friends chose.

On the sentence level, we typically use transition words instinctively. But connecting paragraphs well can take more deliberate thought.

It may be appropriate to end a paragraph with a transition, as an introduction to what comes next. Note the transitions between sentences as well as at the end of the paragraph:

> The White contract is scheduled for signing on the 30th. **However**, some problems have come up that should be discussed at Friday's meeting. **In the meantime,** we can prepare for that conversation **with the following procedure.**

In many cases, transitions should be used to begin a paragraph so it links to what preceded it. Among the useful words and phrases to draw on for both opening and closing a graf are,

> To sum up . . . in review . . . finally . . . in general . . . in other words . . . equally important
>
> To the contrary . . . on the other hand . . . conversely . . . nevertheless . . . in spite of . . . otherwise . . . unfortunately . . . regrettably
>
> Also . . . additionally . . . further . . . specifically . . . for example . . . accordingly . . . moreover . . . besides
>
> Later . . . the next step is . . . recently . . . in the future . . . afterward . . . at that point . . . so far
>
> To illustrate . . . for example . . . similarly . . . conversely . . . accordingly . . . in conclusion . . . finally

Some transitional words and phrases carry connotations that can help convey the tone you want:

> Best of all . . . in fact . . . truthfully . . . of course . . . naturally . . . chiefly . . . inevitably . . . and yet . . . happily . . . it goes without saying . . . surprisingly

In any message that matters (and as you know, I think they all do) check how each paragraph connects to the one that precedes and the one that follows. If you can't make these relationships clear, you may need to rethink your content, and your own understanding of the subject.

In long documents like reports and proposals, use transitions to ensure that the sections connect logically. Go out of your way to clarify the links with phrases that act as transitional devices:

> Here's why . . . the result . . . our conclusions . . . there's more . . . what did we learn? . . . how will this help you? . . . the solution

You can also use whole sentences to introduce a section and tie it into the document's logical pattern. Apply some creativity to these transitions, and they'll really advance your cause:

> Our conclusions are based on the following trials.
>
> We've focused on similar projects for five years and learned a number of lessons.
>
> The sales projections are of particular interest.
>
> Here are the questions most frequently asked—and the answers.
>
> A brief review of the problem's background is helpful.
>
> It sounds great. But . . .
>
> That's what we used to think, too.
>
> Setting up a sequence via a numbered list is another good tool for promoting clarity and holding a document, or section, together:
>
> Four factors weigh most heavily in making the decision.
>
> The process can be completed in seven stages.
>
> Here's the plan for the next eight months.

PRACTICE TIME: KNOW YOUR TRANSITIONS

Find an online article that interests you and scan it for transitional words, phrases and devices. Can you recognize what role each serves? Can you think of alternatives?

One more great benefit to transitions: Consciously used to better communicate a message, they can help you organize your material more easily. In sum, good transitions are essential to convincing written material.

AVOID WORD TRAPS

Buzzwords and Jargon

As you write, keep some important principles of word choice in mind.

Avoid clichés, buzzwords, jargon and just plain overworked phrases whenever possible. Why? They bore, confuse and conceal meaning. Whatever industry we belong to, we typically absorb a specialized repertoire of words and terminology. This is necessary and positive. It enables us to exchange specific information built on common understanding. A lawyer's "inside" language naturally differs from a biologist's, a financial manager's, a graphic designer's and so on.

But industry shorthand can create problems.

Problem 1: Using a private industry code to communicate with a client, a funding agency, a journalist, investors, other stakeholders or the public.

Here's an example from education, a passage (admittedly out of context) from an alumni magazine issued by a major university's Department of English. The article is about how writing instruction must adapt to changing technology.

> Apply this domestic generational paradigm to the English Department and we begin to see how the ethos of space might affect students and teachers, perhaps even an entire discipline.

It's easy to laugh at how people in other industries use jargon, but harder to notice when we do it ourselves. A business example:

> This change will allow us to better leverage our talent base in an area where developmental roles are under way and strategically focuses us toward the upcoming Business System transition where Systems literacy and accuracy will be essential to maintain and to further improve service levels to our customer base going forward.

Q&A: IF YOU WERE WONDERING . . .

Q: With so much business writing dominated by buzzwords and jargon, doesn't that create the industry standard? Why should I invest time writing differently?

A: First, for the same reason that it's good to write clearly and powerfully in general: you gain an advantage over the competition. Being a standout writer gives you more opportunities, too.

Second, various corporate catastrophes over the past decade, from oil spills to CEO personal scandals to fraud revelations, have led everyone to distrust business. To establish or re-establish credibility demands that organizations be honest, transparent, and clear. Writing jargon-laden drivel makes you part of the problem. Writing well makes you part of the solution—whatever work you do.

Problem 2: Using code words with ambiguous meanings that can be interpreted in different ways. This undermines clarity. "Protocol," for example, has different meanings to a diplomat, medical researcher and computer specialist.

Consider the word "overload." To physical trainers, it means building fitness through progressive weight bearing. To computer scientists, it's the use of a single definition for different classes of objects. To some college professors, "overload" means teaching more courses than the base number required. Not to mention that "overload" is also a specific chess tactic, and a Pakistani band.

Of course, context usually tells us which meaning is intended—but if we're talking to someone from a different field of expertise, or the public, this can be a costly assumption.

Problem 3: Using jargon and buzzwords to veil our meaning or avoid having one—such as when we say nothing at all in a supposedly impressive way. Take a phrase like "cost-effective, end-to-end, value-added services." Hundreds of thousands of companies describe themselves this way in print and online: What have they said? Nothing, or worse, because using the same jargon for every service makes them sound identical.

Here's an example from the information technology (IT) world:

> These visible IT capabilities along with IT participation in the project identification process can drive the infusion of IT leverage on revenue improvement in much the same way as IT has leveraged cost cutting and efficiency.

And from another annual report:

The company is maniacally focused on ensuring that all of this software meets stringent benchmarks and product criteria for best-in-class ease of use, simple installation and overall ease of ownership to ensure that mission-critical networks are safeguarded and protected not only by redundancy, but also by the most innovative technology available today.

GOING DEEPER: BUZZWORD SENSITIVITY TRAINING 101

A first step toward stamping out empty rhetoric and buzzwords is to recognize them in your own environment. Here's a beginning list of expressions you should sidestep when possible. For each, think of at least one alternative. (You may find you need to use several words instead of a single one.) For a worthwhile group activity, share results in a small or large group, and extend the list by adding more business buzzwords and good substitutions. Compile a single, alphabetized list of words to avoid—and better choices—to distribute to all class members.

Optimize

Seat at the table

Incentivize

Organizational alignment

360-degree review

Offline

Innovative

Solution

Leveraging

Right-size

Drill down

Functionality

Matrices

Paradigm shift

Synergy

Doubling down

(Continued)

(Continued)

24-7

Push the envelope

Ramp up

Transparent communication

Re-engineer

Cascade down

Outreach

After you do the exercise, download this resource from www.plainenglish.co.uk: *The A to Z of Alternative Words*. It shows alternatives to many common but overly wordy expressions.

Empty rhetoric can consist of meaningless claims with no substance to back them up, a buzzword pile and a stringing together of phrases that any company in any industry can use:

"Leveraging core competencies." "Optimizing functionalities." "Synergistic outside-the-box best practice." There are even online games you can play to come up with such combinations through "buzzword generators." But many businesspeople generate the meaningless combinations with no humorous intent whatsoever.

How do you avoid the jargon trap?

It can be challenging. Here are some tactics:

1. Know what you really mean and figure out how to say it most clearly. When you're drafting generalizations that have no true substance, face it and think: How exactly would I explain this to my brother, or my friend, using simple language that requires no translation?

2. Be as concrete as you can. What is truly original or different about your product? What does it do? What do *you* do, what can you really offer?

3. Find the facts and use them. "97% of our customers told us they'd buy our product again" is a lot better than "we've got a phenomenal satisfaction rate" (provided you can actually cite such a study).

4. Go for evidence of some kind. "We've been recognized for innovative products three times in the last five years by the Consumer Advice Board" is more

convincing than "we are the most innovative." "We have partners in 23 countries on five continents" works better than "we're really international."

It takes thinking to figure out what you want to say and the best way to say it. Spouting vague generalities is the easy way out. Determine not to take that path.

THINK GLOBAL: RECOGNIZE IDIOMS

Using overworked words and phrases for "domestic" audiences is like white noise. It fills space and drowns out perception. But for audiences whose native language is not English, or who need the English translated, using clichés, idioms and slang can be disastrous. Many commonly used expressions mean something different when translated—or mean nothing at all.

Since so much of what we write will be read by an international audience, it's even more important to take care with clichés and jargon. Moreover, today most organizations' internal audiences include many non-native speakers. So you must often find alternative ways of expressing an idea rather than taking the first one that comes to mind.

Here are a few idioms that can confuse readers whose first language is not English.

Against the clock

Draw the line

By word of mouth

Face value

Lose track of

Make a stand

Zero in on

Set the record straight

Out of place

On the shelf

In a nutshell

Get to the bottom of

Let something ride

(Continued)

(Continued)

    Gain ground

    Bear in mind

    Explore every avenue

    Across the board

    Change of heart

    At every turn

Even this smattering suggests how entrenched many idiomatic expressions are in our thinking. The idea of eliminating all of them, even from a short document, is challenging. But **an awareness of clichés and idioms will help you improve your writing, particularly when your audience is diverse or the document will be translated.**

Once again, the antidote is to get behind the meaning of what you want to say and find the clearest, least ambiguous way to put it. Look particularly for multiword expressions and write more basically.

Will the writing lose color and interest without idioms? For native English speakers who read well, yes. For all others, the loss of color matters much less than clarity. This is yet another example of how you must shape your writing to your audience.

AVOID TONE TRAPS

The Meant-to-be-funny

Humor is a tremendous asset for a speech, a presentation, a conversation. Unfortunately, unless you're a talented and confident humor writer, it's a risk to use it in writing.

A piece of writing lacks the advantages of personal interaction. There is no facial expression to underscore or counter the words, no subtle body language to suggest your true meaning, and above all, no tone of voice to communicate the real message.

This is a particular drawback with using irony and sarcasm. There's no way to indicate that you're "just joking" and no way to soften the message. What would be funny in person can easily come across as insulting or cruel. Especially because e-mail (like social media) is infinitely forwardable and accessible, a moment's entertainment can have unforeseeable consequences.

So the rule: In business writing, avoid the temptation to make fun of someone or something others might care about. Don't joke at someone else's expense.

Prejudicial Wording

Don't undercut your message by building in a negative slant, consciously or not. Suppose, for example, you receive an e-mail that begins,

> As I already told you . . .
>
> This is to reinforce our conversation . . .
>
> You did not provide . . .
>
> You are apparently unaware that . . .
>
> I am at a loss to understand . . .
>
> Don't fail to let me know . . .
>
> As you should have foreseen . . .

Obviously, you'll be on full defensive even before reading the rest of the message. The lesson: Avoid this tone and wording. It's not a productive way to address people, no matter what their relationship to you.

Amazingly, however, companies will often write to customers in a similar off-putting manner:

> This is to inform you that we are unable to ship your product at this time . . .
>
> Our policy clearly states that purchases are only refundable if . . .
>
> For your information, we no longer provide support services for . . .
>
> Please understand that we cannot make exceptions . . .

The substance of a message may in fact be negative, as in the foregoing examples. If this is the case, then take special care to present the information in as positive a way as possible.

SUCCESS TIP: REIGN IN YOUR EMOTIONS

In business, the line between expressing passion and emotion can be a fine one. Your colleagues, superiors and subordinates certainly want to feel your conviction, enthusiasm and confidence. But these qualities must appear to be

(Continued)

(Continued)

based on an objective reality—not personal investment and feelings.

Obviously, it's bad to lose your temper at a meeting, act defensively, sulk or cast blame. In the business world, like the political, such behavior marks you as the loser. Results can be even worse if you send a hostile message. It can circulate or rankle forever.

Never let what you write show anger. Never criticize anyone in writing (unless it's part of a structured, planned evaluation process). Work hard to maintain a balanced, reasonable tone. Avoid words that can be negatively interpreted, don't sound judgmental and monitor your messages so they don't betray any attitude, emotion or feeling that will work against your interests.

Am I recommending that you act hypocritically? Not really. You want to build better relationships, not worse. When you're tempted to send a harsh message, take a minute to think about how you'd feel if you received it. This pause can be a critical part of your editing process.

The first statement, for example, might (if the facts justify it) be phrased,

> We're delighted that you've ordered our Product #65, but sorry that because it's proved so popular, we are unable to fill orders as quickly as we'd like. Each #65 is individually crafted . . .

Here's how one smart retailer responded, in part, to a return:

> We'd love another opportunity to please you. Please accept this offer of free shipping on your next purchase in our catalog or online at . . .

Note that if any company produces a flow of impersonal these-are-the-rules-and-we-don't-care-if-you-like-them-or-not messages to its customers, then policies should be reviewed. The marketplace is too competitive for this approach.

The Pompous and Pretentious

We often see overblown, pretentious language that combines long words with awkward construction. This undercuts a message. It also fails to communicate when used in place of real substance.

Here's an example—It's the third sentence of a long lead paragraph from a *Wall Street Journal* opinion piece called "Toward Sustainable Capitalism," by former Vice President Al Gore and his business partner David Blood.

> At the most basic level, however, capitalism has become the world's economic ideology of choice primarily because it demonstrably unlocks a higher fraction of the human potential with ubiquitous organizational incentives that reward hard work, ingenuity and innovation.

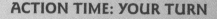

ACTION TIME: YOUR TURN

Rewrite the preceding sentence paying attention to word choice, tone, and sentence structure. See if you can express the same thought more effectively in half the length.

How to avoid writing like that? To recap: Use simple, short words; simple, straightforward, short sentences; simple, clear construction. And remember the clues that tell you to look for a fix: Read it aloud, notice repetitions (in this case, for example, three words ending in -*y* occur in the same line). Check the Readability Index as covered in Chapter 4 (which will tell you the sentence has 38 words, requires a 12th-grade reading level and 0% of readers will understand it).

Many different signals can tell you that it's time to rewrite.

The Cold and Impersonal

People today value messages that feel authentic and personal. Whether you're writing a memo explaining a company benefit, a promotional piece selling a product or a letter responding to a complaint, make it personal. Often this means taking the "you" viewpoint:

For example, rather than,

> The new policy on filing for overtime claims is . . .

try,

> To file an overtime claim, you need to know . . .

For pitching a product,

> The newly designed Inca 247 offers a number of features to help the graphic designer.

doesn't work as well as

> Inca 247 saves you 20% of your graphic design project time and . . .

This tactic ties right in with your need to instantly engage readers and pull them through your document. Remember, when people decide whether a message is worth reading, self-interest rules.

VIEW FROM THE FIELD: USING LANGUAGE THAT CONNECTS WITH PEOPLE

I don't know the rules of grammar . . . If you're trying to persuade people to do something, or buy something, it seems to me you should use their language, the language they use every day, the language in which they think. We try to write in the vernacular.

Our business is infested with idiots who try to impress by using pretentious jargon.

—Advertising pioneer David Ogilvy,
quoted by Kenneth Roman in *The King of Madison Avenue: David Ogilvy and the Making of Modern Advertising*

A PROCESS FOR EDITING YOUR OWN WORK

Many people are wary of editing, as if it requires some rare mystical skill. But just as with writing, a strategic approach can guide you through.

Knowing you will improve your document and fix problems later is liberating. It frees you to be more spontaneous and even experimental when developing a first draft. This is true whether you're a get-it-all-down-at-once type of writer, or one who crafts each sentence thoughtfully.

Here is how to think about the editing process.

1. Plan your time to allow for editing. On a typical project, many professionals allocate a third of the available time for planning, a third for drafting, and at least a third for editing and rewrite. If you're developing a big project, build in a good amount of time for editing at the end.

2. Give it some space. When a document is important, try to put it aside for a week, or a few days. Distance helps you be objective. When you read the draft after a lapse, errors of tone and substance will pop out, as well as technical mistakes. Even a significant e-mail should be stashed for a few hours so your eyes are fresh and your emotional antennae are up.

3. Switch roles. To be your own editor, approach the piece as if you've never seen it before. Don't be influenced by how hard a particular section was to produce. In fact, many fiction writers follow the advice, "Kill your little darlings," meaning that passages to which they are especially attached are suspect—probably distracting from the piece's overall intent—and should be cut.

> *I like to cite chapter and verse with all the proper punctuation laid in. If nothing else, it's a demonstration of both your IQ and your writing skills. How can you trust someone who doesn't bother to spell correctly or can't manage to lay out a simple declarative sentence?*
>
> —Kinsey Milhone (fictional private detective in *N is for Noon* by Sue Grafton)

4. Print it out. It's tempting to edit onscreen, but material reads differently in print form and mistakes become easier to spot. Of course, you need not do this with routine e-mails. But consider it with letters, reports, blog posts, website copy and more.

5. Plan to edit important material in successive stages. When you make changes, they usually require further changes. New mistakes are often introduced and must be spotted. And every time you review your new version, you'll find more opportunities to improve the language and make the content more persuasive.

6. Get a reader. Backup is invaluable—scout your environment for a colleague, partner or friend to read your important documents and provide honest feedback. Find out how your message is perceived. And extra proofing is always an excellent thing. Offer to perform this service in return.

Now let's look at a practical editing strategy to use, complete with some professional tricks of the trade. Note that a garden-variety e-mail might need just a quick run-through, while a major document such as a proposal, or a résumé, demands careful step-by-step attention. But do commit yourself to at least re-reading everything you write with an eye toward improving content and fixing mistakes.

Practical Editing Stage 1: Review Your Substance

Start by focusing first on the big picture—content and tone. Conveniently enough, you can recap the same checklist that led you through the planning and writing processes:

Goal: What comes across to the reader—does the gist of the message embody your goal, the reason you're writing?

Will what's included accomplish your purpose?

Are the points relevant? Anything missing?

Is there too much information? Does anything distract from the goal?

Is the sequence logical? Convincing?

And really important: What is the overall impact on your company, and you, of broadcasting this information? As companies post more and more content on their websites in the interest of transparency, misjudgment is common.

It's a problem on social media sites, too, for individuals. People post information (and pictures) for an audience of peers, but may lose job opportunities when employers check them out.

Audience: Is the content right for that audience? The level of detail, and assumed knowledge base? Have you considered possible audience sensitivities?

Tone: Appropriate to your goal and audience? Can anything be misinterpreted? Is the tone right for the relationship, and for relationship building? Courteous and friendly? Positive in spirit?

 ACTION TIME: EVALUATE AND REWRITE

Read this message from a company's technical communications department to the rest of the organization, and evaluate—based on the content—where the writer went wrong in terms of goal, audience, tone and structure. Try rewriting this document. What should the writer have said? What should he have left out? What information seems to be missing?

Subject: Videoconferencing

For your information, the Technical Communications Center offers a Video-conferencing Service. Next are some guidelines that should be followed when facilitating a videoconference.

1. The enclosed videoconferencing package should contain the following:
   a. Three Registration Forms
   b. Guide to Videoconferencing
   c. Videoconference Listing for the Current Year

2. When you have received this package, it is important to fill out a Videoconference Registration Form. This form must be filled out completely. All information on this sheet is pertinent to the booking.

3. The Videoconference Registration Form should either be mailed, e-mailed or faxed to our office. Because dates book quickly it is in your best interest to return the forms to us as soon as you can to insure the booking of your videoconference.

4. Once the Communications Center has received the forms, we will investigate the dates and times you have chosen and the status of your request will be confirmed.

If you have any questions please do not hesitate to contact me at xxxx.

Message structure: Well organized? Clear, engaging lead? Strong close, with a call to action if needed? Is the response you're asking for perfectly clear?

By now you should have a good idea of what cuts to make in your document and any additions you should develop. Move on to sharpening your language.

Practical Editing Stage 2: Improve Words and Structure

Take out your red pencil. You'll need one if you're editing a printout, or make changes on screen (using the "Track Changes" tool if your document is important or you're collaborating).

Do the content cuts. If you haven't already removed any extraneous ideas, cross out or delete them now.

Add any new and necessary information or ideas.

Scan the result to see how the sentences and paragraphs hang together. Check your transitions and add new ones as needed so everything connects and flows. Look at paragraph length—find break points for those that run more than three to five sentences long.

Identify where the document needs improvement in any or all of the following ways:

- Check the Readability Index—too much passive? Words and sentences too long? Hard to understand?
- Read it in whole or part aloud to check the rhythm—or have someone else read it and listen for the stumbles
- Look for repetition of every kind: words, sounds, sentences that create a monotonous rhythm

After making all the changes, proofread. Use your computer's grammar and spell check to pinpoint mistakes, but don't rely on this help entirely. Your computer won't know that you meant "sole" rather than "soul," for example, or that you've used a specific structure to highlight a fact.

Especially don't rely on any device's auto-correct feature, which can create notable bloopers. Whole websites are given to such mistakes and while they're funny, they can be damaging too.

A proofing trick that professionals sometimes use, if they've read material so many times they can hardly see it, is to read it backwards, beginning from the end. You can pick up typos and repeats that you wouldn't otherwise notice.

One more tip: If you customarily edit on printouts rather than on screen, it's a good idea to use proofing symbols, a shorthand that writers and editors employ to communicate with printers and each other. Just Google "proofreading marks," and you'll find a number of demonstrations. The marks are easy to learn and make the proofing process more efficient, and a touch more fun.

GOING DEEPER: WHEN AND IF YOU NEED HELP WITH GRAMMAR—SOME USEFUL RESOURCES

You may want to review the basics, address specific problems in your writing or know where the resources are when you need help. Great books are available and also excellent online advice and reference material. Here are some choices. Check out the ones that sound promising to find those that resonate for you.

Books

Robert Allen, Editor, *Pocket Fowler's Modern English Usage* (2006)
A classic, updated with new entries on the language of e-mails and the Internet.

Karen Elizabeth Gordon, *The Deluxe Transitive Vampire: The Ultimate Handbook of Grammar for the Innocent, the Eager, and the Doomed* (1993)

This book does a better job than you might imagine of making grammar fun.

Constance Hale, *Sin and Syntax: How to Craft Wickedly Effective Prose* (2001)

A guide to English prose drawing on pop culture for a really up-to-date take on language.

Richard Lanham, *The Longman Guide to Revising Prose: A Quick and Easy Method for Turning Good Writing Into Great Writing* (2006)

A specific system for revision you may or may not like.

William Strunk and E. B. White, *The Elements of Style* (2000)

The classic case for simple writing revered by all writers.

William Zinsser, *On Writing Well* (2004)

A fine manifesto on clarity, and you get the message in just the first few chapters.

In Print or Online

The Associated Press Stylebook (http://www.apstylebook.com)

Merriam-Webster's Collegiate Dictionary (http://www.merriam-webster.com/dictionary)

Roget's Thesaurus (http://thesaurus.com)

Online

The A to Z of Alternative Words

http://www.plainenglish.co.uk
See "Free Guides" for this helpful, downloadable pdf showing good substitutes for long words and phrases and other useful writing guides.

Eleven Rules of Writing

http://www.junketstudies.com/rulesofw/
Surprisingly concise problem-solver.

(Continued)

(Continued)

Grammar Girl—Quick and Dirty Tips for Better Writing

http://grammar.quickanddirtytips.com/proofreading.aspx
Tips and advice in a friendly Dear Abby format.

Guide to Grammar and Style, Jack Lynch

http://andromeda.rutgers.edu/~jlynch/Writing/
An alphabetized list of problem areas.

Guide to Grammar and Writing/Interactive Quizzes

http://grammar.ccc.commnet.edu/grammar/quiz_list.htm
Teaches by quizzing you.

The Online Grammar Guide

http://www.world-english.org/grammar.htm
Another alphabetized list of problem areas.

Plain Language "Examples Database"

www.plainlanguage.gov/
A payload of terrible but true "before" examples with the illuminating rewrites, a must-see especially if you're looking toward government work.

College/University Writing Help Sites

University of Calgary/The Basic Elements of English Grammar Guide
http://www.ucalgary.ca/UofC/eduweb/grammar/

Capital Community College Guide to Grammar & Writing
http://grammar.ccc.commnet.edu/grammar/composition/editing.htm

University of Chicago Writing Program
http://writing-program.uchicago.edu/resources/grammar.htm

University of Illinois Center for Writing Studies
http://www.cws.illinois.edu/workshop/writers/

Purdue University Online Writing Lab
http://owl.english.purdue.edu/owl

Sentence Sharpening Techniques

Here are examples of what to look for when editing your own writing or someone else's, and how the problems can be fixed. You already know many of these strategies from Chapter 4, where we talked about writing the draft. Here's how to apply the ideas in the editing stage and turn your document into a winner that reads quickly, clearly and powerfully.

For each example, try to improve the sentence yourself before reading the revised version. If you come up with a different rewrite, compare it to the one presented. Remember, there's always more than one way to rewrite.

1. Substitute short words for long ones—unless you're making a particular point, can't find a short one or a short one doesn't work as well.

> The new managers are embarking on a fundamental shift in accounting methodology, in the hope of circumventing financial embarrassment.

vs.

> The new managers will introduce a new accounting method to avoid financial embarrassment.

2. Strip everything that doesn't add to your meaning—ideas, phrases, words—so your sentences are briefer and punchier.

> All these ideas are excellent and you can find an approach that works for you to supplement the practical strategy we'll pursue here.

vs.

> These ideas are all excellent. Use them to supplement the strategy we've described.

> The research Ellen has done so far is a major element of the department's progress.

vs.

> Ellen's research is a major reason for the department's progress.

3. Cut as many of the redundant words and phrases as you can.

> This is truly a very good time to think about the newest ideas for innovating a new product line for spring.

vs.

> This is a good time to plan a new spring product line.

4. Replace lifeless, dull verbs with lively, active ones, dumping those extra phrases that clutter our writing.

> I suggest we have a meeting to discuss the issues that may put our company's image at risk.

vs.

> Let's meet to talk about the risks to company image.

5. Or just take a few seconds to think of a better, more to-the-point alternative.

> We ought to get ready for the bad publicity.

vs.

> We must brace for the bad publicity.

6. Replace the "of" and "to" and "for" constructions where possible.

> The plan for the department is to restructure in order to apply the best principles of management.

vs.

> *Easy reading is damn hard writing.*
>
> —Nathaniel Hawthorne

> The department plans to restructure so we can apply the best management principles.

> Mark is of the opinion that the council will reconsider the facts of the matter.

vs.

> Mark believes the council will review the facts.

7. Cut down on the phrases that contain too many words ending in *-ed* and *-ing* and *-ion*.

> Giving the audience the responsibility of interpreting your writing is a bad idea.

vs.

> Don't make the audience responsible for interpreting what you write.

> Jane provided us with the information that Jerry has submitted his resignation.

vs.

> Jane told us that Jerry resigned.

The intention of providing the information is to provoke a reconsideration of the guidelines.

vs.

We're providing the information because we want the guidelines reconsidered.

8. Avoid too many "is and "are" sentences. Particularly beware of sentences that begin "There is" or "There are."

There is a section describing the new technology inside the report.

vs.

The report includes a section describing the new technology.

9. Look for stock phrases that are wordier than they need to be and simplify them. For example, why say

We came to the conclusion	better: We concluded
At the present time	better: Now
We're in a position to	better: We can
The question as to whether	better: Whether
We wish to bring to your attention	better: Please note
Owing to the fact that	better: Because

10. And, cut the empty filler—the use of jargon and buzzwords, and the pretentious. As in:

With risk weighted profitability metrics implemented in a consistent manner across the organization, both financial and staff resources can now be optimally allocated based on maximized overall business performance.

I'm not even going to try to translate that.

To simplify, sharpen, tighten and enliven your writing is definitely a challenge. Fortunately, the payoff is real. People will find you more interesting, credible and professional.

Look at editing as a game. You don't need to memorize rules or even systematically attack a piece of writing based on all these guidelines. But follow the clues that tell you when something can be more clearly said, and think about how to say it better.

Every writer has a personal set of repeat problems. Start recognizing your own and consciously make fixes. You'll soon accumulate your own set of solutions.

About Editing Down Long Copy

Sometimes, you'll work through a document and find you've occupied more space than is allocated, or more than your subject is worth. Trimming it back can be hard.

First, apply the guidelines: Cut everything inessential to your goal—ideas and information, words, perhaps whole sentences and paragraphs. If you've shortened your message as much as you can and it's still too long, think about whether you can pull out some material and supply it as an appendix. This works well with a report or proposal, for example. If you're writing an e-mail, the subject might be divided into two or more messages.

One helpful approach is to think about exactly what you need to get across and then, without looking at what you wrote, draft a new version. It will probably be much stronger as well as closer to the length you want.

But resist the temptation to just condense everything you write into a shorter space. This approach often saps all the interest from a piece. Journalists prefer to sacrifice whole sections of a story rather than lose an interesting quote or sidelight that brings their story alive.

You need not necessarily deliver everything you know about a subject in a document; it's much more effective to deliver less, more powerfully.

In the next chapter, we'll begin to apply the writing guidelines to specific media. First up: e-mail, a channel that is an overlooked make-or-break success factor in most industries. Mastering this short-form message system will give you a head start on the longer, "important" documents common to the business world.

PRACTICE OPPORTUNITIES

I. Diagnose and Rewrite

Individually or in small groups: Review the following paragraphs, considering both stages of editing: the Stage 1 big picture (goal, audience, tone and content) and Stage 2, improving clarity and language. Rewrite each example. Then check the Readability Index (see the end of Chapter 4) to compare the old and new versions and be sure you're satisfied with your version in each case. Finally, proofread: Use your computer's grammar and spell check to pinpoint mistakes, but remember not to rely on this help entirely.

A. From an interoffice e-mail

Dear X Department Staff:

On June 18, at 2 p.m., a meeting has been scheduled to follow up on our previous conversation of May 10 and I would ask you to make arrangements to be in attendance. It is anticipated that approximately two hours will be necessary to cover the agenda thoroughly and review the various recommendations that were previously made. Please advise me of your availability.

B. From an advertorial

With risk-weighted profitability metrics implemented in a consistent manner across the organization, both financial and staff resources can now be optimally allocated based on maximized overall business performance.

C. From a corporate white paper

Design happens at the intersection of the user, the interface, and their context. It's essential for interface designers to understand the gamut of contexts that can occur, thereby ensuring they create designs that are usable no matter what's happening around the user.

D. From a pharmacy wall plaque

The price for which your prescription will be dispensed will be provided upon request and upon your presentation of such prescription for pricing or dispensing.

E. From a management report

The office manager made an independent decision to implement the new policy in hopes that this adaptation would help the staff be more efficient and functional.

II. Sentence Rewriting (Nobody's Perfect)

Here are some sentences that I wrote for this book—and upon review, rewrote. Figure out how you would express the thoughts better. Work individually, then compare results in small groups and agree on the best solution for each example.

A. Even if writers could restrict themselves to writing only for traditional print form, they'd have to take account of fundamental ways in which on-screen reading (whether computer etc.) has changed reader expectations.

B. It's a box that appears immediately after spell check.

C. All the approaches are excellent and you can find one that works for you to supplement the practical strategy we'll pursue here.

D. Have you considered any sensitivities your audience may have?

E. All the graphic tools are even more important because many people are resistant to on-screen reading.

F. Note that the longer sentences give the writer the ability to make connections between actions.

G. Giving the audience the responsibility generates either misinterpretation or indifference. You never want your readers to wonder "Why is she telling me that?" or substituting their own reasoning for your own, even non-consciously. Ambiguous connections generate misinterpretation, or indifference.

H. Nevertheless, if you write better sentences, combine them effectively, and use the structured thinking principles covered in the last two chapters, you're on the way to a powerful, flexible writing capability that will serve you well.

III. Write a Memo to Yourself

Review the areas covered in this chapter—good paragraphing, using transitions, avoiding the various word traps and applying strategies to edit and sharpen writing—and examine some examples of your own work. What specific opportunities can you identify to improve your writing? Draft a memo about this to serve as a reference guide and help you sharpen your writing in the future.

Chapter 6

E-MAIL

YOUR EVERYDAY CHANCE TO BUILD A PROFESSIONAL IMAGE

LEARN HOW TO . . .

- ➤ Use e-mail for your strategic purposes
- ➤ Apply the structured thinking process
- ➤ Build in a tone that fosters relationships
- ➤ Create messages that support internal communication
- ➤ Network more effectively

In 2009, worldwide e-mail traffic totaled 247 billion messages per day—81% of which were spam. By 2013 the number of messages is projected to be 507 billion messages per day, almost double, despite growing use of social media.

—Research by The Radicati Group (http://www.radicati.com/)

START WITH STRATEGIC THINKING

E-mail is serious business in today's workplace, and no wonder: It's the nerve system that connects us, the way we communicate in all directions, no matter what the nature of the organization.

Despite the inroads of Facebook and other social media tools in some business circles, e-mail is how we generally interact with colleagues, supervisors, subordinates, collaborators and services. When we deal with people outside—from clients and prospects to suppliers, partners and industry contacts anywhere in the world—e-mail is usually the route of choice.

In fact, we typically turn to other communication channels only when we must: if in-person contact is essential, for example, or when the occasion demands more formality or even faster speed.

What could happen in a given company if everyone wrote good, clear, appropriate e-mails, day in and day out? I am sure that efficiency and productivity would rise. Customers would buy more and behave more loyally. Relationships inside and outside would improve.

While I don't know anyone who's done research to prove this yet, effective communication does connect to the bottom line, as we saw in Chapter 1. So since e-mail is the dominant communications medium, I rest my case.

But more to the point, what will happen if *you* write strong e-mails each and every time? Your work life and career prospects will improve—perhaps dramatically. Supervisors, colleagues and customers will find you capable, logical, credible, persuasive and professional, probably without knowing why.

You are what you write. The caliber of your e-mails adds up to create a total impression, and you have the power to make it a positive one. Not to mention that your e-mails will get the responses you want much more often, whether you're asking people to meet with you or supply resources or refer you to an employer or client.

The same principles apply if you're communicating for business purposes through other e-channels, including social media, so learning to write successful e-mails is time well spent. And, the planning, writing and editing process is exactly the same as for major documents like proposals and business plans.

So here's how to write e-mails that work for you.

Strategy 1: Commit the Time to Craft Your E-mails Well

Do this without exception, because you can't know which messages are important. E-mail was the first medium with that most special and frightening feature: limitless forwardability. You may address a progress report to your immediate supervisor, but he or she might send it right on up the food chain. You may dash off a casual message to a buddy, who ends up forwarding it to half his address list, or includes it as part of a long message thread to people unknown and inappropriate.

So never write anything you'd be embarrassed to find on the CEO's desk, a billboard, or the front page of a newspaper. Don't write anything you won't want dug up years from now, either, when you're up for CEO or running for office. E-mail has another special feature, it's indelible. It may sleep but it never dies. Invest in planning, drafting and revising every message so it reflects your best writing in every respect. What you *don't* write can matter as much as what you *do* write.

That said, I acknowledge there are occasions when timing counts more than quality. If your boss calls from China to say he's signing a contract and needs the research results e-mailed *now,* don't labor over your wording. But here's the good news: The practice you give yourself when less pressured makes handling emergencies a snap.

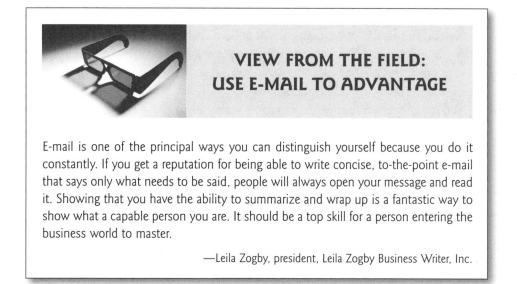

VIEW FROM THE FIELD: USE E-MAIL TO ADVANTAGE

E-mail is one of the principal ways you can distinguish yourself because you do it constantly. If you get a reputation for being able to write concise, to-the-point e-mail that says only what needs to be said, people will always open your message and read it. Showing that you have the ability to summarize and wrap up is a fantastic way to show what a capable person you are. It should be a top skill for a person entering the business world to master.

—Leila Zogby, president, Leila Zogby Business Writer, Inc.

Strategy 2: Know When an E-mail is the Right Medium—and When it's Not

While "traditional" advice says to use e-mail for short messages and stick to one idea, in fact no one follows such rules. However, never forget that many people don't really like reading long documents on screen and resist scrolling. They tend to skim e-mails and will rarely print them out. So complicated messages full of ideas or instructions don't work well. Of course, you can attach a complex document—provided you're pretty sure the recipient will open it. Or you can link to online materials to provide backup detail.

Look for a communication channel other than e-mail when

- The occasion calls for more formal documentation, with a potential legal aspect or a need to go on record. There are times you should protect yourself with a print document, like when you're signing a contract, making a complaint, filing a claim or delivering a performance review.
- You're asking for something that has a personal angle: a donation to a good cause, or a reference, for example. Depending on your audience, e-mail may

be fine but in other instances, this demands a letter, or phone call. Whatever written form you choose, the message must be crafted to represent your best writing. E-mail may be easier to send—but that doesn't mean it's easier to write it well.

- The person you're addressing is e-mail averse. It's important to consider, for example, that many wealthy investors and donors to charitable causes are over 65 and, especially if they no longer work in office situations, may use e-mail minimally at best. Important audiences need to be addressed in their own terms. And even some much younger people prefer more formality. At the other end of the scale, the youngest generations are starting to sidestep e-mail in favor of social media like Facebook.

- Your message should be delivered privately or in person. Don't criticize or fire someone by e-mail, send anything you don't want shared or use it to break off a relationship. It's not only cruel and cowardly, but apt to backfire on you in major ways.

In general: Don't make e-mail a substitute for in-person contact. It's not a great relationship or team-building tool as compared to face-to-face interaction or even telephone calls. Like all written communication, it doesn't come with clues to meaning like facial expression, tone of voice and body language. So never negotiate by e-mail, or use it to engage in give-and-take situations. The medium's impersonality is leading some companies to mandate weekly e-mail-free days, forcing employees to pick up the phone or walk down the hall.

Strategy 3: Draw on Your Own Natural Responses to Tell You How to Shape Your Messages

Are you impatient with meandering e-mails of dim purpose, or that require time to decipher? So is everyone. This tells you that relevance, conciseness and clarity count.

And all the human interaction factors do too: sincerity, honesty, courtesy. We're the same people in the work setting as we are

SUCCESS TIP: SOME "ALMOST NEVERS"

Your business e-mails should almost never convey emotions, negative feelings, sarcasm and cute stuff.

Never send an e-mail when you're angry. It's something people won't forget or forgive and is guaranteed to bite you back. Take especial care if you're writing to someone you dislike—you might ask a friend to check your message. Sarcasm, irony and most humor don't belong in e-mails because they depend on facial expression or tone of voice to be understood. Write nothing that can be misinterpreted. And put the emoticons way back on the shelf if you want to look professional. The same with exclamation points, though a case can be made for them in texting, which offers few options for expressing enthusiasm, and their use is creeping into e-mail as well.

outside of it. Most of us want to feel included, respected and appreciated—liked, and maybe even cared about.

You've probably noticed that even the briefest work memo can convey subtle emotions when you're on the receiving end. Every message you send includes such a subtext, intended or not. Practice awareness of what you communicate in the emotional dimension. Think "golden rule" and you'll accomplish your goals and build good relationships far more easily.

Q&A: AVOIDING E-MAIL TROUBLE

Abbreviations: Y Not?

Many people are unaccustomed to the abbreviations that are second nature to frequent texters and instant messaging. They may fail to fully understand your message, misinterpret it, disregard it, or read it resentfully. None of these outcomes is good.

An additional large number of people understand the abbreviations fine—but do not like to see them in another medium, even e-mail.

Together, both groups probably include a lot of people important to you, such as clients, future employers and supervisors. Therefore, it's sensible to avoid abbreviating in general.

Attachments: When?

A concern for computer viruses is among the reasons a fair number of people make it a rule not to open attachments. But when you have a lot to say, it's challenging to write a short e-mail. In the case of a report or other lengthy document, it can be impossible.

The best solution is: Know your audience. Ask if necessary whether your recipient will open an attachment and prefers it. If the answer is no, then incorporate the material in the body of the e-mail but use formatting to distinguish it from the e-mail message—for example, draw a line between the message and report, and give the report a clear headline. And make the rest of the document as readable as possible with subheads, some white space and so on.

Readers on the Go: How to Accommodate?

It's very possible that your e-mail will be read on a tiny screen while the reader is at the airport, in a taxi or eating lunch. Your best strategy is nevertheless to write in complete sentences, not fragments, and avoid abbreviating. But use your awareness of iPhone and BlackBerry readers to keep messages short and tight.

WRITE E-MAILS WITH A STRUCTURED SYSTEM

To write successful e-mails—as with every written communication—approach the task systematically. This process will become second nature with surprisingly little practice. The process is explained in detail in Chapters 2 and 3. Here's how it applies to e-mail:

1. Define your **goal** as closely as you can, and consider your **audience** and its **characteristics**.

2. Figure out what **substance** will accomplish that goal with that particular audience and put the elements in a logical order.

3. Decide what **tone** is appropriate to that audience, taking account of the person's status, personality, your relationship with him or her and the nature of your goal.

4. Based on the first three steps, figure out a direct, clear **opening**. For e-mail, that's the subject line, salutation and first one or two sentences.

5. Follow through with the **middle**, which typically contains technical information, backup for your request and/or the reasoning if you aim to persuade.

6. **End** strongly, making it clear what follow-up you want.

7. **Review, edit and tighten:** Business e-mails (and I would say all your e-mails) must be concise and error-free with correct spelling, punctuation and basic grammar. Poor writing interferes with comprehension and makes you look incompetent and uncaring.

Now let's apply this framework to a workaday e-mail.

You notice that you're not included in a flow of reports relating to a major department project, one you're not directly involved in but would like to be.

Here's how you should plan your message, preferably writing down the answer to each question as I do in this example.

Goal? Immediate, to be added to the distribution list. Long range, to be better positioned for interesting work that's important to the organization.

Audience? Primary: Your supervisor. Secondary: Possible higher-echelon executives who may make the decision.

Audience characteristics? What do you know about these people? You're writing for a range of personalities, but since they are all managers, you can safely assume they have a few things in common: self-interest in "getting the job done" and, one might hope, grooming new talent.

Tone? Must be very respectful. Even if your manager is a pal, you're asking for something, and his/her bosses may not even know you. But you don't want to sound artificially formal.

Substance? The question to always ask: What can I say that will make my case with this audience?

VIEW FROM THE FIELD: TRY TO HIT THE E-MAIL MARK

It annoys me when an e-mail goes on and on, especially when it's a solicitation—getting a long complicated e-mail from someone I don't know and am not engaged with is a fast way to make me hit the delete button. So keep it simple. If you need to elaborate, send an attachment or have a conversation. Once in a while I get an e-mail that's fast, right to the point, doesn't include a lot of rhetoric or misspell my name, or approaches me in some way the person knows will be relevant to me. That shows they did their homework and figured out what's in it for the audience.

—Laurie Bloom, Director of Marketing & Communications,
Rivkin Radler LLP

Looking at the situation through the other persons' eyes always provides your best clues. *If you were the supervisors, why should you grant the request?* Don't write an e-mail asking for something until you have an answer, because that's essential to deciding what to include, and what to leave out.

Knowing the company also tells you whether your request is a hard sell or not. Is information flow generally good, or is there a knowledge-is-power mentality? Are there rigid guidelines on pecking order entitlements, or flexible ones?

If you assume your request is an easy sell, you could simply say,

Dear Jack,
I'll appreciate having my name added to the Carter Project distribution list. I'm interested in seeing how it goes. Thanks—Jane

But this would be a mistake. You can't really predict whether the recipients will see the change as insignificant or as a departure from protocol. So you need to make a case. Think about possible advantages to the other parties. For example:

- The information will help you with your current work.
- You possess some special background or experience that means you might make a contribution.
- You hope to be involved in similar projects down the line and this will help you prepare for that.

ACTION TIME: YOUR TURN

Follow through with Steps 4, 5 and 6—writing the opening, middle and end—to create a memo you think will work. Then check out my Draft 1 to see one approach.

Draft 1

Subject: Request to be added to Carter Project distribution list

Jack:

I'd like to ask if I can be added to the information distribution list for the Carter Project.

Since I'm currently working on several smaller-scale but similar projects, seeing how the challenges are handled will be helpful and could save me significant time. Also, the chance to review the materials will enable me to sharpen my thinking so I am better prepared to handle future large-scale initiatives.

As you know, I have a background in the medical imaging industry, so I might possibly have some useful thoughts to offer on Carter.

Thanks so much.—Jane

This brings us to step 7, editing and revising. Here's how I'd rewrite my own draft after reviewing and thinking about it.

Draft 2

Subject: Information request, Carter Project

Dear Jack:

I'd appreciate it very much if I can be added to the Carter Project distribution list.

I'm working on several similar smaller-scale projects right now, and seeing how the challenges are handled will be a big help. Also, reviewing the materials will help prepare me for future large-scale projects when those opportunities arise.

Thanks so much for considering this request.—Jane

Is this version better? Why did I make these changes? Here's the reasoning, step-by-step, along with guidelines that apply to all e-mails.

Subject line. *Focus them tightly, or your recipient may trash your message without reading it.* The subject line in Draft 1 is long and wordy—only part of it will probably show up on the reader's screen. It needs to be tighter and more direct. Also, a good subject line enables you or the recipient to easily retrieve an e-mail in the future, which can be very valuable.

Salutation. *Pay attention to tone in salutations.* In Draft 1, using the name alone is abrupt, not appropriate to a request, especially when you're addressing a superior.

The lead. *The first sentence in large part determines whether your message will succeed. Take time with it.* Draft 1 begins okay in that it gets right to the point, which, almost always, you want to do. But it's a little obsequious, asking for permission to make a request. So I took out "I'd like to ask" and substituted words that set an appreciative tone.

Message substance. *Always aim for just the right amount of content to make your point—not too much and not too little.* Draft 1's substance works reasonably for the purpose but on more careful consideration—which is easy once you have the draft in front of you—paragraph 3, offering to help on the project, seems a bit arrogant. So I cut it, though should a conversation result from the e-mail, it's a good point to hold in reserve.

The close. *End strongly by underlining your request, or whatever other purpose motivates your message, as specifically as possible.* In Draft 1, the very general ending doesn't really close the natural circle of your message. In this case, you're asking for a response to a request; at other times, your close might say, "Let me know when you're available to meet with me," or "I look forward to hearing when the new system will be ready."

Writing style. *Aim for simple, direct language that moves naturally to pull the reader through.* Draft 1 overall sounds rather stilted and clumsy. To instantly discover where the language needs attention, read the message aloud. Wherever it's hard to read smoothly and rapidly, look for ways to reword.

You can also find wording that interferes with speed by searching out repetitions—for example, there are two phrases using "to" in the first sentence. Paragraph 2 also fails to meet the reading-aloud test and sounds "hedgy." You may notice the word "help" appears twice, but that's okay, because that's your subject—asking for help.

Do you write telegraphic e-mails leaving out words and relying heavily on abbreviations? Break the habit! You'll get better results with cohesive messages that don't require readers to fill in what's missing or figure out what you mean.

Tightening the message. *A major goal of editing is to make complicated sentences simple.* So always look for alternative ways to say the same thing more directly and plainly, eliminate unnecessary words and rephrase the thoughts. I did this with Draft 1, sentence-by-sentence, and ended up cutting about 25% in the process. Notice that once you cut words back, it becomes obvious that they aren't needed. You can always check your editing this way: If eliminating words or thoughts makes a message read less well or seem less convincing, don't do the cut, or look for another way to say what you mean.

Review Chapters 4 and 5 for a full rundown on almost grammar-free editing techniques that enable you to improve your own writing.

Review the total message for the big picture—what's coming across? In the case of our example, is Draft 2 respectful and polite? Have any negative feelings crept in? Does the content appear to make the case with clarity and logic? Does the message as a whole seem to proceed logically? Are the transitions good? Is there anything that can be interpreted as being against the writer's interests?

Also important: Does the message read quickly and easily? The faster your writing reads, the better it works and the more convincing it becomes. Contemporary means short: words, paragraphs, sentences and documents.

Compare Drafts 1 and 2 to see how much faster the second one flows, how much more convincing it seems and how it projects a professional image for the writer while being very respectful.

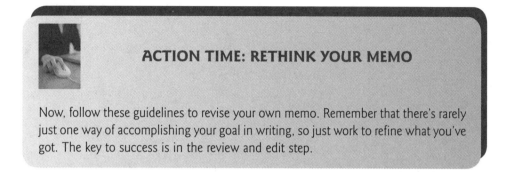

ACTION TIME: RETHINK YOUR MEMO

Now, follow these guidelines to revise your own memo. Remember that there's rarely just one way of accomplishing your goal in writing, so just work to refine what you've got. The key to success is in the review and edit step.

Are you reluctant to take time for the kind of planning and editing I recommend? Know that if you can achieve what you want with your first draft you're unique: Professional writers don't expect to and nor should you. There's an old adage that writers like: "A writer isn't someone who writes, but someone who rewrites."

And know that if you don't invest the energy, you're gambling against your own success.

The good news is that just a little practice will put you way out in front of the field—and once you've built the habit of writing it right, you'll find it doesn't take much time at all.

BUILD IN THE RIGHT TONE

Here's a kind of challenge you may face whatever your career field, and it's not unlike the challenges you deal with when doing group projects in school.

As project coordinator, it's your job to pull together a team report. The group consists of your peers and a few subordinates, and each has been working on a different section. The deadline is approaching and you need to be sure the pieces come in on schedule.

Here are two possible ways of writing the e-mail.

Version 1

Subject: Assignments due!
Everyone on Martin Proposal Team:

As you know, I expect you to deliver your assigned part of the Martin proposal on Wednesday, April 3, by 2 p.m. via e-mail. Unless I hear otherwise from you, I'll expect you all to meet the deadline. Thanks.

John

Version 2

Subject: Due April 3: Martin proposal sections

Hi team—

I look forward to having all sections of the Martin proposal on my desk by Wednesday at 2.

An e-mail attachment will be fine. If you're having any last-minute problems pulling your part together, give me a call ASAP.

The plan calls for me to review everything by the end of the week, so please be available to answer questions. Marian needs all the pieces in hand by Monday so she can edit the full proposal and make it cohesive in time to meet the client's April 12 deadline.

I know we'll have a great proposal and a good chance of landing this contract. Thank you Mark, Jane, Eric and Marie for all your hard work on this.

Sincerely, John

Which version would you rather get? I assume it's the second one, so let's analyze why.

There's nothing wrong with Version 1 technically. The spelling and grammar are correct, and it's clear and to the point.

The glaring difference from Version 2 is in the tone and its probable effect on the recipients.

The subject line in Version 1 is vague, and at the same time threatening. It makes the writer sound like a teacher calling for essays and expecting the worst. The negative voice sustains throughout.

Version 2, on the other hand, takes the trouble to project a positive attitude and a team spirit. It gives a context for the proposal process, so the deadline doesn't seem arbitrary. It offers help with problems—better to find out any hitches now rather than later, no? It conveys enthusiasm for the result, reminds everyone that something important is at stake and extends appreciation to each team member as an individual, treating everyone equally.

If you think the difference is trivial, consider: Which writer would you rather work for? Which would you work harder for, on this and future projects? Based on the messages, which person would you want to team with again?

Yes, it's essential to structure your messages well and use your editing and proofing tools to craft your language. But achieving the right tone is equally critical. ***The complaint that employers most often make about how younger staff members write is failure to adopt the right tone.*** So let's explore where tone comes from and how to control it.

Thanks to text messaging and the modern business tempo, with a boost from Twitter, many people have learned to get to the point quickly with the least possible number of words. But what can get lost in this minimizing is tone. Most noticeably, both respect and warmth are often glaringly absent.

Getting the tone right starts with how you think through your content.

In our e-mail example, Version 2's writer obviously thought not only about what she wanted, but her recipients' needs and reactions. If I were in their shoes, she asked, what might I want to know? If I'm having a problem, what should I do? What would inspire me to a last final best effort? Can I feel that all my overtime work is appreciated?

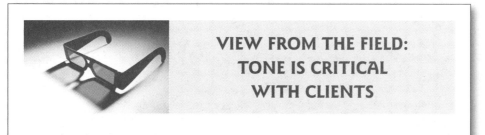

VIEW FROM THE FIELD: TONE IS CRITICAL WITH CLIENTS

Many people I supervise use the wrong tone when they write to clients. If a client owes you a response, that's never an excuse for an e-mail that sounds like you are barking orders. Start off requests with the magic word, please; end any request with thank you; and always indicate that you are prepared to help facilitate whatever response you need. If an e-mail to a client on any topic sounds like something a parent would say to a child, a drill sergeant would say to a new recruit, or your boss would say to you—it needs to be rewritten.

—Arik Ben-Zvi, managing director,
The Glover Park Group

As every good manager knows, there's everything to gain by making people feel included and important. Taking the time to write the thoughtful message is an excellent investment.

Many managers have trouble projecting warmth. But if you begin by looking at the situation from the other person's viewpoint, it will usually happen naturally. Consideration shows. But you may also have to consciously think about how to frame the message from the other person's point of view. For example, writing, "If you don't send your work in by Friday you'll mess up the whole team project and it will be late" is very different from "Please send your work in by Sept. 5 so we can fit it into the final project and meet the deadline."

You can also choose language that reinforces the positive tone. What helps establish a friendly, persuasive and even motivating tone? Writing tactics, such as

- Saying "please" and "thank you"
- Using polite salutations and closing words
- Using contractions ("I'm happy" vs. "I am happy")
- Using the word "you" a lot—cutting back on "I"
- Adopting a consistent "you" perspective, the what's-in-it-for-me
- Using positive language and avoiding negatives
- Using names in the message body
- Generally conveying enthusiasm and confidence

Suppose you're sending a report to a client and must write a cover note for it. You might say,

> Frank—here's the January progress report that you wanted. Regards, Ben

This short message sounds abrupt, barely courteous and inappropriate to the relationship. It uses a "buddy voice" at best. What would work better? Perhaps the following:

> Dear Frank,
>
> I'm pleased to provide the attached report for January. If you have any questions, I'll be happy to answer them and can also provide more details if helpful.
>
> Best regards, Ben

Is Version 2 unnecessarily long and wordy? True, it doesn't contain much "real" information. Nevertheless, circumstances call for it. It sounds like the writer took the time to craft the short message carefully, which in itself shows respect, and it seems thoughtful. It is the tone a client expects from a supplier and, particularly, from someone who's not at the top of the pecking order.

In all honesty, a recipient might not actually notice your careful e-mail—but he or she will definitely notice one that's careless, breezy and blunt. Keep in mind that many clients are probably considerably older than your own age cohort and more formal to some degree in their lifestyle and expectations. Even if they are young, they typically want the respect the relationship demands—and by the way, the same is true if you have a young boss.

Let's look at one more example, a thank you note—famously difficult to write well—and how sentence structure affects the impact.

> Dear Joan—thanks for inviting me to the networking event. I had a good time. Also I met a client prospect.—Regards, Ned

Not very convincing, is it? Here, we can fault the writing style. Ned's sentences are choppy and stilted, reminding us of a fourth-grade textbook. He forgot the sentence rhythm technique of alternating short sentences with long ones (see Chapter 3). He could have written,

> Hello Joan—
>
> I want to thank you for inviting me to the Celex networking event. It was great to meet so many new people who are part of our industry, and I even have a prospective client to follow up with. Thanks again for thinking of me, I very much appreciate it.
>
> Sincerely, Ned

An even better way to voice appreciation is to be very specific. Here's an e-mail I was happy to get from a business client.

> I just wanted to say thank you for inviting me to the luncheon today. I really enjoyed the group. The presentation was interesting, but the highlight was one of the better question and answer sessions on the subject I have heard at any session. And I am extremely grateful for your introduction to numerous people, making sure that they knew what I did. You do go out of your way to help, and it was appreciated. Thanks.
>
> Best regards, Lewis

USE E-MAIL TO SUPPORT INTERNAL COMMUNICATION

E-mail offers you an extremely effective tool for managing and even improving your relationships with coworkers and supervisors and, in your immediate school environment, with other students and professors. Some of the examples we've looked at show why it always pays off to think through your goals and audience needs.

Depending on whether you're writing to a superior, a subordinate or a peer, the content of an e-mail may vary even when you're writing about the same subject because each of these people needs different information and has different self-interest. The tone might also vary—but only somewhat.

It's always best to write with courtesy and consideration regardless of the hierarchy. Use your everyday communication flow to build trust, good will and credibility. Build in a "caring" spirit, which may mean personalizing the message with a brief comment about a mutual interest, an important event in the other person's life or anything else that's not out of line.

And you can apply your writing methodology to problem-solve your working relationships. Sometimes, you can work wonders by expanding your audience analysis to ask a question beyond what's-in-it-for-me. The question is: Where is this person coming from?

Consider what you know about the individual personally and in terms of his or her own work situation. How does your boss fit into the company? Is the position secure? What kind of person does he or she report to, and what pressures might be coming to bear?

For example, Elaine, a new fund-raising administrator in a major charitable foundation, found herself continually at odds with her direct supervisor, a woman 20 years older than herself. During all their interactions, Elaine found Dorothy impatient and abrupt. She also made many decisions that Elaine disagreed with and believed were bad for the department. Eventually, Elaine hated coming to work but didn't want to leave the job. She asked herself: What might be making Dorothy behave this way? Where was she coming from?

Once she consciously considered the question, Elaine realized that her boss was actually in a difficult position: She'd recently been promoted to a job with larger responsibilities that could prove a reach for her, reporting to a supervisor clearly impatient for results. Reporting to Dorothy was a bevy of ambitious young people—Elaine included—who didn't like her and didn't conceal the fact.

Looking at the situation from Dorothy's point of view, Elaine further realized that as one of these young people, she herself was probably coming across as judgmental—silently disapproving of her supervisor's decisions.

Elaine decided to see what would happen if she showed Dorothy full support even when she didn't fully agree with her. During in-person exchanges, she communicated that she understood that Dorothy's role was to "see the bigger picture" and make appropriate decisions. In her e-mails, Elaine relaxed her tone and took care to convey receptivity and a positive spirit. She drafted every message taking account of Dorothy's problems and response patterns.

The result: Elaine netted a substantial turnaround in her relationship with her boss, who began to trust and rely on her more. As it happened, Dorothy was transferred out after a few months, but Elaine outlasted her.

Of course, it isn't always possible to achieve this. Unquestionably, you may at times work for or with people who are genuinely bad-tempered, unfair and frustrating. Looking at their problems and your own response patterns may in such cases not help much.

But remembering that one of your ultimate job responsibilities is to help your boss look good to his or her superiors will always work to your advantage. In fact, it's pretty much a universal that all people will respond well when you make them look good and/or feel good about themselves, as touchy-feely as that may sound.

Take this idea into account in your face-to-face interaction and writing if you want to build relationships and support.

THINK GLOBAL: E-MAIL KNOWS NO BOUNDARIES

Because e-mail (and all electronic media) leaps oceans and crosses national borders so readily, we forget that we're communicating cross-culturally. This can be a problem because even in its more formal moments, the American style tends to sound brusque and discourteous to people whose primary language is not English. So take care to be very polite and considerate. Try to be aware of other countries' specific cultural norms, for example, whether requests are best made directly or indirectly; and whether it's in order to express personal interest in your recipient.

More tips for internationalizing what you write:

- Use short common words and short declarative sentences
- Cut the jargon and idioms
- Use lists when appropriate
- Phrase everything as straightforwardly as you can
- Avoid passive structures and those with "get" and "have"
- Don't pile up long strings of nouns
- But avoid writing in ways that sound unnatural in American English (though the messages will often feel rather stark)

Remember that most businesses today must also consider internal audiences whose native language is not English, so the guidelines often apply.

USE E-MAIL TO NETWORK MORE EFFECTIVELY

E-mail can be critical in scoring opportunities, and in building and maintaining relationships, so examples of messages to support networking are included in some of the preceding chapters. But e-mail is especially important when you're looking for career opportunities, so let's apply the ideas to this situation.

Suppose you want to tap your school's alumni network for advice on your career path, and perhaps even some direct job leads.

Your goals are clear, so think first about audience. Why might a graduate of your school take the time to talk to you? Here are a few reasons.

- You have common ground in graduating from the same school
- You have some common experiences
- Many people like "giving back"
- Being asked for advice is flattering and reinforces people's view of their own accomplishments, especially if they're relatively recent graduates
- General networking and good will—"you never know" if someone might prove a good contact in the future

Tone. Your tone should be respectful and appreciative. You are, after all, asking for a favor you're unlikely to return.

Content. Remind recipient of your common bond. Bring it alive in some way. Make yourself sound worth helping because you'll likely be successful, and a person who'd be good to know.

Here are two examples that someone I know received from fellow alumni requesting informational interviews, reproduced as received (except for details changed in the interest of privacy). Which works better?

Sample 1

Subject: White University career network

Dear Ms. Lewis:

I'm a senior at White, majoring in science and anthropology. I was hoping you could tell me a little about your job—what does an average day entail and how did you get to where you are today? Im interested in what working for a non profit is like.

Thank you and I hope to hear from you soon.

Sally

Sample 2

Subject: Possible informational interview

Dear Ms. Lewis,

My name is Jessica, and I too graduated from White. I obtained your name and contact information from the White Career Network.

I am writing to request an informational interview. I am very interested in pursuing a career in high-level research and analysis, I hope on an international scale. As a result, I would very much like to learn more about the work you do for FLU and your prior professional experiences.

Just to let you know a little bit about myself, while working on my degree, I was president of the International Club and active with the Speaker Committee.

I spent a full year as an undergraduate in Dubai, and interned at the National Association for Freedom.

I am ready to utilize my international background, and as I am brand new to this career path, any advice will be greatly appreciated.

I will be in your area on Thursday and Friday, July 27 and 28. If you are available either of these days and willing to meet with me for 30 minutes, I will be most grateful.

Thank you for your time, and I hope to speak with you soon.

Sincerely,
Jessica

Which e-mail would you probably respond to? If you agree that Jessica's e-mail is better than Sally's, think about why.

To begin with, Sally didn't take the trouble to carefully draft or proofread what she wrote. It comes across as off the top of her head and a bit illiterate, suggesting she is (1) not so smart, (2) not respectful, (3) not really appreciative or (4) all of the above. Further, her note is very unspecific, so it's hard to understand what she wants to know. She shows also that she didn't trouble to make a good match between herself and her hoped-for information source.

Jessica, on the other hand, clearly thought the connection through and made the relevance of Ms. Lewis's experience to her own goals plain. Her gratitude is expressly stated and a few significant details about her background are referenced.

Most important, Jessica sounds like a winner. A person who'd be interesting to talk to for half an hour—by phone if not in person—and worth your time. You'd even assume she'd present well to any contact you referred her to.

All this achieved by a solid, planned-out message that says the person did her homework and knows how to interact? Absolutely.

For good networking, follow through and always write to say thank you—few people do and you'll stand out. If you find an opportunity through your contact, or accept one anywhere, write to let him or her know.

Use the same strategies to connect with people you meet or hear about from other sources as well—the woman you sat next to on an airplane, the man who said he had a colleague you should meet, someone you met at a workshop. Savvy networkers follow through even years later by writing thoughtful, planned e-mails that trigger positive memories and positive responses. Or as appropriate, of course, use social media to maintain or revive contact.

The power of digital communication is there for you when you trouble to do it well.

GOING DEEPER: ETIQUETTE, SHMETIQUETTE—AN E-MAIL CHECKLIST

Do

- Answer in a timely way—24 hours or less. People expect this with a medium geared for speed.
- Don't send unnecessary messages. You need not have the last word, especially if it's just "got the message"; people appreciate hearing less rather than more.
- Include only what's needed and aim for short messages. Speed readers may miss the point when you bury it.
- Use accurate subject lines to identify your message, change it when the discussion shifts and make it audience directed and findable. Use "must read" elements when justified—for example, "DATE CHANGE, Miller meeting."
- Use a strong opening line—bottom line on top.
- Build in a clear close circling back to what you hope to accomplish.
- Use graphic devices if helpful to be clear and stay organized: numbers, bullets, sub-heads and so on.
- Use an easy-to-read typeface in a substantial size—12 point as a rule.
- Use the signature to advantage: Include your social media contact information and whatever else relates to your general or specific audience in a positive way.

Do Not Include

- Emotion—you will instantly be seen as unprofessional and your viewpoint or ideas will be disregarded.
- Anything ambiguous that could be interpreted against your interests.
- Sarcasm and irony because without in-person tone and cues, they can do you damage. Be careful with humor in general.
- Anything you'd cringe to see on the front page of the *New York Times*, your boss's desk or your competitor's e-mail in-box.
- Anything you'd be embarrassed to have forwarded to anyone.
- Jargon and abbreviations beyond the minimal.
- Philosophical ponderings: This is not the medium.

And Never

- Write whole messages in italic, bold or capitals.
- Use smiley faces or other emoticons unless it's a very good friend.
- Forget to edit and proofread.
- Forget to take a big picture view of how your message will (or might) strike a reader.

PRACTICE OPPORTUNITIES

I. Request an Informational Interview

A. Write an e-mail requesting telephone or in-person time with a friend's relative who's working in your chosen career, to ask for advice and possible job leads.

B. Exchange your draft with a classmate for review and editing. Discuss results with each other, and revise if you agree with the suggestions.

Expect to be evaluated on both the quality of your own e-mail and the quality of input you provide to your classmate.

II. Try Writing General Request E-mails

Write to a specific person to ask for a reference, request a special assignment or say thank you for a favor.

III. Group Work: Plan And Write a Communications Policy

A. Together, brainstorm how workplace supervisors should communicate in writing with younger employees: E-mail? Texting? Social media? Intranet? Other?

B. Draft an e-mail presenting your recommendations and reasoning to an older supervisor one of you works for, or once worked for. Begin by profiling the supervisor through asking questions of the group member who knows the person.

IV. Conference Request

Pair up. Student 1 acts as supervisor and Student 2 as a staff member who wants to attend an expensive conference. Student 2: Write an e-mail to "Supervisor" requesting authorization. "Supervisor" articulates his/her reaction to the e-mail—what worked and what didn't work. "Staff Member" rewrites the e-mail based on this reaction.

The students then reverse roles and Student 1 becomes the requestor, asking Student 2—who assumes the role of a client prospect—for an appointment to demonstrate a product.

Both students should be prepared to present their thinking and ultimate written results to the class.

V. Write An E-mail to a Friend Who Writes Poor E-mails

Explain to your friend why he or she should take more care with e-mail, and share the most important points you learned from this chapter about how to write them well.

VI. Questions for Discussion

1. How do you think written communications like e-mails should take account of generational differences? Who has had a problem that relates to this? What did you learn?

2. What words do you typically use to communicate with a friend by e-mail that would be inappropriate when writing to your professor? A supervisor? A client?

3. How can you project a feeling of respect in an e-mail when the situation calls for it? Warmth?

4. In what e-mail situations is it suitable to "be yourself"—with little thought to content, wording, grammar and punctuation?

5. Do grammar and punctuation matter anymore? Why or why not?

Chapter 7

LETTERS

THEY STILL COUNT

LEARN HOW TO . . .

➢ Format, plan and write letters for print and e-delivery
➢ Apply the strategies to specific communication needs
➢ Create job application cover letters

> *I consider it a good rule for letter writing to leave unmentioned what the recipient already knows, and instead tell him something new.*
>
> —Sigmund Freud

WHEN LETTERS COUNT

While you may not routinely write letters to friends and relatives, and might be surprised at how common a practice it was before digital communication, the art is still essential to many business venues. Equally important, you need it for nearly every job application.

Cover letters are usually essential to proposal submissions as well and you may need to write letters to connect with clients, government agencies, suppliers and many other people and organizations.

By "letter," I don't necessarily mean a printed document delivered by the post office. A letter can be e-mailed. But when you're writing for a formal purpose, you must thoughtfully craft and edit the message to meet more formal demands.

Although you may be able to use some "standard" prefabricated pieces in some letters, for the most part, every letter you write must be individual and specific to your purpose. Therefore, we'll focus on how to apply the structured thinking process.

If you find yourself struggling with a particular kind of letter, Google the category (e.g., "letter of introduction") and batches of examples will come up. You can pick up useful ideas and language from these samples, but be cautious:

- Don't bypass the thinking process that starts with "goal" and "audience."
- Don't adopt the old-fashioned, stilted wording and tone of many online samples.
- Don't be tempted to use a pre-made, cookie-cutter letter; it shows, and will fail to accomplish your goal.

Format: Keep It Simple

Let's first get the formatting issue out of the way. The same basic structure will serve for just about every purpose. Use a letterhead or build a serviceable one for yourself at the top of the page, with your name, address and contact information. It doesn't have to be fancy, but if you can print in color, using a sharp color for your name can present nicely. For the sake of personal branding, the letterhead should resemble your résumé's heading.

If you choose not to use a letterhead, then type in your name and address, flush left.

The rest of the document should also run flush left. Start with the date. Then skip a few lines and put in the full name, company and address of the person to whom you're writing. If you don't know the name of the person you're writing to, find out! Skip a few more lines and write your salutation, generally "Dear Ms. X" or "Dear Jane," ending with a colon.

Skip a few lines and start your message in block paragraphs, flush left. Single space the body copy, but skip a line between paragraphs, rather than indenting.

When your message is complete, sign off—for example, "Sincerely"—and be sure there's space for your signature underneath. You can type your name and contact information under the signature space (if the letterhead didn't take care of that) and/ or social media information and direct phone line. If you're writing on behalf of an organization, type your name under the signature space, and your title under that.

That's about it. When you're done, take a minute to center the letter on the page vertically so it looks balanced. If it's a long message, begin page 2 with a line that says something like, "Mr. Bob White/August 3, 2012/page 2." Use boldface to set it off. The heading ensures the continuation won't get separated and lost. If additional material is enclosed or attached, say so at page bottom: "Enclosed: Résumé, three work samples."

The major exception to the style described here is when creative license is called for. Note the solicitation letters that many savvy charitable causes send out these days. They use color, pullout quotes, "handwritten" messages in the margins, subheads, images and whatever else they can come up with to engage attention and get at least part of the letter read.

> *Some Frenchman—possibly Montaigne—says:* I never think except when I sit down to write.
>
> —Edgar Allan Poe

You can take a similar tack in a low-key way to ensure that those who skim rather than read business letters—which is just about everybody today—are pulled along and absorb the most important points. Your tools for this include subheads, bold lead-ins, numbered and bulleted lists of key points, summaries, pullout quotes and underlining.

Use your judgment about deploying graphic techniques: A job application letter should be conservative (unless you're trying to demonstrate creativity); a sales letter, on the other hand, needs to capitalize on techniques that attract and direct attention.

In general, keep letters to one page. If your message is longer and essentially a report or proposal, it's smart to at least work in headings so readers can identify what's important.

What about letters delivered online, such as cover letters for résumés? Usually, it's best to use the same basic format as for print letters. When an occasion calls for a letter, then your document should look like a letter, not an e-mail message.

Characteristics of Successful Letters

Unlike e-mails and very unlike text messages, letters are natural relationship-building tools. They carry more weight than casual, spontaneous-seeming e-mail. Always treat them as a way to make a good impression, or the reverse.

So, it is particularly important to write clear, concise letters that come to the point quickly and move fast. Don't visualize your reader as putting her feet up on the desk and perusing your letter in a relaxed, contemplative manner. Businesspeople don't have those moments any more. Visualize an overburdened, stressed executive who needs to solve problems and find answers. Write to that person.

Make what's-in-it-for-the-reader loud and clear. Apply all the principles of economy—use short immediately understood words (mostly one and two syllables), short sentences (14 to 22 words average) and short paragraphs (three or four sentences *on average*). Keep each paragraph to one idea.

A conversational tone is generally desirable, but many letters need to be somewhat more formal than e-mails. This may move your writing toward a more stilted pattern. Try to counter this by simplifying the language and thinking of concise ways to say things.

Always consider the relationships carefully. Invariably build in respect and courtesy. This isn't always easy: Figuring out how to frame some messages courteously can take some effort. When a client, for example, has repeatedly ignored your request for a conversation, focus on your most important goal: You want the information, sure, but you need to keep the client.

Letters should strike readers as well thought out and constructed. This means making them well organized, carefully edited and visually effective—neat, clean, enough white space, very readable font, graphic balance. Letters must feel personal. Even if you're sending out a mass-audience letter to 100 prospective employers, for example, you must take the trouble to address each one individually.

Always write to an individual. It's off-putting to a human resources director to be addressed by his job title, for example, and if you write a letter that says "Dear CEO," don't expect an answer. Almost always a little research will give you the name—or you can even call the firm and ask for it.

The lead, generally the first paragraph, is critical—and should immediately engage the reader by stating what the letter is about and why he or she should be interested, although you won't say it that way. Throughout, use words that tell readers what to especially notice; for example, "the main idea," "more important to consider," "my most significant qualification" and so on.

The guidelines we followed in earlier chapters for determining your goal, audience, tone, structure and content will see you through every letter, no matter how challenging. We'll concentrate in this chapter on letters for career-building purposes, plus a few general business letter examples to help you apply the ideas.

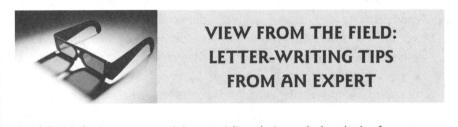

VIEW FROM THE FIELD: LETTER-WRITING TIPS FROM AN EXPERT

Carol C. Weeks, a corporate training specialist who's taught hundreds of government employees and executive assistants to write better business letters, offers these tips.

1. Always start by putting the reader in the picture. So much material begins with "I," and that's not nearly as effective as finding a way to start with "you." For example, rather than saying "I appreciated your taking the time to speak with me,"

say, "Your taking the time to speak with me is appreciated" or "Thank you for taking the time to speak with me."

"You will see my schedule attached" is better than "I'm attaching. . . ." And "Your presentation was excellent" is better than "I enjoyed your presentation very much."

This approach may mean using the passive voice, which you're told generally to avoid, but it gives you a better opening. You can use "I" and avoid the passive in the rest of the letter.

2. Don't use all the jargon that makes so much writing meaningless. "Feel free to call me" says nothing—of course the person feels free to call you. "As per your instructions" is so stilted, "as we discussed" is better. Don't say "Call me at your earliest convenience." It's never convenient. Be specific: "Please let me know by December 15."

3. Take care not to sound condescending. When we reviewed letters written at an urban housing agency, we often saw language like "We will not tolerate people sneaking into the facility." There's never a reason to write like that. It's better to sandwich a negative between two positive statements. For example, "We're pleased to count you as a tenant. Please note that the recreation facility is not open after 10 p.m. Thank you for keeping this in mind."

APPLYING THE IDEAS TO SPECIFIC LETTER NEEDS

Thank You Very Much . . .

Good thank you letters are hard to write: Just ask a communications specialist who works for a nonprofit. Coming up with credible ways to say "thanks for giving" is a constant challenge, especially since the important donors give periodically and gratitude must be expressed differently each time. But every organization knows that future contributions depend on effective thank you letters.

Thank you letters are equally important to you. They're in order when someone interviews you for a job, introduces you virtually, suggests a good contact, recommends you and a host of other situations where an in-person or telephone thank you is inappropriate or impractical.

To work out the characteristics of a good written thank you, consider what you'd like to receive from a charitable cause to which you sent a substantial check. No doubt you'd prefer it to be

- Sincere: conveying a genuine sense of appreciation
- Personal: appearing to be addressed to you, not a mass audience

- Specific: describing how your contribution will help the cause
- Timely: reinforcing a good deed is most effective done soon

Suppose now that you're in the recipient's shoes. You've asked friends and relatives for money to build a library in a Nicaraguan village and received a good response. What could you write in appreciation? Here's one approach, which I'll use at the same time to demonstrate the basic format recommended.

JACOB SLATER
135 Rodeway Place
Washington, D.C. 01234
202–123–5678

November 14, 2012
Mr. Joe Constant
246 River Road
Washington, D.C. 10235

Dear Joe:

Thank you so very much for your contribution to Library Build. Your support for a cause I believe in so deeply means a lot to me.

As you know, when I visited Nicaragua as part of the school's student aid group last year, I was struck by how happy the children were—and adults too—with the few Spanish books we had thought to bring. They shared them with such wonder, we wished we'd brought more. In talking about the trip later, we decided that starting a small library for the village would truly be a gift that would keep giving.

Your contribution is helping to make the idea real for a whole village. We're collecting books right now and a group of us will travel to Perdita in spring to help construct a simple building. Your contribution is helping us buy the supplies we need.

So, Joe, from all the people of Perdita, and from me, thank you for your generosity. I look forward to sharing pictures of the construction with you soon.

Sincerely,
Jake
Jacob Slater
Volunteer Director
Books for Perdita

Does the letter come across as sincere, personal and specific? Do you find it a bit effusive? Would you write it differently? Remember, put yourself in the other person's framework and think about how you'd feel receiving the message.

SIDELIGHT: PSYCHOLOGISTS SAY WRITING "THANK YOU" MATTERS

A number of studies have shown that thanking people makes us feel good and improves relationships. But recently a pair of psychologists (Adam M. Grant and Francesca Gino) studied the effects on individuals who are being thanked. Interestingly for us, the example they chose was to ask people to help a fictitious student named Eric with a job application cover letter. Half the people got an e-mailed thank you back, the rest got a neutral response.

When "Eric" then asked for more help, 66% of the thanked people agreed to give it, while just 32% of those who had not been thanked were willing. The investigators followed up by sending an e-mail from a second invented student, "Steven," asking for similar help. Among the group whom Eric had failed to thank, 25% offered to help Steven; by contrast, 55% of the group that had been thanked was willing.

The lesson: Expressing appreciation not only works to get you more help should you need it, but contributes to how people respond to others asking for help in the future.

—"A Little Thanks Goes a Long Way: Explaining Why Gratitude Expressions Motivate Prosocial Behavior" appeared in the *Journal of Personality and Social Psychology* in June 2010.

The same principle of expressing appreciation applies to many office and networking situations. If someone you work with does you a favor or helps you look good; if a subordinate goes to extra lengths so you can meet that deadline; if a supervisor gives you a special opportunity or if a client refers you to a prospect, it's smart to say thank you. And a written message tends to resonate even more than a spoken one.

Be sure to make your response timely. In fact, if someone connects you with a person you want to meet, it's best to thank the go-between before the meeting happens. You owe appreciation whether the event goes well or not. It's a good idea to write again to report on the meeting itself—or telephone. Better yet, take your matchmaker to lunch.

What if the meeting doesn't actually go well? This raises some interesting questions about what to put in writing. Here's an example.

Sam virtually introduced Angela to a former employer with a job opening in Angela's field. After the meeting, Angela wrote,

Dear Sam—Thanks so much for making it possible for me to meet with Mark White. I saw him yesterday. He was very nice to me, and the job sounds great. Unfortunately,

> I totally blew the interview. By the time we met at 4 p.m., I'd had a really bad day and on top of that, I was unprepared for questions about the gap in my résumé from a few years back. I apologize for letting you down but no one could feel worse about it than me.
>
> I promise to do better next time.—Angela

What do you think Angela's chances are of seeing a "next time"?

Of course, it's always awful to flub an opportunity, but especially when someone else has put himself on the line by recommending you. But it happens. When it does, write yourself out of the worst scenario by focusing on your goal and desired outcome: Here you want to inform Sam that the interview wasn't perfect, sure, but you need to maintain his confidence in you as much as possible. This means there's no point in telling your benefactor that you disgraced yourself and took him with you.

Here's one solution:

> Dear Sam—Thanks so much for making it possible for me to meet with Mark White. I saw him yesterday.
>
> He was very nice to me, and obviously thinks very highly of you. Mark generously spent more than an hour with me and gave me a very good understanding of the open position. At this point, I don't know if he considers me a good match for it, but I'll be very happy if he does.
>
> In any case, I learned a lot about the industry from our conversation and I got some new ideas about how to position myself more effectively for the right opportunities.
>
> So again, thanks so very much for introducing me to Mark and enabling me to have this valuable experience.—Angela

Do you think it's dishonest to send such a message?

Consider that (1) Angela can't know that Mark was as critical of her as she is of herself, and (2) she's not made any false statements. The letter puts things in a way that encourages Sam to feel good about himself, which is only fair. It's clear that Angela values the experience whatever the specific outcome. While she might worry that Mark will tell Sam that she messed up, this is not likely. At worst he's more apt to say something like "Thanks, but it wasn't a good match," so as not to insult Sam's judgment.

ACTION TIME: WRITE A THANK YOU

Think about a connection you'd particularly value if a former colleague could ease the way for you. Assume your colleague made a virtual introduction and you will soon have a telephone conversation with the person you'd like to know. Write a letter expressing appreciation to the colleague, making your message sincere, personal and specific.

After the Job Interview

Should you always write a thank you to the person who interviewed you for a job? Well, only if you're seriously interested in the job, the company, future opportunities or your career. In other words, just about always. It's plain dumb not to give yourself the edge that courtesy and a well-written letter can produce. It's another chance to outdistance the competition and showcase your abilities.

Suppose you've just been interviewed by the assistant manager of a large multinational for a spot in the marketing department. This thank you letter is more complicated to create than those we've been talking about, and should be based on the structure we've practiced with e-mails. Here's how it might work.

Your goal: to advance your candidacy for a highly competitive job.

Your audience: an individual you spent time with and observed—so you know the person's age and something about personality, communication style, company status and so on. That's all relevant, *but*—because this is a highly structured interaction between a prospective employer's representative and you, a candidate . . .

Your tone needs to be formal and businesslike. And just as for a charity's thank you, the letter must feel very sincere.

Content: What will work? One approach:

- A paragraph expressing appreciation
- A paragraph expressing enthusiasm and confidence in your ability to perform
- A good close confirming your availability for further interviews, or to start the job
- And—if at all possible, new information about how exceptionally qualified you are

This is where to draw on your personal impressions: Replay the conversation, visualize the person, and figure out ways to distinguish yourself that the interviewer, and/or the company, will value. It's also the time to think through any points in your favor that you forgot to make in person.

Here's a simple example.

Dear Ms. Royal:

Thank you so much for speaking with me Thursday about the Marketing Associate position at Brandon Inc. I enjoyed our conversation and appreciate your taking the time to tell me about the company and the job.

Your description of the job convinced me more than ever that it is the right opportunity for me, and that my background is an excellent fit with your needs. Thanks to my three years of experience with Malibu Inc., I'll bring a solid grounding in retail marketing practice backed by my course work in White University's MBA Program.

I'd also like to share that over the past five years, I've found additional opportunities to build the communications skills I believe are so important to the profession. I serve as managing editor of White's management newsletter, and have been an active member of Toastmasters International for two years. Recently, I helped win a regional debating competition.

Again, thank you for encouraging my application and I look forward to the next step.

Sincerely,

You've no doubt written letters like this already, and won't be surprised that even a straightforward one takes plenty of time and thought. The more advanced your credentials or experience, the more difficult these letters are to write—and the more important. If you're applying for a creative job, you must really work to show off your originality.

GOING DEEPER: PROSPECTING FOR SALES

Good writing is essential to sales.

Even with stellar marketing materials you can't get away with an inability to write when it comes to client relationships and prospects. The wooing and wowing stage of prospecting demands communication and you need writing to articulate your interest, tell them how you'll improve their situation and keep in contact with them.

You need writing to ask for an appointment, follow up on a proposal and ask clarifying questions—it's often easier to get a response by e-mail than a phone call. And you always need a written trail of confirmation and verification.

And, I find that you can't just sit there and wait for clients any more. They won't come, and networking is not enough. So I e-mail cold-call letters. It works.

> —Adrian Miller, Adrian Miller Sales Training;
> author of *The Blatant Truth: 50 Ways to Sales Success*

Adrian's one-page sales letter:

Dear _____:

Are your sales AND operations functioning at peak performance? Are you sure?

Over the last several years, companies of all sizes have been hit hard with shrinking market share and dwindling profits. While signs of recovery are becoming more evident, most organizations are not positioned for future success in this rapidly evolving economy.

To ensure both greater stability and growth in the future, you must optimize both sales and operations now.

Because every business is unique, there is no cookie-cutter solution. This is where we can help.

These lead paragraphs are followed by sections on "who we are" and "what we do," ending with . . .

Would you like more information?

If you're ready to find out more about how we can help your business move forward with greater stability and success, give us a call. We are good listeners, and we promise not to waste your time with rhetoric and generic "consultant speak."

Sincerely,

Rejection Letters

If you haven't yet been in the position of having to write a rejection letter, you may not believe it, but these are famously tough to write, too. Let's see how the systematic process applies to an entirely different goal.

Suppose you're in charge of the internship program at your organization, and must tell several candidates that the decision has gone against them. The goal here is to write a letter that considers their feelings but unequivocally delivers the bad news. This is important: Beyond the fact that any rejection deserves careful attention—we've all been on that receiving end and the experience stays with us—maintaining the candidate's good will toward the company is high priority.

In line with the concept of delivering the bad news immediately, crafting a lead is not very hard:

> Dear _____:
>
> Your interest in working as an intern for the Ivy Company this summer is greatly appreciated. Unfortunately, we will not be able to offer you a place.

The hard part comes next: What reason can you give? Try brainstorming the possibilities. Here are a few:

> We had a large number of outstanding candidates this year and had to make a tough decision.
>
> More than 100 people applied and we only have room for three.
>
> We needed to coordinate different skill sets to build a balanced team.
>
> We recognize that you are highly qualified but other candidates had specific experience we need.

If any of these rationales strike echoes from the past, it's because colleges as well as businesses use similar terminology, and not lightly: How to word rejection letters can keep admissions officers up at night and the results don't always succeed in spreading good will.

Especially if you're writing to a particular individual, you should also brainstorm any ways to soften the blow or even to be directly helpful. Such an element might give you a good closing. For example:

> We are certain that the company you work at will benefit from your presence.
>
> We invite you to apply again next summer.
>
> We'd be happy to talk with you when you graduate should a full-time position be open.
>
> I suggest you to talk to X at Y Company, which has a larger associate program than ours.

If it's not appropriate or honest to say any of these things, and you can't come up with an alternative, then you might close with simply a "good luck" statement.

ACTION TIME: WRITE A REJECTION LETTER

What can you add to the list of reasons for rejecting the candidates? Or ways to "soften the blow"? Draft a complete letter rejecting an internship candidate. Produce a cohesive, thoughtful message with an effective closing statement. Try for a letter that would make you feel relatively good if you were on the receiving end.

Problem-fixing Letters

In the business environment, letters can be critical to maintaining good relationships with clients, vendors, collaborators, investors and more. Here, tone is really critical: How friendly should a message be, or how formal? How personal should you get? It depends on the situation and the relationship, and on your specific goal. Often it takes some thinking to settle on the right voice.

For example, suppose you head a department and you've learned that a supplier has been overcharging for "fabrications." It's your role to rectify this. A letter is called for.

Your audience: Bob Brown, your contact at the supplier, who has always been pleasant. The relationship is cordial but not personal. Until now, Bob's firm has been reliable, provided good quality products at good prices and accommodated you in difficult scheduling situations.

Your goal: You want the error acknowledged and restitution made. But: You must also consider the longer-range goals. Your options include

1. Fire the supplier immediately—maybe even sue for the overcharge.

2. Let Bob know you're angry and demand an apology.

3. Get the error acknowledged, ensure you are not charged more than you've agreed to again and maintain the good working relationship.

If you review your options dispassionately—which the structure we're practicing is designed to help you do—you'll see that Option #1 is clearly against your interests. You'd need to find a new equivalent supplier and build a new relationship.

Your response should take into account how much trouble that would be. At the least, the effort will be time-consuming and you'll end up with an untested supplier.

Option #2 is tempting, it's always nice to vent—but rarely productive. And you should consider that you don't actually know whether the error was deliberate or a billing mistake. So why not act as if the supplier is honest, which may be the case, and be satisfied with ensuring that it doesn't happen again?

That leads you to embrace Option #3 as your goal.

Tone: The occasion calls for fairly formal business style with a no-nonsense, non-judgmental, very matter-of-fact atmosphere.

Structuring the message: The principles we've established tell us to lead with strength and immediately engage the reader with the subject, organize our points in the simplest way and end with a confirmation or call to action.

ACTION TIME: YOUR TURN

Draft the message you would write before reading the sample version. Make up whatever details you like about the actual error.

Here's one way the situation can be handled.

Dear Bob:

I've learned that your invoice #5742A of July 7 is in error.

The price of #12 fabrications is calculated at $34 per thousand. However, the correct price according to our most recent contract is $31. Thus, on our order for 3,000 boxes, it appears we've been billed $9,000 too much.

Of course, we'd like this corrected immediately. Please confirm that you'll send a corrected invoice.

Acme and Ideal have been working together a long time, Bob, and I hope this matter can be quickly resolved so we can continue to do so.

Sincerely,
Joan

COVER LETTERS: THE GUIDELINES

I've left this subject for last because, in many ways, creating good cover letters is one of the biggest challenges. Knowing how to write good ones prepares you for many other letter-writing challenges.

In business, you may need cover letters to accompany proposals, forms, questionnaires and a host of other documents. Or the letter itself may present the proposal or form. And, of course, you need cover letters to accompany résumés. Here too, there are times when a cover letter must carry the whole weight of introducing you; a résumé may not be desired or appropriate.

Job application cover letters are critical for gaining entry into a business or profession, and, probably, every time you're trying for a new job. Always send a cover letter with a résumé or job application unless the posting specifically says not to. It may be presented as optional, but it's not.

> ## ⬤ SUCCESS TIP: SHOW A GENEROUS SPIRIT
>
> In the business world, when you've got someone dead to rights, and can decimate their position on an issue or disprove their argument, it's often best to show a generosity of spirit. Go out of your way to let the person save face and you'll probably be repaid many times over. You may even want to invent excuses for them, with phrases such as "I know you've been too busy to read all the material on this . . ." or "Congratulations on concluding the X negotiation. I hope there's time now to turn to . . ." Or, "I've identified some additional information that has a bearing on . . ."

Adopt the Right Attitude

Producing a very correct letter is important, and I'll give you the guidelines for doing so, but don't lose sight of the big picture—how you want to be perceived.

Your cover letter should feel totally positive and upbeat. This is not the place to voice reservations about your qualifications or personality. Aim to show enthusiasm, even passion, for the work you want to do, the field or profession, and the specific job opening, as appropriate.

Harder to accomplish: Don't be a bore. It's probable that every job you apply for will be highly competitive, and the organization will receive far more applications than the screeners really want to read. A creative element will gain you favor.

These days, very few employers are looking solely for technical skills, unless they plan to plant you in some hidden back office. The "soft skills"—relating to people, teaming, leading, communicating well—are almost universally valued. Prospective employers want to know who you are, how you'll fit. The cover letter is your chance to tell them.

Remember that the people you're writing to are focused on their own problems and challenges. They work hard to explain what they want. It's your job to match yourself to those needs. If you're doing a "cold" job hunt—writing letters in the hope of unearthing an unadvertised opportunity—you need to figure out what problem the firm might have, and present yourself as a solution.

In both cases, a generalized letter that simply says,

> I'm applying for the position of ABC at your firm . . . my qualifications are great . . . my résumé is attached . . .

doesn't stand much of a chance.

VIEW FROM THE FIELD: THE COVER LETTER OPPORTUNITY

With cover letters I like to tell people, "be authentic." Use language that is comfortable to you and include things that are really genuine. If you're asked about something that isn't genuine, you'll speak about it badly.

Customize cover letters to the job. A generic one does you no service. It must say here are my strengths, what I bring to you. It's an opportunity to sell yourself, so be original to the extent that it applies to the job. It's okay to bring in an anecdote. And it's a great place to tell your story if it's not on the résumé. For example, if you're leaving banking to work for a nonprofit, share why you're doing that. If there's an odd gap in your résumé, if it's not linear, the cover letter is the place to say what brought you to different places.

—Stephanie Shambroom Boms, consultant for strategy, leadership development and recruitment; Yale MBA

Plan for Success

Never dash off a cover letter at the last minute. Most of your competitors spend excruciating weeks on polishing their résumés, and then write sloppy, ill-crafted, thought-free cover letters. Or—maybe worse—they don't include cover letters at all. Either way, probably no one will ever read those painstakingly produced résumés. Everything the audience needs to know is right up front, in the form of a badly written letter, or absence of any at all. Cover letters must embody your best writing: Invest the necessary time to plan, brainstorm, draft and revise.

Remember your goal. A cover letter should introduce you in a more personal, targeted way than a résumé. It need not give a comprehensive overview of your career and qualifications—that's what the résumé is for (if enclosed)—but should aim to

- Present an insight about you that the résumé format doesn't accommodate
- Highlight your most relevant experience or credential and add a little detail
- Suggest some personality, or personal attributes, relevant to the job
- Set the stage for the reader to review your résumé as you would like
- Show why you are the most qualified person for the job

Always, the last point on the list is the most critical: *A strong application demands that you **know** why you are the person that the company should hire.* Have a good answer to "why me," and the cover letter will reflect your conviction and include the facts to back it up. And so will the interview.

Absorb the organization's philosophy and priorities. If you're answering a posting, read it 20 times, it's full of clues about what the advertiser wants and what's important to the company. Look at the company's website and whatever other materials you can access—talk to people who know the firm if you can. Especially if you're sending a cold-call query, try to figure out "what keeps them up at night."

VIEW FROM THE FIELD:
SELL, DON'T TELL

A generic cover letter will hurt you. It must be specific to the job you're applying for, so spend more time researching that company and its products. Write to sell me, not tell me. Get right into the specifics: "My name is . . . I found on Monster that you're searching for . . . I'm eager to have my résumé before you because . . . here's what I can do on this job." You don't have to produce a Disney novel—I'm just looking for somebody

(Continued)

(Continued)

who took the time to understand who we are. But a cover letter can show more energy, enthusiasm and confidence than a résumé—a bit more of your personality.

How to dodge the salary question? Even when a job ad asks for your salary requirements, it's perfectly fine to say "My salary requirements remain open and flexible, as I need to learn more about the responsibilities of this position."

—Doug Silverman, general manager of human resources, Nikon Inc.; president, Society of Human Resource Managers/Long Island

Name that connection. If you have a personal link of any kind to the recipient or organization, say so up front. Name-dropping can work wonders: Who wouldn't rather hire somebody who comes vouched for, even a little bit? So don't be shy if you can come up with anything relevant—for example, that

- Someone the recipient knows suggested you write—a colleague, former employer, professor, friend
- You share a mutual acquaintance
- You saw the person speak at a conference
- You went to the same school
- Your father or cousin worked there

The list is in descending order of usefulness.

It's not just about you: Say something nice about the person you're writing to, and/ or compliment the organization. Few people do this and it can be magical. Examples:

- I know you're a leader in your field because . . .
- I read your book (or article) on X and was fascinated by . . .
- I've followed your career with interest because . . .
- I admire the strategic marketing tactics you introduced . . .
- As someone who follows the business press, I know that Y is the leading company in its market . . .
- I'm impressed by how Y Inc. has created breakthrough products in only five years . . .
- Z told me that working for you was the best experience he ever had.

But don't follow this advice without doing your homework. If you write to Apple, admiring their innovative spirit will get you sleepy sneers. If you want to compliment an organization's ethics, make sure the leaders haven't been indicted lately. Take the time to know what you're talking about and be able to cite some detail—what makes the firm outstanding, what the CEO has a right to be proud of, what her book is about. Find a truly good reason why you want to work there.

Use the language, style and key words of your audience. Cover letters, like résumés, are partial exceptions to the "no buzzwords" rule. Aim to reflect the company's style and focus and get your message across in terms these readers will relate to. This is especially important because many reviewers will scan your letter rather than read it, and may do this digitally. That said, people often don't like to read the way they write themselves, or don't like the biz speak that job ads provoke, so a conversational (but courteous) style is still best. And be wary of adding any jargon of your own to theirs.

Consider using a testimonial. It can be incorporated into the body of your letter, or added as a "pullout" carefully placed on the page with the name, position and affiliation of the person you're quoting. A testimonial can speak to your technical qualifications but at least equally well to your personal qualities—for example perseverance, hard-work habits, people skills, fast learning, taking initiative and so on. This is particularly effective if you don't yet have a lot of work experience to your credit. A professor who likes you is a great source.

Take the initiative for follow-up. Don't tell the reader when to call you—almost always it's better to say that you will call in a few days to schedule the interview. But use common sense: If the job posting says "Don't call us, we'll call you," or a phone number seems deliberately hard to track down, don't try to call.

SIDELIGHT: COVER LETTERS FROM HELL

Never underestimate the staying power of terrible cover letters. Bob Killian of Killian Branding reviews hundreds of applicant letters for creative jobs at his Chicago advertising agency. From these he culls "Cover Letters from Hell." Posted on the company website (killianbranding.com) these letters draw an immense and amused audience.

But it's not funny to be the person gaining such recognition. How to avoid it? Killian says, "Make it efficient, clear, don't bury the lead—most of the things are

(Continued)

(Continued)

commonsensical. Many people using biz speak—the bafflegab of the clichés we make fun of—that's a smokescreen but rarely advances the cause of the writer."

Other mistakes: "Believing that my ideas and intense wonderfulness will come through no matter how I say it. Not recognizing the value of asking someone else to read it before you send it out. Not proofreading and spell checking."

"Young people tend not to hear the sound of what they're writing—always a mistake."

See the company's website for more advice along with this encouraging statement:

"Good news: An error-free letter is now so freakin' rare that the minimal care required to send a letter with zero defects, combined with a few crisply written simple declarative sentences, will, alone, guarantee a respectful reading of a résumé. Maybe even secure an interview."

Technical Tips

Keep the letter to one-page maximum. Less is better. If you're writing a cover letter that will be e-mailed, keep it even shorter—like three brief paragraphs. Needing to be brief is one reason not to waste space on stock phrases, stilted language and obvious statements (like "It is herewith my pleasure to provide you with . . . in response to your recent posting for . . .").

Don't send letters that look mass-produced. If you're mailing an inquiry to 500 prospective employers, personalize and tailor each and every one and include at least something that demonstrates your interest in that specific company.

Use people's names. Addressing letters "To whom it may concern," "Sir" or "Madame" and "Dear Marketing VP" doesn't cut it. Take the trouble to find out who holds the position—now, not five years ago.

Use a formal and respectful salutation. For men, Dear Mr. Wise is appropriate; for women, use Ms., unless you have reason to think the person prefers another form of address (as when, for example, a communication you're responding to is signed "Mrs. Ann Green"). If you're unsure of the person's gender, use the full name—"Dear W. Sutton."

Specify the job posting you're applying for. Write the name of the position in the upper right-hand corner or before the salutation (so you don't have to waste space on that in the actual letter).

Use all the good writing techniques you've been practicing. Short comfortable words, short clear sentences, short paragraphs; concise language with good transitions; lively verbs. This is one of the most impatient audiences you'll have. A good lead is crucial for keeping your résumé out of the trash.

Remember the serial audience. Expect your cover letter to be screened by somebody in the hiring office, a department head, the CFO's assistant, or the new intern. Or the CEO. Fortunately, the letters I'm preparing you to write will work at every level.

Close respectfully and traditionally. "Sincerely" is generally best.

Make it look good. If your cover letter is accompanying a print résumé, use good quality paper, generous margins and white space, a clear typeface like Times Roman in 11 point or bigger and match the heading and style to that of your résumé for a uniform impression. Keep in mind that when you e-mail your application, fancy formatting and fonts may get lost in cyberspace.

VIEW FROM THE FIELD: SIMPLE COVER LETTERS CAN WORK

Recruitment firms and some employers tend to prefer direct, straightforward cover letters:

Just be as simple, clear and brief as possible. Use the first paragraph to say "why I'm writing," and the second paragraph to say "why you should be interested in me." It's fine to begin with "In response to your ad for . . ." or "I'm writing to apply for . . ." Then immediately bridge to how you qualify.

—Rich Young, senior recruiter, Chaloner Associates

How to Craft Custom Cover Letters

Since this book's objective is to equip you to write your own first-rate, customized documents, don't look here for cookie-cutter samples to follow. You'll find plenty online—but you'll also find that most are not very good.

To get you thinking along productive lines, let's look at a specific job announcement. This is a slightly abbreviated version of how a Fortune 500 company (which we'll rename "JA") describes its MBA Human Resources Leadership Program.

> . . . an intensive two-year program consisting of three, eight-month rotational assignments in the human resources functions of a JA business. The program combines job assignments with focused training and leadership opportunities . . .
>
> Candidate criteria: basically 2 years related work experience, MBA, GPA of at least 3.0 and geographically mobile.

That's not much to go on. However, the company website also provides several short videos to inspire candidates. One hints at the general attributes the company wants for all of its competitive leadership training programs: *ambition, a natural disposition to work hard, dedication to making a difference, team skills, global outlook.*

There's also a video specifically about the HR program. Current participants are featured talking about their work *bridging communication gaps, getting into the hearts and minds of people, interacting with people worldwide, being a talent champion and being willing to move out of comfort zones.*

How would you present your case to compete for this opportunity?

First, brainstorm all your obvious matching points. Make a list. This might, for example, include

- Your MBA from a school known for its marketing focus
- 3.5 grade point average
- Three years experience that can be interpreted as related work
- Yes, you're willing to go anywhere

Okay, you meet the formal criteria but clearly that's not enough. So . . .

Second, ask yourself: What in your background speaks to the skills that are specified—and just as important, the skills that are implied? These can be listed as

- Ambition
- Hard-work ethic
- Making-a-difference orientation
- Good teaming
- Leadership potential
- Relating well to people

- Global viewpoint
- Flexibility
- Enthusiasm for HR work
- Ability to take initiative

Also, the company no doubt wants assurance that you'll really appreciate this opportunity, are prepared to make the most of it and will welcome challenge.

You must come up with concrete facts and evidence to show you possess the desired skills and attitude. If the opportunity is any kind of a match for your credentials and personality, you can definitely do this. If you find it hard, try a version of the visualization technique described in Chapter 2. Imagine you're being interviewed for the job (perhaps by one of the managers featured in the video if provided) and imagine the questions you'd be asked. Or role-play the situation with a friend asking the questions. Write down all your possible answers.

Three, now study your list and check off your best selling points and evidence. Mull these over and do some freethinking to find ideas for the lead—and don't rule out any that seem nontraditional or far-fetched.

Before I offer some creative approaches, let's say that a simple "classic" lead will often serve you fine. As some of our experts quoted in this chapter say, straightforward and "correct" may alone help you stand out. So you might lead your letter to "JA" like this, with variation to taste:

> I'm writing to apply for a position in your MBA Human Resources Leadership Program, which I was extremely interested to discover on your website. I believe my work experience, education and personal qualities thoroughly equip me to make the most of this outstanding opportunity.
>
> I will be awarded my MBA from the White School in May . . .

However, when you face a lot of competition, it's often worth taking pain to stand out from the field. Imaginative presentation can make the difference. This is also true when you're trying for a job that's a stretch.

Here are a few different approaches to the "JA" ad to demonstrate how to think through your strategy. *The examples will suggest some useful language, even if you don't like the overall pitch or find them inappropriate.* Note that in some ways these general-type job postings are hardest to do. When the employer gives you a lot of information, you can key your response off the specs.

An engaging lead requires hard thinking. But when you settle on one, the rest of the letter begins to fall into place. Notice how short these examples are. If a résumé is attached, you don't need more. If you're applying without a résumé, you'll have to compose a middle section—a few paragraphs—that summarizes your top matching points with the job you want. But try to keep a readable style rather than listing 20 bullet points or condensing your whole life into a page. (More about this in Chapter 12, "Presenting Yourself.")

Example A

When I was 9, I sold more Girl Scout cookies than anyone in the county—even though my family was small. When I was 15, I talked 30 classmates into a waterfront cleanup program. In college, I founded an International Studies Club and while earning my MBA, created a Speaker Program that drew the region's business leaders to our doorstep.

In my two years in the Talent Management department of a leading regional manufacturer, I was twice commended for improvements in the recruitment system.

Now I'm ready to work harder than ever and learn from the best in human resources, the profession that fits my nature, experience and education.

I know that JA is leading the way toward new models in talent management and economic development worldwide. I look forward to learning more about your Leadership Development Program in Human Resources, but am already sure that it's my ideal opportunity: a chance to grow, meet new challenges and contribute to the profession that creates the meeting point between global business and individual people.

I hope you will invite me to talk about the program with you.

Example B (note testimonial at end)

Your description of JA's Leadership Program for MBAs inspired me to speak with three White Business School alumni who have joined your staff. What they told me resonates with my highest career hopes: to learn from the field's best people while building my leadership skills, interacting globally, and practicing out-of-the-box thinking to solve tough problems.

My career to date has prepared me to make the most of this opportunity. Beyond my intensive MBA and undergraduate studies in management and psychology, I have

- Developed my communication skills through elective programs in writing, speaking and presentation
- Produced a comparative analysis of personality evaluation systems, chosen for White Business School's "Best Resources" annual

- Chaired a student advisory board to help MBA program directors align academics with shifting workplace models
- Handled four full HR-related internships in three years, giving me field experience in a range of industries

I'd be delighted to explore my candidacy for the Leadership Program with you.

John Black is among the most dedicated students I've had the pleasure of teaching. I was able to count on him to introduce interesting angles for classroom discussion, produce substantial original research rather than just routinely fulfilling assignments, and to relish the complex challenges that confront today's HR practitioner.

—Professor Jane Umber, Talent Management class, White Business School

Example C

When I was 14, my father lost the job he'd held for 24 years because the company closed down his department. I sensed how tragic this was, though he tried to hide that from us. But a company HR manager intervened: He spent hours with my Dad, talking through his work history, qualifications and long-ago aspirations. The bottom line—my father agreed to obtain some specialized training, and the company rehired him in a new capacity that worked out well.

So while other people cite a great doctor or entrepreneur as an inspiration, I've always remembered how a good HR manager made a big difference in my family's lives by doing his job well. As my résumé indicates, I've held this idea throughout my school years and prepared every way I can think of for a career in Human Resources. I've chosen my course work, my extracurricular activities, internships and summer jobs to broaden my perspective on managing talent to maximize organizational effectiveness—and help people.

I look forward to an opportunity to discuss why I am a perfect fit for the Human Resources Leadership Program.

Example D

As an enthusiastic reader of many Human Capital journals, I know how challenging today's global business environment is and how much the human resources profession can contribute. It is the HR specialist who is called on to manage the people side of complex multinational organizations, find and retain the right talent, prepare workers for a new world and anticipate needs that won't exist until tomorrow.

I consider HR the most exciting profession of all and my goal is to contribute to it.

My résumé outlines how I've prepared to make the most of the JA Leadership Program. Beyond meeting your criteria, I bring five years' professional experience handling a spectrum of personnel responsibilities in two different industries. I take pride in being known as the go-to person for problem solving, someone who can find common ground between diverse viewpoints.

On the concrete level, I was credited in my most recent role for increasing job ad response rates by 37%, while reducing advertising costs by 55%.

I'd like very much to explore how my experience and interests correlate with this extraordinary opportunity to grow.

Example E

In my Talent Management class last year, as a first-year MBA student at White, I was assigned a case study on handling human resource issues on the international level. The subject was JA's challenge in establishing an operation in Beijing. I was so impressed with the innovative strategies developed by the team that I decided right then that JA was the company I wanted to work for . . .

About these examples: They may not suit your personal style, goals or experience, but may prompt some ideas. Ideally, a cover letter makes readers want to know more, and leads them to notice the "evidence" of your claims when they read the résumé.

Example A paints an image of a person who showed initiative from an early age, demonstrating leadership qualities, people skills and the desired mind-set toward meaningful work and globalism. The lead itself shows off an original cast of mind.

Example B leads by showing a bit of initiative and serious interest because the writer made an extra effort and sought out participants to talk with. Some of the language in the online recruitment material is echoed. The letter goes on to list some "extras" that may or may not be covered in the résumé,

SUCCESS TIP: FIND YOUR STRENGTHS BY THINKING ABOUT . . .

- Your personal history—things you did, learned, hoped for
- School experience: elementary, high school, college, graduate programs in every aspect—academics, sports, clubs, volunteer work, interest groups
- Qualifications: technical capabilities, evidence of leadership and team building, awards and recognition, achievements

(Continued)

but grouped together, testify that this candidate has some special assets. The teacher testimonial is included to show how you might use one.

Example C offers a personal insight into the applicant's reasons for wanting the opportunity and stresses his strong motivation. (Of course, never invent anecdotes like these.)

Example D is more matter-of-fact but suggests a big-picture orientation and a depth of experience that will make the candidate stand out (and which may or may not be found suitable). Note that this candidate uses the "I'm looked to as . . ." statement, and cites a quantified achievement, always great for résumés as well as cover letters.

Example E demonstrates a lead that is simple but more engaging than "I am writing because . . ." When you can make any kind of personal connection to the company, whether a person, an experience or an affinity, use it right up front in the lead.

The idea in sum: Go for the evidence that you are who the organization is looking for, that you're perfectly suited to the job, and

(Continued)

- Personal attributes and "signature strengths": Fast learner? Resilient? Multitasker? People person? Creative thinker? Big-picture viewer? Detail oriented? Good negotiator, or salesperson? Problem solver?
- "Crossover strengths": If you're trying to launch yourself into a new career field or role, and don't yet have a related track record, figure out how your proven capabilities can be transferred to the new work
- Any accomplishments you can quantify
- Any significant people who can back you up with a testimonial (think not just of teachers, but club advisers, the manager of a volunteer activity and others who can talk about your personal qualities with sincerity)
- Good causes you've worked for; these are "hot" today (but be cautious about citing controversial ones)

that everything you've done prepares you for it. The proof truly is there, in your life and experience, provided the job is a reasonably good match—you just have to articulate it.

Cover letters and résumés must supplement each other, or when appropriate, be crafted as a single document. For more ideas on how to showcase yourself effectively, see Chapter 12.

Right now, let's move on to some big challenges, the materials that keep the business world humming: Proposals, reports, business plans and presentations. All require persuasive writing, so first we'll explore effective persuasion techniques from a range of vantage points.

PRACTICE OPPORTUNITIES

I. Practice the "You" Orientation

Find a job application letter you wrote at any point in the past and review it. Can you think of ways to substitute "you" for "I" throughout, especially at the beginning? Rewrite the letter taking "you" into account, as well as the other principles covered in this chapter and the preceding ones.

II. Write a Letter for Bob

Take the role of "Bob," who represents the company where that incorrectly billed its client in the situation described in this chapter. You've received the letter specifying the error and determined that a new accounting clerk had used the wrong price index. Write a letter to your customer, Joan.

III. Respond to Rejection

You've applied for an associate job you wanted, at a company where you hoped to find a foothold, and just received a rejection letter. You're very disappointed but know it would be smart to send a response, because you're planning to try for a full-time job there after completing your degree. Write a complete letter.

IV. Manage a Client

Assume you're an accountant. A client has provided a carton of information you've had to sort through, and you find it doesn't contain some of the major items you asked for: tax returns for the past three years, documentation about technology expenses and correspondence with the IRS about tax shortfalls. Write a letter to the client requesting these materials within three days.

V. Apply to Your Dream Job

Find a posting that at this point represents your dream job once your degree is awarded. Though you're not yet ready to apply, draft the strongest cover letter you can think of making your case. Be sure to

- Brainstorm your history, experience and all qualifications that might relate
- Analyze and interpret the job description and other employer material
- Figure out what you'd bring to the job beyond the bare essentials

- Know why you are the best possible candidate and why the organization should hire you
- Come up with some imaginative leads and evaluate whether they are appropriate

VI. Group Discussion

What's the best rejection letter you ever got? What made it good? And what was the worst one? Where did it go wrong and how did it make you feel?

Share with classmates. Collaborate on a list of bad rejection letter characteristics, and a second list of characteristics that define good ones.

VII. Draft a Letter about Writing Letters

Your department head has noticed that some embarrassing letters are going out to clients and prospects and wants to assemble a short how-to guide for everyone's reference. She's asked for staff input on guidelines to include. Consider what you've learned in this chapter, and the preceding ones, and draft a letter presenting your best advice. Use graphic techniques to make your message clear and readable.

Chapter 8

WRITING TO PERSUADE PART 1

THE TOOLS AND TECHNIQUES

LEARN HOW TO . . .

- ➤ Deploy the tools of persuasion and advocacy
- ➤ Use writing techniques to promote your viewpoint
- ➤ Make the most of your graphic presentation

> *Perhaps the most common problem . . . is that a well-intentioned and informed writer simply fails to get the message across to an intelligent, interested reader. In that case, stilted jargon and complex constructions are usually the villains.*
>
> —Warren E. Buffett

Your everyday writing enables you to demonstrate your professionalism and open doors. Of course, you also need to know how to handle opportunities once they're in hand. Among your likely challenges are creating "long-form" documents such as reports, proposals, presentations and business plans. This and the following chapter will show you how to apply the principles of good contemporary business writing to these materials.

All the techniques you've been practicing for "short-form" communication such as e-mail and letters apply. But with the longer documents, more may be at stake, so they demand more planning, more thinking, more crafting.

Often these documents must be written to persuade, whether to an idea, a viewpoint, a course of action or an investment. Your academic program probably includes courses in marketing, negotiation and other relevant subjects. Everything you learn in these courses applies to persuasive writing.

Look also at the world around you to see persuasive strategies at work. Ads, commercials and solicitations of every sort bombard us in every medium. Cast an analytic eye and ear toward these sales pitches. Notice how they engage your interest and sway you to a cause. Think about how the strategies can be adapted to your own writing needs.

Here, we'll focus on ways to write persuasively with a resource of practical ideas from professional specialists. The tools of persuasive writing are the tools of advocacy. A number of the ideas apply to other media such as speeches, and to times when you are called upon to present or defend a viewpoint.

THE TOOLS OF PERSUASION AND ADVOCACY

The ability to advocate for a cause, whether it's a company's new service or a nonprofit's mission or your own enterprise, is a critical ingredient of today's communication. It involves understanding other people and authentic interaction, not just technical skills.

First, some general concepts to take into account.

Believe in your story. Ask a master salesperson, a public relations executive or an entrepreneur to name the one essential of persuasion and they're likely to say it's personal conviction. To sell something you must believe in it. Some documents call for an objective tone, and in such cases, overenthusiasm may not work. Proposals, for example, should in general feel objective and reasonable, rather than showing emotional attachment to your recommendation. But even in such instances, a quiet conviction should shine through. And it's always right to project a passion for what you do if you're aiming to pull people into your orbit.

Know your story. Drill to the core so you don't get lost in the detail. Unless you focus on your central message and base content decisions upon it, you may miss the mark. Challenge yourself to think like a scriptwriter pitching a producer—you've probably seen it done on film and television and it often works that way: The pitch must boil down to a few sentences that distill the heart of the project—what it's about, who the main players are, why people will care. In fact, scriptwriters try—whatever the subject—to crystallize their theme in three words or less (e.g., "love redeems," "crime doesn't pay" or, in line with shifting mores, "smart crime pays").

Keep in mind that even a 50-page document is ultimately a message. Because it's a major message meant to influence decision making, it may require a lot of backup detail and support material. Nevertheless, it must present your story in a cohesive, simple to follow, convincing way.

Know what you want. Be clear on the result you want the document to achieve and be sure your goal is realistic. You're unlikely to change 100 years of tradition with one proposal, no matter how good. And be sure what you want is 100% clear—the action you endorse, the amount of money you need and, for yourself, your own bottom line.

Clarifying the goal makes content decisions easier throughout the planning process. If you want funding, bottom line numbers and proving your own capabilities are important. If you want to talk someone into a new customer relations strategy, you may need to explain its successful use elsewhere, what will improve, staff training needs and more.

SIDELIGHT: A NEGOTIATOR ON GAINING AGREEMENT

It's a scientific fact that the brain makes decisions in the emotional area 100% of the time. The business writer who understands that spends her time crafting words to create vision, which drives the decision the writer wants. The great negotiators of the world work hard at creating vision for the other party because people make decisions because they see something—"I see how that works and I'll do it." They may see the future, and how a problem can be solved.

Here's the system for negotiating that I train people to use.

1. Create vision in an adversary's world based on mission and purpose.

2. Ask, what problems must we overcome to succeed in this negotiation?

3. What preconceived ideas do we have going in, good or bad, that encumber us? Emotions like excitement, for example, would hinder us.

4. Examine our assumptions about what the other side may be carrying in—for example, did we fail to deliver on time two quarters ago and are they still angry?

5. What do we want to accomplish from this negotiation? I always want a decision, even if it's a rejection.

6. What should we do next? In the case of a reader, what should the reader do next?

To me a writer is negotiating. It's about painting pictures with words to create vision—being conscious of the purpose of this paragraph, this sentence. A writer invests effort into bringing about agreement to what he's saying or delivering.

We often destroy vision by overloading the knowledge.

—Jim Camp, CEO/founder, Camp Negotiation Systems;
author of *Start with No and No: The Only System of
Negotiation You Need for Work and Home*

Know your audience. See things through your readers' eyes. Like a letter, a proposal, business plan or report succeeds when framed in "you" terms, not "I" or "we." These documents are not about you or even your company. They are about the reader's needs, problems and hopes. If you're responding to an RFP, mine it for clues—analyze the questions asked and the reasons behind them. If you're assembling an in-house proposal, center it on the problem your recommendation will solve.

Think too about where your primary readers' self-interest lies, what they know about your subject, how they are likely to feel about it, what elements they will resist, their hot buttons, the arguments and evidence they will find convincing: Hard data? Anecdotes? Expert opinion? Historical context? Impact on the bottom line, or on people, or company image, or personal reputation?

Focus on benefits, not features. This is the mantra that drives marketing and advertising. A feature is a fact, such as a car's high horsepower engine, a skirt's A-line pleating, a customized training system. The benefit is what the feature will do for you—for example, the hot car will make you feel young and powerful; the skirt will help you look slim so you feel attractive and confident going to the party; the training program will teach your employees exactly what you want them to know without wasting their time and your money.

Effective marketing sells benefits, not features. Figuring out benefits takes some work. Look at your product from your customers' perspective, and ask, what will this feature do for me? Why would I want it? Why would I want to change the services I buy—or my opinion? Take account of this thought pattern in all your marketing messages.

Write with a particular person in mind. Just as this helps focus your everyday messages, it helps focus substantial documents. Pick someone you know who typifies the audience you're addressing. Visualize that person as you write, and you'll have a good sense of his or her level of knowledge, concerns and probable questions. It's easier to gauge what might be clear to one individual than a sea of unknowns.

Write with a sincere effort to inform and educate. Never patronize your readers or allow that sense to permeate your documents. Think about the reasons you hold a certain conviction and how you can share that reasoning with others. Providing information may be important. Bringing the reader along with you through the facts that led you to a conclusion, or a logical sequence of ideas, can open their minds.

It's especially powerful to give people facts and ideas that lead them to draw their own conclusions. If that sounds hard to do, try to provide as much as you can to guide them, step by step, toward the "right" conclusion so that when you express it yourself, your readers are ready to agree. That's a good target to aim at for all persuasive writing.

SIDELIGHT: A PSYCHOLOGIST'S ADVICE ON ADVOCACY

To communicate your viewpoint or effect change, first listen and look for common ground. Make a genuine effort to understand the other person's point of view and identify things that you can appreciate. When people feel listened to and understood, they are more open to another's perspective. Then when you engage in a discussion about alternative possibilities, the person is more likely to be receptive to your perspective.

You must be genuinely respectful and authentic—people are very intuitive and will sense any effort to manipulate them. Be sensitive to their frames of reference and speak in a language they will understand. Talking to a technologically oriented person when you're a businessperson, for example, can be like speaking English to someone whose language is French. When you're advocating, it's up to you to adapt your language. You have to translate, put your proposal in a language that takes into account the other person's way of looking at the world.

Don't stop listening. Pay attention and don't make assumptions. If you get caught up in your own ideas and forget the other person, you lose your connection. Always show respect for the other person and don't focus so much on trying to sell your point of view that you forget to do this. Remember, people are more responsive to what you offer when they feel respected.

Concrete examples help, such as how well something worked for other people. But the examples must draw on something real and feel like something the person can see himself doing. Acknowledge your reader's concerns, and even when you seem far apart, thoughtful language can help bridge the gap: "I wonder if you've ruled out . . ." or "I understand that . . . but let's look at what might work."

—Susan H. Dowell, psychotherapist

Tell the story in an organized, natural way. For a long document, you need an outline. If you're developing a business plan, you may not need to start from scratch, since sample templates are readily available. You can, for example, find sample business plans relating to various industries online at Bplans.com.

For business proposals and reports, however, you may not find helpful models because each is more or less unique. In such cases, take account of your goal and audience analysis—just as you practiced with e-mails and letters—and brainstorm what the document should include.

Assemble a list of sections. Then juggle your content list into a logical order taking care to put what's important and interesting up front. The backup stuff most people find dull, like research data, should go in back so it's there for those who want it but it doesn't slow reading down to a crawl. But this depends on the audience: If you're preparing a document for a CFO, data and financial analysis should probably go up front.

SIDELIGHT: ORGANIZING LONG DOCUMENTS

You can solve organization problems with long documents the same way as for short ones. (See Dr. Haber's "Sidelight: An Easy Organization Technique" in Chapter 3.)

Create a map of what you'll write about by coming up with a sentence that represents your main point. Then, determine what your key word is, which will help you identify the sections of your document. Each section will usually contain a singular example of your key word. (Sometimes, your document might be so complex, that you may have several key words.)

As an example of how this planning works, if you're writing a report or technical document that has a point of view—for example, the company should do X or Y—the body of the document must contain a key word such as "justifications" or "reasons." Get all the ideas down to prove that point. It's not sufficient just to enumerate the reasons—you need to come up with sufficient supporting details for each reason.

To take a different example, suppose your main point is, "We should give more breaks because it will improve productivity in various ways." You have to prove that. How will it improve productivity? Use the key word "ways," and for each way, you need to thoroughly explain how that way will improve productivity. Good writers support their ideas by coming up with good supporting details. If you assume your audience is hostile, it forces you to come up with more supporting ideas.

Once you have the ideas, organize them and decide which to begin with, and how much information to include. Most managers complain that they either get too much or too little information. Think of your audience and you'll know how much detail they need, and which reason, if that is the key word, is most important.

What if the document is very complicated and you can't come up with the key word? Try starting the other way around—the "back-door" approach. Write down the topics you want to cover. Say you come up with three problems, and you have solutions for each. Then you know that your main point is, "I'm going to tell you about three problems and possible solutions for each."

—Dr. Mel Haber, president,
Writing Development Associates

Remember that people make decisions based on emotion. Then they justify them with reason. Good salespeople know this, and the advertising world has relied on the concept for generations. That's why you see ads that show cute babies to sell investment opportunities and car commercials with happy families enjoying the time of their lives.

Recent research supports this premise. Neuroscientists are tracking how the brain functions during decision making, and the new field of behavioral economics studies buying behavior. A key finding is that people generally make decisions based on emotions, often almost instantaneously, and then bolster them with reasoning.

The concept has far-reaching implications. It suggests that whatever you're marketing, consider people's emotional attachments and anticipate reactions. This may mean identifying the problem that keeps them up at night and what frightens them. Or at the other end of the emotional scale, linking to things that ring positive bells and trigger good associations.

Another corollary is that people buy more readily, and find arguments more persuasive, when they like the person delivering the message and feel they are on the same wavelength. The best salespeople work hard to encourage other people to talk, and then listen carefully. This enables them to identify the problem the other person wants to solve and to respond appropriately, while at the same time building rapport.

The idea of emotionally based decision making is starting to influence big-picture management thinking, communication practices, and fields from marketing to finance. It merits serious attention when you aim to persuade.

ACTION TIME: YOUR TURN

Do you agree that people make decisions, from life choices to minor purchases, on an emotional rather than a reasoning basis?

Pick three decisions you've recently made, such as choosing a school, selecting a smart phone, making a donation to a specific cause, pursuing volunteer work or making a major purchase, like a car or computer. Carefully analyze the process you followed and assess what motivated your decision.

Does thinking this through lend support to the emotion-first concept? Does it affect your outlook on using persuasive techniques?

And: Research emotional decision making for a more in-depth view and think about whether the concept makes sense to you, and to what degree.

Create trust. When you're selling something through a piece of paper, whether print or virtual, it's automatically a challenge. One of the first rules of selling is to get in the door so you can connect in person and show that you are credible, knowledgeable, likeable and so on. It's a chance to establish common ground through factors such as a mutual acquaintance, a shared sports interest, or where you live and went to school. Good salespeople pose the right questions and read the other person's responses, including body language, to gauge concerns and present their service or product as the solution.

But you can't do that with writing. A proposal, for example, has to stand on its own. So you must establish credibility and trust. Your techniques include supplying the right information, which might include credentials, related experience, examples of similar work, testimonials and hard evidence of accomplishment proved by data, photographs, graphs and other visuals.

And, build trust by strong, accurate writing and good presentation. *A business plan or proposal in itself is important evidence of how you work.*

VIEW FROM THE FIELD: A JOURNALIST'S ADVICE ON HOW TO TELL YOUR STORY

The challenge in my work is to integrate diverse kinds of information and explain everything clearly. It must be engaging, so we ask, what part of the story is most interesting? The test results? History? Related news? Writers must be aware of the range of tools and choose the most appropriate.

Figure out what you would tell your husband or daughter—the "Hey, Martha" moment. For the lead, ask, how do I begin the conversation? What would pique my own interest? That's your beginning point, but know your audience—what they care about, their values.

And know yourself: How good a guide you are to what's interesting, and your biases and prejudices. Consult other people so you have different perspectives on what's interesting. For example, we know that some kinds of shopping advice may be very interesting for women, but less so for men. Appeal to different demographics with a broad spectrum.

Write with clear, declarative sentences so language doesn't get in the way of a message. Headlines and captions must be interesting and work with the message, but not repeat the information. Avoid jargon wherever possible and if something won't be familiar to readers, interpret it for them.

> To bring things alive for readers we'll illuminate interesting points with information nuggets. And for investigative articles, like one on financial traps coming out of the recession that caused people to lose their houses, we'll use personal stories about people who were hurt or helped. We also dig into the research for a broader context and to find something people don't know.
>
> Never skew information to make your point. Everything is helped by transparency and credibility; find the other side.
>
> —Robert Tiernan, managing editor, *Consumer Reports*; former editor, *Newsday*

Acknowledge other viewpoints. It is much more credible to refer in an objective way to opposing ideas or approaches rather than dismissing them by omission or disparagement. You can absorb the other side into your argument if appropriate. For example:

> As recently as last year, Strategy X was the standard way of doing things. But today, new technology empowers us to choose a more efficient, less expensive model.
>
> Certainly, investing in Opportunity A offers some immediate advantages. Opportunity B, however, gives us a long-range potential in a new market and will ultimately pay bigger dividends.
>
> Three other products are available to clean clay floors. However, Miracle Wax J is the first and only one to restore their original color.

Try, try, try not to bore. If you've done a project and are reporting on the results, or you're recommending an operational change, or asking for money to fund your start-up, the message isn't boring to you—and it must not bore your audience. Remember, when it comes to communication, we live in an opt-in world. Successful complex messages must be carefully crafted.

Once you've determined the right substance, you have two basic tools to deploy:

> Good writing, which engages and persuades through concise but vivid language, and effective graphic presentation, which is critical to how long-form documents are received.

VIEW FROM THE FIELD: TECHNIQUES TO BUILD TRUST

The first step is always to start with your goal and work backward from there. Too often people in business skip that step and jump right into tactical or narrow-focus questions.

A lot of times companies will throw in a lot of spin—a cardinal mistake—and will try to cover five points. Whether you're writing an op-ed or speech, if you're trying to persuade an audience, make a single argument—know your core argument and then support it with evidence.

The most effective technique for business, politics, nonprofits, is credibility. Build trust with your readers by acknowledging valued points of the other side. This has disappeared from politics, which is why people are cynical and frustrated. It's much more successful to take account of an opponent's points or rebut them: "Yes, you have a good point per se, but here's why ultimately it's not convincing."

—Dan Gerstein, president/founder of Gotham Ghostwriters;
political strategist, analyst and commentator

WRITING TIPS WHEN YOU NEED TO PERSUADE

Apply the Basics

1. Keep it simple. As with all media, short words, sentences and paragraphs are best. Stay with basic sentence structures, though it's good to alternate between simple ones (John ordered the computer) and longer more complex ones (He claimed, with little justification, that it was a good idea).

There are additional reasons why the generic KISS rule (Keep it Simple, Stupid) applies to documents meant to persuade. *Simplicity conveys authenticity and transparency.* The converse is true as well. If you employ $2 words when the nickel versions will do, and write in difficult long sentences and dense paragraphs, what you present is less credible. Beyond giving people material that they're less likely to read, you create the impression that you're hiding facts. And, that you don't understand your own story very well.

Remember, no matter how complicated your message is, it can and should be presented in simple, clear writing.

2. Build for speed. Your goal is to make your whole document read as fast as you can. Rhythm is important. Apply the "say-ability" test: Read what you write out loud and where you hear that sing-song sound, or stumble, look to rewrite and then retest.

Connecting every thought to what precedes and follows is critical. Good transitions create the binding that holds your piece together and reinforces the logic of your argument.

Check the discussion in Chapter 5 for how to use transitions between sentences and paragraphs. Try building them into every sentence—you can always cut some later when you edit. The strategy will force you to make sure your thoughts do in fact proceed logically.

> *If you ask readers if they understand what you write, they'll say "No problem." But if you test their understanding— which we recommend—it will force you to reconsider your writing and focus on the parts people have trouble with. By working to make it clearer, you'll develop a more useful document.*
>
> —Annetta Cheek, board chair, Center for Plain Language

The payoff for strong transitions is that your presentation will appear cohesive, your arguments logical and your conclusions inevitable.

3. Cut ALL hype. Do not use empty, inflated descriptions of your product, company or yourself. To say, "We are exceptionally sophisticated strategic innovators" or "We are noted for excellent teaming skills" or "We take pride in our unique craftsmanship" says nothing to your busy skeptical readers. They want proof.

To demonstrate innovation, cite some actual examples of how you solved problems. To talk about teaming, you might give examples of how your teams are assembled and the skill sets coordinated. To show craftsmanship, include images and show off your specialists. You can also bring in third-party testimonials from happy customers and other people you've worked with and for. Case histories are effective and engaging.

Ask, how can we prove our main points and qualifications to get this job or recommend a course of action?

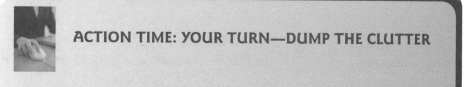

ACTION TIME: YOUR TURN—DUMP THE CLUTTER

When we write An Important Document, the process seems to trigger our most old-fashioned instincts toward the formal and pretentious. Resist! Here are some phrases that are not only too wordy, but interfere with the reader's ability to

(Continued)

(Continued)

absorb the big picture or even get through the document. How would you replace the following?

At this point in time

In consideration of

In a position to

Reach a conclusion

In view of the fact that

It is important to note that

Notwithstanding the fact that

The manner in which

Following the conclusion of

In the event that

Contrary to the assumption that

In mitigation of

In a very real sense

The purpose of this document is

Collect your own list of language clutter from what you read over the next week and make a list of substitute words. Train yourself to notice your own wordiness and use better alternatives.

4. *"Show don't tell"* is the fiction writer's mantra. A version for the business world: *"Show don't sell."* This guideline encourages you to think about what will bring your message alive and the elements that will help it work.

Incorporating stories and anecdotes is one way. They're hard to pull out of the air on demand, and need to be true. So collect them over time—from stories friends or colleagues tell you, articles and your personal experience. Most useful are stories that center on people to illustrate a point, a success, a problem or best of all, a solution. Notice how good journalism presents big problems and trends through personal stories. *Wall Street Journal* reporting excels at this. Editors call this technique "storifying."

Another way to apply the mantra is to *figure out specific examples to support your case.* Concrete examples resonate and shore up abstractions. So tell readers how some other company made a strategy work, how a similar investment paid off, how the recommended course of action is in line with another successful change. Graphs, charts and relevant photographs are excellent "show me" pieces.

Just as valuable, the show-don't-sell concept gives you interesting ways to spice up your language. *Painting pictures with words and providing familiar frames of reference* are among the fiction writer's best tools for bringing the abstract alive. You can use these techniques to good advantage, too.

Similes are figures of speech that make comparisons using the words "like" or "as":

> Eliminating System A without replacing it would be like removing the pillars that hold up a bridge.

A metaphor is a more subtle comparison that doesn't use "like" or "as":

> The region is a crazy quilt of farmland, suburbs and urban patches loosely knit together and these days, fraying around the edges.
>
> We see far too many businesses that paint their tails white and run with the antelope.

Analogies are also comparisons and can lend reality to an abstract idea or help explain something technically difficult. To express a key theme of this book, I could say,

> It's critical to write well, because although few people seem to notice when you fail to, they may nevertheless respond negatively.

or

> Bad writing is like bad breath. People won't mention it, but they may keep their distance.

Communicating through visual ideas is especially convincing. A website that advocates against bottled water states,

> Bottled water produces up to 1.5 million tons of plastic waste per year.

A television commercial for a water filtration system, on the other hand, says (paraphrased):

Americans drink enough bottled water every year that laid end to end, the bottles could stretch around the world more than 100 times.

Whether the second statement is true or not—bloggers take issue with the math—it's certainly more powerful.

Writers work very hard to come up with original metaphors and images. While it's definitely not an easy task, the impact can be worth the effort when you're pitching something that matters.

Don't overlook the basics of vivid language and tight writing covered in Chapters 4 and 5. Use vigorous verbs to carry a feeling of action. Try to use the present tense as much as possible—"This tool performs a variety of functions" is better than "This tool will be able to perform a variety of functions." Cut back on all those extra words and phrases: "This system can be adapted to . . ." works much better as "This system adapts to . . ."

Keep away from trite wording and jargon. Edit ruthlessly and borrow extra eyes from friends or colleagues and eliminate every error and misspelling.

Formal business documents are a good reason to explore a thesaurus for word choice. Find one you like in print or online—or simply Google the word and a ton of options will appear.

VIEW FROM THE FIELD: WHY GOVERNMENT HIRES GOOD WRITERS

In international work, you need to communicate with people in different time zones so writing is really the only way to do it. And we're the government, so we also need a documented paper trail for the record to show why we did something.

My job is to enable people to make good decisions, and to do it without my being present. We communicate a lot verbally, but not everyone is at the meetings. Even if they were, given the amount of information flow, they won't remember everything I say. So I need coherent, clearly written documents that give people everything they need to know.

Getting people to come together around a document to agree on major conclusions can, if it's concise and clear, generate the underlying decisions needed. For an internal audience, if I'm presenting research, I need the takeaway and justification for what I believe to be the case.

So writing is very important to me when I hire people. When I interview, I ask, "How would you explain this to our vice president who will make a decision about it? And how would you explain it to a group of curious students?" I walk them through different groups and it's quite telling to see how people would write for different audiences.

—Alicia Phillips Mandaville, director of development policy, Millennium Challenge Corporation (U.S. foreign aid agency)

Simplicity Rules

If you ever think that a subject is too complex to communicate simply and clearly, consider the financier Warren Buffett. He's become justly famous not only for his success in making money, but also for the way he writes about it. He's looked to as a model by most Wall Streeters on both counts.

Review his annual reports (easily accessed online) to see how he makes financial material understandable through sentence structure, choice of words, analogies and stories. Together with a folksy, we're-all-real-people tone, these techniques produce documents quite different from the usual annual report.

You can learn a lot from Buffett. Here's an excerpt from his July 26, 2010, report.

Charlie and I hope that the per-share earnings of our non-insurance businesses continue to increase at a decent rate. But the job gets tougher as the numbers get larger. We will need both good performance from our current

SUCCESS TIP: PRACTICE THE ART OF INTERVIEWING

When you need information from a specialist, a collaborator, your boss or anyone else, treat it as an interviewing opportunity. The same skills will help you lead teams, negotiate and sell— whether a product, service or yourself. The key to a good interview is good questions: They elicit better information and give you the fastest route to rapport—people find them engaging and are usually pleased by your interest. Here are some useful strategies.

1. Know what you want from the interaction and gauge this against how much time you'll have. If it's only a few minutes, focus on what's most important.

2. Prepare: Find out about your subject or the person and craft "level 2" questions that get

(Continued)

(Continued)

past the surface: The more you know the more you will interest the other person, and the better the quality of response.

3. Communicate what you want to learn clearly and especially if the subject is sensitive, set parameters so the other person feels comfortable. This is a good way to "open."

4. Interact conversationally, rather than interrogating. Some give and take establishes a sharing atmosphere— but don't talk too much or dominate.

5. Ask for clarification and seek depth (but try not to stem a natural flow). Ask, what do you mean by that? Can you explain that another way? Can you give me an example? What you're saying, in other words, is. . . .

6. Listen carefully. Watch for real enthusiasm (or other strong feelings) and follow the trail if appropriate. Sometimes this proves more productive than your original idea.

7. However, if the interviewee takes off on a long unproductive tangent, look for a chance to politely redirect with a comment such as, "Thank you. Could you tell me now about. . . ."

8. Work on your questions. Avoid those that will draw a "yes" or "no" and try for open-ended ones. For example, according to the situation:
   What's important about this?
   What do you wish people understood better?
   How did you figure that out?

(Continued)

businesses and more *major acquisitions.* We're prepared. Our elephant gun has been reloaded, and my trigger finger is itchy.

Buffett's simplicity shows the benefits of making it easy for the reader. Beyond being clear, the document is more enjoyable than you'd expect. Moreover, it conveys that the message is sincere and heartfelt.

Buffett also sets a wide stage to good effect. To give readers a broad context or perspective is in itself an effective technique of persuasion. Use words to make a vision or concept real for readers and you will not only convince, but may even inspire. Working in personal experience helps, too. From the same annual report letter:

No matter how serene today may be, tomorrow is *always* uncertain.

Throughout my lifetime, politicians and pundits have constantly moaned about terrifying problems facing America. Yet our citizens now live an astonishing six times better than when I was born. The prophets of doom have overlooked the all-important factor that *is* certain: Human potential is far from exhausted, and the American system for unleashing that potential—a system that has worked wonders for over two centuries despite frequent interruptions for recessions and even a Civil War—remains alive and effective.

We are not natively smarter than we were when our country was founded nor do we work harder. But look around you and see a world beyond the dreams of any colonial citizen. Now, as in 1776, 1861, 1932 and 1941, America's best days lie ahead.

The more concise, easy to read and lively you make your document, the more it will achieve for you. The more you bring information alive by communicating vision, telling stories and crafting vivid language, the more convincing it becomes. There's only one Warren Buffett. But like him, you can practice good writing strategies to communicate your message. I'm willing to bet he plans his writing carefully, and edits it closely.

(Continued)

How would you know that it works?

What do you see as the biggest problem you face? How does it affect you?

What else should I have asked you?

Of course, in-person interviewing is best. Telephone is second best. If the person writes responses via e-mail or other media, you'll typically get more guarded, academic-sounding responses. Whatever the situation, remember that relationship building matters in the long run.

THINK GL🌐BAL: WATCH THOSE WORDS

When writing for international audiences, all of the basic rules—simple words, straightforward sentence construction, correct grammar—apply. But it's even more important to consider your word choice. Will your readers understand your intended meaning? Do the words you're using exist in their language, and do they translate appropriately? Perhaps you will need to include definitions that are unnecessary for American audiences.

Not that far back, for example, one nonprofit leader found that when she explained that her organization's mission was to support "high-impact entrepreneurs," she was met with blank stares by people in Brazil and other developing nations. These countries simply did not have a term in their respective languages for being an "entrepreneurial" businessperson. The word had to be explained, in both written documents and in face-to-face presentations.

You must also have an incredibly critical eye when it comes to identifying jargon. Every industry, every business has its own set of go-to words or phrases. And yet, these words often lack meaning—whether in the original English or an attempted translation—and can easily be replaced. When you work with international clients, you may find that they don't understand the jargon, but are reluctant to admit it. So, when writing or editing any document, be sure to ask yourself, is there another shorter, easier way to say this?

—Victoria Canavor, program manager, TechnoServe
(an international economic development organization);
MBA, Kellogg School of Management

GRAPHIC GUIDELINES FOR DOCUMENTS

It's tough to pull people through long-form documents. You need your full tool kit if you want to create documents that are readable, inviting and enticing. Your competition will certainly take trouble with appearance, and so must you.

In some industries, extraordinary skill goes into the visual appearance of proposals. They devote whole creative teams to this effort.

Whatever your goal, represent yourself with a document that makes a good impression. Design a title sheet—simple is fine. Build in headlines for sections and subheads, and lots of white space to rest the eye. Short paragraphs are especially helpful. Use a very readable typeface even if it's less slick and "modern" than one that's trendy.

GOING DEEPER: A GRAPHIC DESIGNER'S ADVICE ON GOOD PRESENTATION

The general rule for just about all documents, in print and online, is Keep It Simple and Keep It Clean. Here are some guidelines.

About Typeface

The point is readability and accessibility. So . . .

- ✓ Consistency counts. Don't mix two different serif faces—those are the ones with the squiggles at the ends. Stick with one font. But you can mix a serif face with a sans serif (squiggle free) face. For example, Times New Roman or Garamond for body copy works well with Arial for heads and subheads.
- ✓ Sans serif can also be used for body copy if you don't have a lot of it or a pretty face counts, like in an advertisement.
- ✓ Size matters: In general, keep to the 10- to 12-point range.
- ✓ But size is subtle: Fonts have different "x heights"—meaning that the bottom part of a lowercase letter in one face will be higher than that of another. The higher one is more readable. For example, Helvetica has a higher x height than Berkeley. So if you're using a small type size—like 8 or 9 points—Helvetica is a better choice. You can check this effect visually.
- ✓ Caps and italics are hard to read, so use them only for emphasis or headlines. This is true for bold as well.

✓ Don't justify: Run copy for most purposes flush left and rag right—justifying forces text into unappealing letter spacing, and makes readers feel uptight. Rag right is calming.

Break It Up

Use all the tools available for creating air and space.

✓ Let your lines breathe: Don't cram copy in so the lines run too close to each other. If your column is wide, try adding space between lines (if you have control over this, use at least 2 points between lines such as 9 on 11, or 10 on 12). On your computer, see how it looks for your purpose if you add 1½ spaces between lines on documents rather than 1.
✓ Keep substantial margins on left, right, top and bottom—generally no less than an inch; yes, even on résumés.
✓ Use bullets and indenting deliberately as a way to break up space.
✓ When using subheads, leave more space *above* the subhead to separate it from the body copy than the space left *after* the subhead; it offers a better visual break.
✓ Headlines: Be consistent in using caps or upper/lowercase and making them flush left or centered—don't alternate.

For Proposals and Other Big Documents

✓ Take the trouble to make proposals inviting. This will increase the likelihood of winning the bid.
✓ Be sure proposals reflect your brand identity. Use the colors associated with it.
✓ Choose fonts and arrange your pages for instant readability.
✓ Build in LOTS of white space and page breaks—wide margins, subheads, pullouts, indents, bullets, colored boxes, a rule element, images. Designers love white space because of what it says to the audience. People associate white space with higher value and quality, luxury, simplicity, sophistication, calmness, design savvy, concern with esthetics and thoughtful attention to their preferences.
✓ Use relevant graphics and keep to a single style: Don't mix and match cartoons and photographs, for example; and keep visuals in line with your graphic image.
✓ Clip art: Stay away from it! If you have no image resources or nothing relevant, get your message across with color boxes and other variables.

Spark up graphs and charts with color. Think about a more intriguing way to present them than plain and static. Try to build in a feeling of motion and action—see the difference between the "Boring" and "Not So Boring" examples.

—Tina Panos, president, Panos Graphic Services

(Continued)

(Continued)

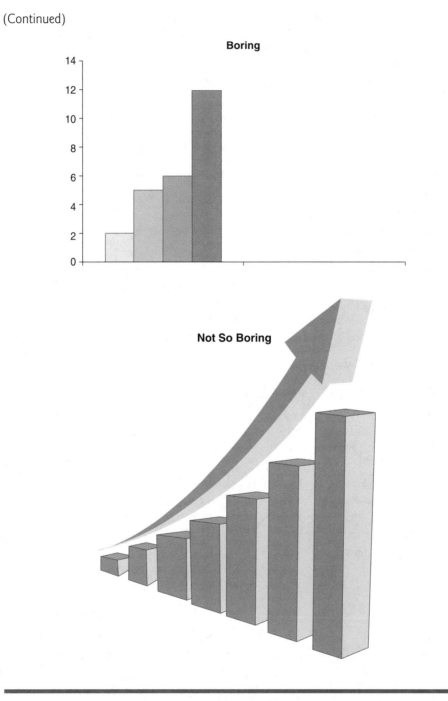

In the next chapter, we'll move on to explore how to apply the principles of persuasion to the important business documents you may need to create for yourself or an employer.

PRACTICE OPPORTUNITIES

I. Analyze the Advertising Around You

Review three print ads, three television commercials and three online ads. Answer the following questions and write about your observations:

A. Who is the target audience (or audiences)?

B. What persuasive techniques can you identify?

C. How effective is each pitch?

D. What differences can you observe in the tactics used in the three media?

II. Read and Analyze Warren Buffett

Find and read at least three pieces of Buffett's writing, easily available online. Identify all the persuasion techniques you can identify, and try to add more not covered in this chapter. Share your findings with a small group of classmates and assemble one master list with examples.

III. Questions for Discussion and Writing: Persuasion and Ethics

Here's a statement by Warren Buffett, part of a cover letter to his company's directors. It accompanied his letter to stockholders.

> The priority is that all of us continue to zealously guard Berkshire's reputation. We can't be perfect but we can try to be. As I've said in these memos for more than 25 years: "We can afford to lose money—even a lot of money. But we can't afford to lose reputation—even a shred of reputation." We *must* continue to measure every act against not only what is legal but also what we would be happy to have written about on the front page of a national newspaper in an article written by an unfriendly but intelligent reporter.
>
> Sometimes your associates will say "Everybody else is doing it." This rationale is almost always a bad one if it is the main justification for a business action. It is totally unacceptable when evaluating a moral decision. Whenever somebody offers that phrase as a rationale, in effect they are saying that they can't come up with a *good* reason. If anyone gives this explanation, tell them to try using it with a reporter or a judge and see how far it gets them.

If you see anything whose propriety or legality causes you to hesitate, be sure to give me a call. However, it's very likely that if a given course of action evokes such hesitation, it's too close to the line and should be abandoned. There's plenty of money to be made in the center of the court.

A. Analyze: What do you think of Buffett's position? How would you feel if you received this message from your CEO? Does it feel like Buffett believes in what he's saying, rather than just giving lip service to a moral directive? How does the way he writes carry sincerity (or fail to)?

B. Note that not long after Buffett wrote this letter, one of his top executives (and probable successor), David Sokol, was accused of unethical behavior (buying substantial stock in a company that Berkshire Hathaway was about to acquire). Sokol resigned but Buffett's initial response, which didn't express much outrage, was widely criticized. He later called the violation of the rules and company ethics "inexcusable." Does this set of events alter your view of Buffett's letter? What does it suggest about the relationship between written ideals and actions in business? Other spheres?

Research the events and statements this situation generated and write an opinion piece, in blog or op-ed style, about what the episode "means" or how it should be seen.

C. Do you see any dangers in using persuasive techniques to accomplish business purposes? What examples of unethical use come to mind in what you've observed or have read about?

D. Identify a specific example of unethical use of persuasion strategies you find interesting in any realm. Analyze why you believe the tactics were unethical. Then present your thinking to the class or group in three to five minutes. After hearing from all participants, collaborate with the group to draft a set of guidelines for the ethical use of persuasive techniques.

IV. Write a Persuasive Letter or E-mail

Select something you feel strongly about from your school, business or personal life. It can be an idea, such as why companies need to enforce strong ethical guidelines or give new hires more access to leaders, or why the person you're writing to should buy a different computer, take a particular course, read a book, build an aquarium—whatever. Write a persuasive memo to the relevant person using as many of the techniques covered in this chapter as you can, including the graphic guidelines. Then list the techniques you incorporated and identify the corresponding examples.

Chapter 9

WRITING TO PERSUADE PART 2

CREATING BUSINESS DOCUMENTS

LEARN HOW TO . . .

➢ Write an Executive Summary
➢ Prepare a business plan
➢ Write a proposal
➢ Develop PowerPoint presentations
➢ Plan effective videos

> *Writing leads to wealth.*
>
> —Jeffrey Gitomer, Chief Executive Salesman,
> in *Little Green Book of Getting Your Way*

Every major document poses its own demands and challenges. I can't cover them all in this book, but want to give you a resource of ideas and strategies to draw upon. In this chapter, I'll focus on aspects of the major documents you're most likely to write. Business formats have a lot in common, so read everything even if you don't now anticipate needing guidelines for all—or any—of these materials.

THE BIG ES—THE EXECUTIVE SUMMARY

The Executive Summary (ES) is a critical element for many kinds of business documents: business plans, proposals, white papers, reports, grant applications and more. The busier everyone gets, the more vital a role the ES plays. In many cases, it will be the only part of the document your key audience reads. If they like it, they may read the rest—or take action based on the ES alone.

So leave plenty of time to develop this piece. Don't pull out excerpts from the full document and tack them together. Use the summary to tell a complete, self-contained story. It must fully articulate your idea and clearly recommend a course of action, or convince readers that you have a great idea so they keep reading. You must make a clear recommendation and support it with evidence.

Every element of the document should be covered, but give center stage to what the reader will most care about. If you're writing a business plan for a new venture, focus the Executive Summary on communicating your idea vividly. Say why it's important and to whom, what difference it will make, why it will be profitable, how you'll go about it, who will carry out the idea and why the team is qualified.

And, aim to accomplish everything in one to two pages—rarely is a longer summary called for or welcome.

Marshal your writing tool kit to make the ES as interesting as you can. This is the place to recreate your own excitement as an entrepreneur ready to seize the day, or as the dedicated adviser prepared with a solid, innovative recommendation for a client or boss.

Use all the skills you've been practicing: Write clear simple sentences, use action verbs and avoid passive-sounding constructions like "a decision will be made at Stage 3." Instead of phrases like "we will provide evidence to support this," craft statements like "The evidence supports this." Opt for vivid, simple words. Be consistently positive; phrases like "we hope that" or "it's possible that" have no place here.

Craft a strong lead based on what is most important for the reader to understand and what is most interesting about the idea. Check that the piece is "say-able"—read it aloud and to friends. Some advisers suggest reading it to a teenager to see how easily the document can be understood and what questions come up.

Expect to edit through a series of revision cycles. If your first draft (or two) is too long, as it probably will be, look for redundancies in thought and word. Cut empty phrases as well as hype to tighten the writing. Polish, polish, polish. But don't edit the life out of it.

Beyond all the technical effort, try to immerse yourself in your own conviction and the excitement that drove you to prepare this document. Speak from inside your own commitment.

VIEW FROM THE FIELD: THE EXECUTIVE SUMMARY AS ADVOCACY

My goal in writing an Executive Summary is generally some form of advocacy: to get my point across, to influence, to make a compelling argument that can be fully trusted. Very often your audience has limited time so it needs brevity—but the Executive Summary should also show a solid organization and logic in respect to a business issue. The most successful Executive Summaries are self-contained. You may get approval based just on the ES.

It's good to show your audience that you know what came before and use it for context. Don't discredit it. And it's sometimes appropriate to make one recommendation but show other possibilities. This lends credibility, and people like to have a choice.

Move with gentle guidance into key findings or data points to support the recommendation, putting the most compelling ones on top. Know your audience: If you're appealing to the CFO, you may want to arrange your data points to address return on investment, cost saving and other financial aspects. Think of your audience's core responsibilities to help you plan your arguments and prioritize what you say.

Avoid flowery language and too many superlatives. I like to use language that shows an attempt at objectivity, focusing on the facts of the situation. The Executive Summary is not the time to put your heart on your sleeve. Err on the side of formality. Decision makers expect a level of seriousness when you ask for buy-in—chummy doesn't work. And accuracy is really important: It's a first impression thing. People will focus on a typo rather than your argument.

—Lisa Cuevas Shaw, executive editor,
SAGE, responsible for business, management,
marketing and public administration book programs

The Executive Summary: An Example

Here is the lead portion of an Executive Summary created for a new business venture, part of a business plan for fund-raising purposes. This is approximately one third of the complete ES.

> The Long Island Art Incubator will give the region's creative people a place to work, learn and collaborate while building businesses based on their talents.

For the first time, people focused on creative expression—whether fine artists, artisans, inventors or hobbyists—can subscribe through paid membership to a center that intentionally integrates all the resources they need to advance their work and their business acumen. In a well-located building serving as the Art Incubator's home, they can access

- Private studio and co-working space
- Equipment not individually affordable
- An energizing community life
- Classes on cutting-edge creative techniques
- Training in entrepreneurship and practical business strategies

A critical mass of 20,000 creative people now lives and works on Long Island. Although settings such as art leagues, arts councils, universities and museums offer some training opportunities, no facility exists that can serve these valued individuals and thus the interests of the region.

Usually associated with technology, incubation is a proven way to accelerate the successful development of emerging companies. Incubators that thrive bring entrepreneurs together in an intentional manner so they can interact, while drawing on resources that will help them stay accountable to their business growth goals.

Like technology entrepreneurs, creative people tend to generate valuable ideas but do not know how to implement them. Just as incubation enables technology specialists to explore viable ideas and turn them into marketable products, the Art Incubator will give this opportunity to creative specialists.

An incubator for creative people has special potential. By focusing our most creative minds on problems in the marketplace and community at large, it will contribute solutions in the form of valuable, innovative products and services.

—Courtesy Dianne Parker, CEO, *Executive on-the-run* Ltd.

The remainder of the Executive Summary covers key considerations, marketing objectives, expected accomplishments and required capital.

WRITING BUSINESS PLANS

In addition to formats and guidance you can access through your course work, good help with business plans is available online and in person. Small Business Development Centers (SBDC) are available in every state and offer experienced counseling customized to your goal. Advisers will sit with you and help you craft a strong document, possibly over a number of sessions. Because they're thoroughly familiar with the local business scene, they can also help you make valuable connections.

Many locales also have retired executive groups who are happy to advise you. The U.S. Small Business Administration (SBA.gov) is a good source of advice and templates, and a host of websites supports entrepreneurs, offering some free services and others for a fee.

Drafting a business plan is no small task—don't be surprised if it takes weeks or months. For some people, it's an evolving lifetime endeavor. Business advisers believe that a business plan created to guide a business's development should be reviewed and updated every year.

Fortunately, in addition to the persuasive writing techniques covered in the preceding chapter, you can draw on the same principles that work for writing everyday materials when you develop major documents. As an example, we'll review the first steps of how to prepare a business plan.

Begin by clarifying your goal. Do you want to secure investors to fund your business? Or are you drafting an "internal" plan to guide your own business thinking or lay out a blueprint for you and your partners? You may at times create business plans for organizations that employ you, perhaps to map a path for a new business idea, expansion or product. Many major companies use business plans to guide their activities and chart the future. Business plans can do the same for individual departments and units.

Different goals lead to different decisions on content and to some extent, style. In every case, aim to tell the whole story as clearly and completely as you can. A business plan is not a request for an interview. *Certainly in the case of a request for funding, if you can't clearly explain what you want to do and how you will do it in writing, the hearing is over.* You won't be asked to orally interpret what you wrote.

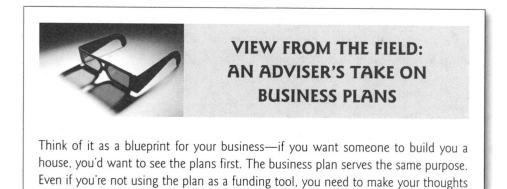

VIEW FROM THE FIELD: AN ADVISER'S TAKE ON BUSINESS PLANS

Think of it as a blueprint for your business—if you want someone to build you a house, you'd want to see the plans first. The business plan serves the same purpose. Even if you're not using the plan as a funding tool, you need to make your thoughts

(Continued)

(Continued)

materialize on paper because it forces you to think methodically about your operational plans, market prospects, competition and value adds.

Aim for brevity and elegance, as for all business writing. Avoid flowery language. Consider the audience—if you're looking for investors, for example, use formal language but avoid industry jargon and technical terminology. Do not use the first person ("I"). Look at business plans by others in your industry.

Treat each section as a mutually exclusive piece if you're submitting the plan to a lender. Everyone may read the Executive Summary but the other pieces will be distributed to various people. The Executive Summary is of the utmost importance. It's like the preface to a book, or a movie preview—it should capture the entire essence of your plan in less than one page and spark readers' interest.

To be truly good at something, you must love it, so showing your passion is always a plus. You can also sound objective—passion and objectivity need not be mutually exclusive.

—Ritu S. Wackett, business analyst, Farmingdale State College,
Small Business Development Center (SBDC)

Once you're clear on your goal, **consider your primary and secondary target audiences.** When your aim is to be funded, you're talking to financial specialists—whether bankers, investors or angels.

These are probably people you don't know and may not meet. You can safely anticipate, however, that they are bottom-line oriented; busy and impatient; conservative in outlook; and more than smart enough to detect omissions and flaws in your argument and financials. Their business may be risk taking, but they want to be sure you're a good bet.

Take into account that the concerns of a venture capitalist, who looks for return on investment (ROI), are different from those of a banker who's evaluating a small business loan and wants to minimize risk.

If you're writing an internal business plan, a primary goal is to spell out roles and responsibilities and how you'll work together.

Choose tone according to the medium and your decisions on goal and audience. While the business plan may be the most "formal" document you'll write, it should not be stiff, wordy, dull and technical sounding. On the contrary, considering how busy and impatient your readers are, it must move fast and actively engage. It must feel objective. It should also sound upbeat, even when you specify existing competition or unpredictable factors.

Your writing must be more "correct" than for everyday communications: full sentences, fewer contractions, absolutely no mistakes. Especially if you seek funding, remember that your readers belong to conservative professions and require seriousness on the part of those who want to use their money. Wouldn't you?

If you work for an organization, check out earlier plans, especially well-regarded ones. Note the format, tone and content to which management is accustomed and responds.

The next step is to figure out your content. "Standard" formats are readily available online or from your textbooks. You can start with one that's geared to your industry and adapt it to your idea.

VIEW FROM THE FIELD: BUSINESS PLAN AS REALITY CHECK

If you're a business owner, a business plan is like having an in-depth dialogue with yourself about where you are, what you want the business to be, and how you're going to get there, in specific business terms. You first have to figure out what your vision is for your business—the big picture—and then translate that into specific goals and how you're going to reach them. During this stage, telling the vision to someone you can have a dialogue with helps you clarify it to yourself as well as others.

I advise breaking the business plan down into five essential pieces: Leadership, sales and marketing, operations, administration and finances, and innovation—the last because I think you need that culture to survive in an up-and-down economy.

But the biggest question you have to answer is, who cares? Who wants this product or service? How many want it? Who is serving them now? If you can't answer that, even if you do everything extremely well, the marketplace won't get it. A lot of business owners don't understand why the world doesn't get their idea. The business plan is a huge reality check that helps both the business owner and potential funders understand why the marketplace should care.

The writing must draw people into the story from the first page and be very accessible, and authentic—make people believe you're really connected to what

(Continued)

(Continued)

you're saying. Funders and other stakeholders want to experience the vision and concretely see how you're going to get there, especially whether it's profitable. Don't try for a conversational tone. You're not basically trying to build a relationship—you're trying to draw the reader in and then prove a point. People want to see the proof.

—Dianne Parker, CEO, Executive *on-the-run*, Ltd.

Of course you need not write the plan in the same sequence in which it will appear. In fact, you shouldn't. The Executive Summary is best left till last, at which point you know exactly what to get across. Together with the Business Description section, the ES is your chance to explain your idea as effectively and convincingly as you can. Whomever you're writing for must first be interested in your idea; then they'll check the financials, and then if still interested, read more.

Brainstorm what will prove your case. Ultimately, you must tell your reader exactly what the opportunity is, what problem it will solve, who needs your solution and what is special about it, how you will reach your market and the size of the market you credibly anticipate.

To help decide what that should include, try mental role reversal: What would your prospective investor want to know? What would he or she ask? What objections can you anticipate? Speak to those things.

Investors, for example, require detailed and accurate financial information including your needs, the costs, your operational plan, marketing analysis, projections over three or more years, return on investment and so on. They will evaluate whether your idea is viable and profitable.

More often overlooked: The importance of demonstrating who you are. Convey that you are credible, honest, knowledgeable, trustworthy, realistic, competent, respected and a good manager. It's good to show that you're a big picture thinker and at the same time, firmly grounded.

You should also demonstrate flexibility—the ability to cope with new situations should obstacles and problems arise. Are you resourceful and resilient enough to deal with setbacks should the market shift, regulations change or a major customer decamp?

Solid information about your management team is equally critical. ***Don't shortchange the professional biographies and leave them to the last minute.*** Be sure they demonstrate the skills, track record, education and personal qualities that equip the key people for their roles and explain how the team will work together.

Classic Business Plan Outline: An Example

Writing a business plan rarely calls for inventive formatting. You must meet reader expectations and needs, which means as always "know your reader," and take care to include the right information and make it easy to find. However, adjust presentation to purpose as necessary. Here is one standard way to organize a plan.

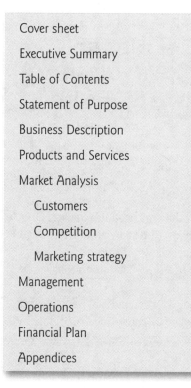

Cover sheet

Executive Summary

Table of Contents

Statement of Purpose

Business Description

Products and Services

Market Analysis

   Customers

   Competition

   Marketing strategy

Management

Operations

Financial Plan

Appendices

PROPOSAL WRITING

Whether you're pitching for a project or applying for a grant, proposals have to be first rate to stand a chance. There just aren't many huge piles of money sitting around without a horde of applicants buzzing

SUCCESS TIP : USE A FOLDER SYSTEM TO JUMP-START BIG PROJECTS

When a major writing project looms, ease your path by collecting ideas, thoughts, and resources in file folders, either real or virtual—or both. (If you use paper, note that colored ones are better than plain manila. You can color-code by subject.) Divide the project into sections. If you're working on a business plan and follow the "classic" outline shown, you'd make up 10 folders. Then, as random useful thoughts come to you, write them up and put them in the applicable folders. Do the same with materials like financial statements.

If you've allowed reasonable time for the project, you'll end up with a batch of ideas and information for every topic. The writing will feel less formidable and you'll have good material right at hand. The system also keeps you organized. Best of all, this simple write-as-you-go method builds your thinking much more forcefully than if you sit down and try to create the document from scratch, all at once.

around, pitching for a share or the chance to do the job. Lean times tempt less qualified applicants to try for every opportunity, so in many fields, competition keeps rising.

We'll focus on the not-for-profit and government sectors, but keep in mind that most of the concepts apply to the profit-making world as well.

If you're responding to an RFP—request for proposals—you may be aiming to win a grant, or at least, get to the next step of the application process. Who's your audience? It's your business to find out as much as you can about the organization and people who will review what you write.

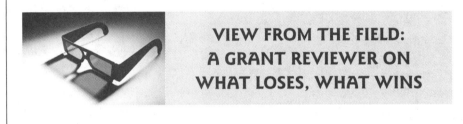

VIEW FROM THE FIELD: A GRANT REVIEWER ON WHAT LOSES, WHAT WINS

What annoys me most is that people just do not answer the questions. They talk around the issues and don't get to the heart of things, the core interest of a donor or funder: Why should we give money to you and not another organization that's doing similar work?

Many grant applications are particularly light on the organization's impact. One, for example, asked for more money to do more work in the same area. They talked about how horrible the problem is that they deal with but not the agency's impact. I asked about it: "You've been using the money for 15 years—what difference have you made?" They talked themselves out of the funding.

Don't just cite numbers to show success—saying "we trained 500 people" isn't going to make me invest in your organization. I want to know what happened to those people a year later. It can be hard to track results with figures but you can show them anecdotally.

I notice bad writing, I don't notice mediocre writing, and I do notice good writing—when you see something written well it has stars around it, sparkles. Good writing stands out.

Given that the application shows capacity and evidence that the organization can do the work, good writing gets the grant.

—Ann Marie Thigpen, director,
Long Island Center for Nonprofit Leadership at Adelphi University

You can glean what you need from the organization's website and other materials, particularly the RFP itself and any guidelines issued with it. Your research should reveal much about the giver's orientation and style, which proposals have won before and many specifics, like whether the group prefers collaborative proposals, public—private initiatives and so on.

Perhaps the most important tenet is to take the organization's mission seriously. Whether they represent foundations, government agencies or non-governmental organizations (NGOs), proposal reviewers typically feel quite passionate about that mission. Of course you should apply for grants from sources that align with your own activities and goals. But watch for the subtleties that distinguish a particular organization's mission and write a proposal that dovetails.

Also, make some general assumptions about the reviewers. It is safe to assume that reading and evaluating a stack of proposals is a challenge even when there are many screeners.

As you write a proposal, imagine this scene: A group of people gathers around a table at the end of the day. The table is piled high with applications that they previously read in the corners of their day or night. Whether they're busy professionals or board members conscripted for the job, they can't go home until the proposals are discussed and consensus is reached on which requests to fund.

The review process doesn't always look like this, but is usually similar in spirit. What kind of proposals should you send these tired people?

Proposals that get to the point quickly and succinctly and clearly. And another lesson you've learned before: Don't be boring. Storify: Use anecdotes about people to make the need real and illustrate accomplishment. Create a vision of what will be better should the money become yours.

Crystallize your communication: Eliminate all words you don't need. Use simple language so your ideas shine through. Don't repeat material to pad out the proposal, or because reviewers may only read Question 7 and need grounding in what you said elsewhere. If you concentrate on answering the questions properly, you'll find that repetition isn't necessary. In fact, if you do repeat, take it as a clue that you're not answering the questions as you should.

The finished proposal's organization must exactly correspond to the RFP. True, breaking it up this way may make it hard to build a cohesive, flowing narrative, but it can be done. Each part should stand on its own, be presented consistently and contribute new information so that the parts add up to a complete, compelling story.

VIEW FROM THE FIELD: BUSINESS PROPOSALS THAT GET YOU IN THE DOOR

Winning proposals don't focus on you so much as on the clients. You need to really know them, what they're going after and why. First, I look at all the hot buttons mentioned in the RFP. I like to repeat them throughout and get them into the cover letter. If the RFP says, "Here are our goals and what we hope to get out of this project," great. If not—dig, through interviews or research.

We establish a theme for the entire proposal. For example, if it's a redevelopment project and the main thing they want is more jobs, our theme would be creating jobs and we'd carry it through the captions, images, and photos in addition to the cover letter and technical scope section.

The cover letter is very important. If it doesn't appeal to the clients, they won't go further. We establish guidelines: The first paragraph restates the client's goals so from the beginning, it's not about us, and you show your understanding. The second paragraph introduces the team members, not just who they are, but why the client should care—have they worked with the company before? Have relevant experience? Then we follow through looking at the RFP and the evaluation criteria, showing how we meet them and how our characteristics benefit the client.

We're matching our story to theirs.

Then we refer to what is unique about our proposal—shortened timeline? Coming in under budget? Ideally, something that makes us special. And don't forget to include contractual matters, such as "This contract is good for 180 days . . ."

The letter should be clear, concise, one page when possible and two at the most. The proposal must read well all the way through and be integrated. Use an active voice, keep sentence length to 15 words or less; be positive and remove unnecessary words. Write it so you can bring it home to someone who's not part of the industry and check if they understand it. Our proposals are reviewed by committees, so they must be understood by the layman. The graphics are extremely important. Try to engage.

The goal is to get interviewed! The proposal's quality makes the difference to getting shortlisted and interviewed.

—Christine M. Cesaria, marketing production manager,
VHB Engineering, Surveying and Landscape Architecture, P.C.

COVER LETTER FOR A PROPOSAL: AN EXAMPLE

A proposal always demands an individual, well-thought-out cover letter. Here is the closing section of one written to compete for a major construction project.

Unlike pure bike planning firms, our firm knows what it takes to get to construction and we will therefore help ABCDE find feasible solutions for the White River trails.

Enthusiasm and Dedication

We have a passion for bicycle projects. For us they are not a side business, they are a stand-alone practice area. Furthermore, our team includes avid cyclists and bike advocates. Our enthusiasm translates into focused attention to quality and service, and we take special pride in and ownership of these assignments.

On behalf of the project team, thank you for this opportunity to present our qualifications for this interesting assignment. We hope to have the opportunity to discuss our experience and approach further. Please feel free to contact me at xxx-xxx-xxxx should you require any additional information.

Very truly yours,
Christine M. Cesaria, VHB Engineering,
Surveying and Landscape Architecture

Grant Application Strategies

Make telephone calls. Talk to the grant administrators. Ask questions about how to best present your request—the level of detail they'd like to see, data to include, even whether a particular project is a good candidate. This enables you to perfect your pitch, closely tailoring it to expectations.

It is a rare funder that will mind hearing from you, as long as you speak with intelligence. Making awards is a grueling business for funders as well as for the applicants. They're happy to help you meet their needs. Moreover, the interaction works toward building a relationship. We choose to work with and invest in people we trust. And as I said in the previous chapter, emotion plays a big role in decision making.

Telephone calls are your first choice, but if you must write to pose questions, present your best image through your best writing.

Focus on the problem. Be sure to clearly state what problem your solution is intended to solve, why it's important, its dimensions.

Focus on outcomes. Funders often complain that many grant applicants fail to provide enough information on outcomes—what will be accomplished if the money is awarded. Outcomes must be meaningful: "We will train 50 farmers to use the new agricultural method" is a so-what statement. But this is not: "We will train 50 farmers and show them how to train their peers. Each will train an additional 25 per year and they in turn will share their training. Within two years, the program will reach half the co-op's farmers and yield a collective crop increase of 15 to 20%."

Focus on the action. Sometimes outcomes are well defined, but don't connect to activities and the methods expected to bring them about. Let's say a program's objective is to help failing students improve their math grades by 20%; but the application says only that this will be accomplished by presenting 15 workshops. What will the students learn, who will teach them, what innovative strategies will be adopted? Can you show a track record for the methods?

Don't get lost in detail. Stick to what is central to your story. But be as specific as possible in your financial analysis. Like bankers, funders don't like not knowing how you'll spend their money.

Keep the proposal consistent. If various people work on different sections, be sure someone is responsible for tying it all together and checking that the style is uniform.

Remember that funders like projects. Your nonprofit may desperately need financial support for its office and salaries, but few funders like to award money for operational expenses. They prefer new program components and new projects that help people and make an impact by contributing to their own mission.

Set the stage for future applications. Understandably, many nonprofit organizations cannot afford expensive follow-up studies to prove a program worked. When you're responsible for managing the grant, look for tracking options at the very beginning and build them into the work. For example, field workers can be asked to make note of clients' input on how they were helped.

And always, report back to the funder on results, whether that's a formal requirement or not. Many requestors fail to do so and wonder why their new applications fail.

VIEW FROM THE FIELD:
PROPOSAL ADVICE FROM
A PROGRAM DIRECTOR

We start with knowing the audience and the language it speaks. We aim with all our writing to be very clear and direct. Saying it in simple terms is important. People often want to overexplain things in a proposal but then the less clear it becomes. Thread in too much detail and you lose directness and intensity. Put in too much mechanics and people start to get lost in the machinery.

There's an art to finding the most direct way to say something about a sophisticated idea in a short amount of space. Usually we have 10 pages to explain what we'll do with millions of dollars.

The underlying structure we use:

- Rationale
- Political context
- Why it's important
- Why we're the best to do the work
- What the work will actually be
- Timing
- Results we expect

I recommend outlining what you're trying to do, so you go into a document with a road map of how it all fits together. This tells you where questions will arise and what research you have to do so you have a game plan. The document may not end up much longer than the outline. This process helps people distill the ideas and concepts down to bullet points—then they have the luxury of adding detail and can figure out the sequence people will understand. An outline also lets us brainstorm with other people, who many times are overseas, so it's easy for them to contribute and you build buy-in in advance.

Always, put the bottom line up front. If you're asking for something, whether in a letter or proposal, come out with it right away. Be unambiguous. It gives the reader a unifying idea of what the document is about.

This is important also because of another element, how you want readers to think of you. They learn about the team, and the project, by how the document is written. You want to be seen as straightforward, direct, easy to understand. You need them to trust you and feel they can get a very direct answer in a quick amount of time.

—Erin Mathews, director of Iraq Programs,
the National Democratic Institute (an international development agency)

PRESENTATION: CREATING AND USING POWERPOINT DOCUMENTS

PowerPoint and similar programs have evolved into two different uses:

1. As a presentation aid, for which it was designed

2. As a basic vehicle of communication in the business world. For which it was not designed

Unfortunately, it is rarely well used in either capacity, which has led to a lot of impassioned criticism. But, realistically, it is a core tool in many business programs and use proliferates. So creating good PowerPoint is a valuable skill. Good writing strategies can help you produce better results for both uses.

PowerPoint for Presentation

Too many presenters allow this medium to become the message. They shape their content based on a predetermined format rather than developing a solid presentation that uses PowerPoint as an adjunct tool.

PowerPoint is best seen as a way to add visual dimension to a speech. A speech is a direct interaction with an audience. Just thinking in terms of your goals and audience tells you that, whatever the subject, you must

Engage the audience: This means sharing information they need, want or will find entertaining, and delivering it effectively.

Persuade the audience: This can mean inspiring them, educating them, moving them to think, reconsider or do something.

Involve the audience: People don't like passive listening in large doses. Perhaps they never did, but these days they have many alternative, interactive resources and are less inclined to sit still for a monologue if they have a choice.

Generate follow-up: You may want your audience to care about something, take action, think further and/or remember your central message—and you.

Create a positive image for the messenger: You want to be seen as authoritative, professional, creative, articulate and so forth, depending on your field and role; also open-minded and reasonable, and preferably skilled in interpersonal relations.

Does it work, then, to provide a full deck of dense copy with boxes and circles and charts and lists and arrows with fonts that can hardly be read at 10 feet, let alone from the back of a room? And do you successfully present when you read from the screen in a darkened auditorium so that the audience keeps its eyes on the screen? If your subject is anything except how to live for 200 years and stay healthy, you've got one badly bored audience.

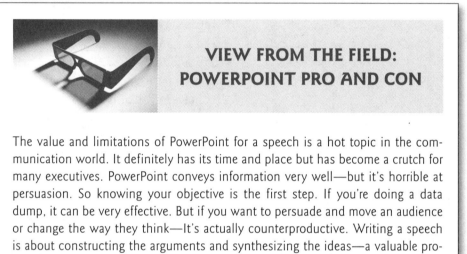

VIEW FROM THE FIELD: POWERPOINT PRO AND CON

The value and limitations of PowerPoint for a speech is a hot topic in the communication world. It definitely has its time and place but has become a crutch for many executives. PowerPoint conveys information very well—but it's horrible at persuasion. So knowing your objective is the first step. If you're doing a data dump, it can be very effective. But if you want to persuade and move an audience or change the way they think—It's actually counterproductive. Writing a speech is about constructing the arguments and synthesizing the ideas—a valuable process. PowerPoint can be like creating a cheat sheet rather than doing the hard work—like building a lean-to instead of a house, where the data points are second to the arguments.

—Dan Gerstein, founder/CEO, Gotham Ghostwriters; political adviser, analyst and commentator

The key to presenting well with PowerPoint is to plan and write your presentation as a speech. A speech needs an engaging opener, a single major focus, a clearly presented sequence of ideas and facts (not too many of either though), a strong close and these days, planned audience interaction at given points.

What role does that give PowerPoint? Use it to

- Add visual color and interpret the meaning of information—relevant images and photographs, and easily absorbed tables, charts and graphs that leverage the medium's ability to show change over time or helpful comparisons.

SUCCESS TIP: HOW TO PREPARE YOUR OWN SPEAKING NOTES

If you need to deliver a speech word for word because the occasion calls for it or you must not forget a thing, here's a simple trick for preparing your script.

Type it up to reflect how you'd read it with natural pauses. Start a new line at each pause. Take, for example, this excerpt from a memorable speech by President John F. Kennedy:

> And so, my fellow Americans:
>
> ask not what your country can do for you—
>
> ask what you can do for your country.
>
> My fellow citizens of the world:
>
> ask not what America will do for you,
>
> but what together we can do
>
> for the freedom of man.
>
> Finally,
>
> whether you are citizens of America
>
> or citizens of the world,
>
> ask of us the same high standards of strength and sacrifice
>
> which we ask of you.

This method allows you to deliver the message much more powerfully. It also enables you to look up frequently and maintain almost steady eye contact with the audience. And if you use this approach, you won't need to hold long lines of copy in your head as you speak and will feel much more relaxed.

- Provide cues to keep yourself on track when speaking. Slides can be as simple as a headline: "What we learned from this research" or "Questions." Steve Jobs of Apple is famous for using a few simple words with splashy, imaginative graphics.
- Reinforce important points you want the audience to focus on. Visual learning is very effective provided the material is simple and easily absorbed.
- Provide ready-made handouts—which gives you a chance to circulate your contact information if you're scouting for clients.

Aim for simplicity in both content and language. This medium obviously needs your most conversational, say-able style. Expect to draft a speech and then cut, amplify and refine in stages, based on the say-ability test. Read it aloud and fix all the stumbles and hard-to-say parts. Rehearse. Build in stories and anecdotes to perk people up and reinforce memory.

As you develop the content, think about how to use the visual dimension to enhance and support your message. Or think about it after the speech is in place. Also build in places for questions or discussions to keep people involved.

The less you can refer to notes and maintain eye contact with your audience the better. Choose the least obvious way to check your script that you can handle. Keep in mind that since you know more about the subject than your listeners, they won't notice what you leave out, so don't obsess over remembering every point.

Don't try to tell people everything you know. And read your audience as you go so you can adapt to what sparks their eyes, and speed up the parts that glaze them.

PowerPoint for Business Communications

PowerPoint has become the communication tool of choice in many business environments. It's used extensively to share information and guide discussion at meetings, both in person and increasingly, through virtual media. It also is employed as the medium of record.

Such uses can present a major challenge. If you spend all your time and energy turning information into visuals that fit a limited format, the message can easily get lost and the information distorted. If you use bulleted lists heavily, they're only shorthand, and just don't work for some kinds of information where context and connections matter.

If all or part of your purpose is to distribute printouts, then you can cram a lot of data onto your slides. They may be readable when printed out and distributed—but that doesn't mean people will understand them. Perhaps the ultimate incomprehensible slide, discussed below, was produced by the U.S. Department of Defense in 2009. Widely circulated, it revealed that the military, like many industries, depends heavily on PowerPoint for decision making. Many people were amazed that life or death decisions could be based on an indecipherable slide, raising intensive questions about the medium.

But what are you to do if an employer or client expects you to use PowerPoint as a basic means of sharing and recording information? You may be told directly to ignore good rules of writing.

HOW THE DOD LOST THE POWERPOINT WAR: AN EXAMPLE NOT TO FOLLOW

The Department of Defense prepared the slide on the next page for top-level military and political leaders, as an aid during deliberations on how to handle the war in Afghanistan. The single slide was charged with presenting every aspect of a very complicated scenario. It looked, as the New York Times *said, more like a bowl of spaghetti than a guide for planning strategy.*

(Continued)

Afghanistan Stability / COIN Dynamics

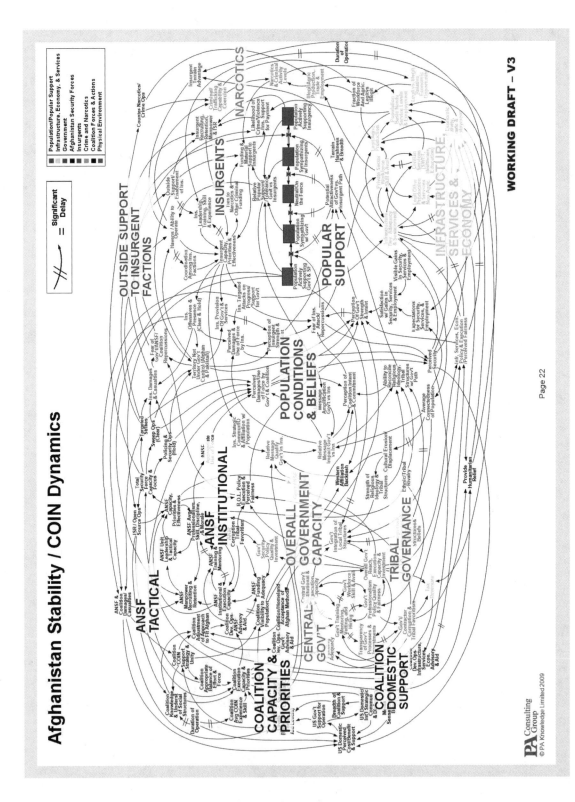

WORKING DRAFT – V3

PA Consulting Group
© PA Knowledge Limited 2009

Page 22

206

The slide circulated on the Internet and in major newspapers, and brought to light some quite hostile feelings about PowerPoint. "It's dangerous because it can create the illusion of understanding and the illusion of control," a brigadier general told a reporter. "Some problems in the world are not bullet-izable." A movement to ban PowerPoint in the DOD was set underway.

There are lessons to be learned here, but I'll let you come to your own conclusions.

In that case too, don't plunge immediately into slide making. Instead, decide what you want to communicate. Take the time to understand the topic or problem in depth and your main message points. Figure out how things relate and connect. Then plan your slides, keeping them simple, and once they're created, check how well you can explain each one.

The result may differ somewhat from the PowerPoint that people are used to seeing. However, you are apt to get positive reactions even though viewers may not know why they liked the presentation.

Also, you'll be far better equipped to answer questions than if you'd concentrated on turning out a batch of data-jammed slides.

GOING DEEPER: HOW TO WORK WITH POWERPOINT

I always start by profiling my audience, understanding their core needs and expectations. And if I want things from the audience, what are they?

My next step is to go with pen and paper. A lot of people start with a blank computer screen and the tools, PowerPoint or whatever they're using, but I believe that's limiting in building a story line and coming up with content organically.

So I develop a storyboard, thinking about it like a filmmaker—what's the overall plot line? The key messages or takeaways? What are the scenes that will build up to deliver that? I think about the logic of the ideas and how to translate them into visual representations. When that's well developed on paper, I go to the computer screen, and that's where some principles of slide design become more relevant.

(Continued)

(Continued)

I think audiences do one of two things: read what's on the slide or listen to your words. You want them to listen, which means using fewer words and more images to depict complex content graphically.

When I've written the presentation's initial draft, I spend most of my time preparing to deliver it—I present to a colleague or stand in front of the mirror. This leads me to simplify the slide content even more. If you learn your message, you rely less on the slides to remember your notes, and the audience focuses on you. The final step is to refine the content, which usually means simplifying, stripping what's unnecessary so the key messages speak louder than the detail.

Keep in mind that PowerPoint is not always the right tool, as opposed to spoken word alone, or a written memo or video. People might not perceive there's an option, but I think they're actually hungry for innovation. They want to be communicated to in a way that suggests they are unique and understood, and that you're not just defaulting to what you've done with other audiences. I think people are hungry to move away from death by PowerPoint. But deal with expectations early on.

When you're preparing slides to distribute as a handout, the concepts are the same in that you want the audience to listen to you, so put less on the page and know your story really well. But if you're handing out a presentation without delivering context and it must stand alone, it's different. Then you're writing more of a document in slide format and people need time to sit down and read it. If it's then used for presentation, you must translate it to simplify content and deliver more verbally.

Favorite resources:

TED.com (great examples of speakers using slides to support their talks)

Slide:ology (Nancy Duarte, O'Reilly Media, 2008) and www.duarte.com

Presentation Zen (Garr Reynolds, New Riders Press, 2008) and www.presentationzen.com

—Clint Nohavec, senior consultant,
Deloitte; MBA, Kellogg School of Management

HOW TO PLAN EFFECTIVE VIDEOS

With new technology that makes it easy to produce and disseminate video, the medium is everywhere. It's becoming more and more important as an adjunct to websites, blogs, social media résumés and many other venues.

It's popular to assume that production values no longer count. In fact, some public relations agencies have found, literally, that video shot by the mailroom clerk draws more viewers than expensively produced "traditional" video. People often do seem to find unfocused video with shaky movement more "authentic" than the carefully created kind, at least on YouTube.

But generally such video needs to be short or immensely entertaining, lest we lose patience with it. More important: When you're using video for business purposes, be cautious. No matter where you show it, your clips speak for the organization. Huge numbers of viewers don't necessarily provide a benefit you want.

Whether you're a job seeker using video to introduce yourself on your social media résumé, a consultant interested in making your website more personal and engaging; a company president using it on the home page to explain the firm's mission or apologize for a disaster or a CFO using video to review company financials for distribution to a worldwide audience—in every case, you need a clear idea of your goal. And you need a script.

This applies even if the whole video consists of you as seen by an unmoving camera. At the very least, see video as a speech. And a speech needs a good lead, informational middle and an effective end. It needs to be smoothly and convincingly delivered, so you must know exactly what you will say and rehearse. You can't read the script on camera, but you can use written cues.

Or if you're a confident speaker, just as for a speech, you can use talking points to wing it. The advantage of video versus a live performance is that you can do the "bad" parts over and edit the best takes together.

If you're creating a more ambitious video, you need a storyboard to represent the main points and how they connect. This can be done simply, as described for PowerPoint. In addition to video clips, you can include stills and graphics. This takes planning. You'll need to marshal what's available to work with and decide what else you can feasibly add to the mix.

Another way to plan is to create a two-column script with a line down the middle. The visuals go on the left side, which reminds you of their dominant role in this medium, and the words go on the right. For example:

VISUALS	V/O (VOICE-OVER)
C/U (close-up) of JB	Hi. I'm John Brown and I'd like to show you how my team won this year's debating conference in Miami.
WS (wide shot) of team giving presentation	We took a long road getting there and learned a lot. Here's how we got ready.
Stills/team practicing	
Cutaways of notes, papers, faces	I can't believe how much work it took. Every day we spent 3 hours . . .
C/U Ellen	

The core concept is that with video, you don't just script words, you also must script the visuals, in tandem. You need something on the screen for every second of voice-over. Of course, you'll have to edit everything together neatly, but these days, if you have the time, the software is there and the skills can be learned.

Unless you're creating the kind of simple, straight-on video where the camera stays on you and you talk through it, perhaps demonstrating something, words and images must be juggled to tell the story. Video specialists aim to use few words and let what's on the screen say as much as possible. The narration is used to bridge between scenes and ideas, and explain what can't be translated into visuals.

However, those few words must be carefully chosen. Try for very accessible language, short say-able sentences with good rhythm. Fragments work fine, since in spoken language, formal sentences can actually sound unnatural and jarring. *Don't fill the script with wall-to-wall words. Silence is the videographer's version of white space.* It allows viewers to focus on the images and hear the ambient sound—for example, the team members rehearsing—or absorb the music if there is any; music is one more dimension for effective video. Music can underscore emotions and unify the presentation.

The very smallest camcorders, or even your smart phone, can work amazingly well for many purposes, thanks to the digital revolution and fast-improving technology. But they carry some important limitations.

One is sound quality. With tiny machines, this has lagged far behind the level achieved for visual recording, and research says that people have far less patience for bad audio than for bad picture. Especially if you're selling something, or delivering any message that people don't need, *pay attention to the sound quality.* You may need to use auxiliary equipment for this. And you may need to use a camera that allows you to plug in a mike.

A second limitation is lighting. If you watch a professional video crew at a shoot, you'll notice that excruciating time is spent setting up the lights. It's the critical factor in getting good, real-looking, interesting pictures. You are unlikely to have a lighting specialist, but know that simple front-on lighting gives you a flat (and unflattering) image. Worse, though, is backlighting—where the source comes from behind the subject. This obliterates all detail and produces, at worst, a silhouette. So (1) watch for where you position your subject and the angle you shoot from, in relation to the light, and (2) consider a supplementary camera light when your video matters.

One more caveat—try to not rely solely on what the industry calls "talking heads" to deliver your message. Use imagination to come up with visual ideas so the camera doesn't just stay focused on one person. When you can't do this or don't have the resources, keep it short. That generally means less than two minutes.

Planning, shooting and editing video takes hands-on practice. So if you want to use it, spend some time experimenting and see what works. For helpful advice, try the websites of journalism schools.

In the next chapter, I'll turn the spotlight to the online world, starting with websites.

PRACTICE OPPORTUNITIES

I. Group Project: Invent and Propose a New Course

Collaborate on ideas for a new course that would add to your capabilities and help you compete in the job market. Pick one, then brainstorm what you would learn. Divide up the responsibilities and collaboratively write a formal proposal to your school's director explaining what you recommend and why. Review the techniques of persuasive writing and use those that apply to create a convincing proposal.

II. Group Project: Build a Business Plan

In a small group, adopt an idea for a new local charitable cause you agree would be of value (e.g., cleaning up a park; collecting used clothing for a children's shelter; an after-school tutoring service). Talk the project through and draft a business plan for it, to help raise funds. Decide what elements need to be covered and the central focus of your story—the need that the new organization will fill, who will benefit, the extent of demand, who will be on the team and so on.

III. Write an Executive Summary

Collaborate on an ES for the charity based on the business plan.

IV. Plan a PowerPoint Slide Deck

Drawing on methods suggested in this chapter, create a storyboard for a presentation your group will deliver to raise funds for your good cause. Use either a paper and pen or computer, but fully develop your plan and content.

V. Graphic Interpretation

Pick a cause you personally believe in and come up with a visual idea to express the severity of the problem or need.

VI. Group Project: Plan a Video

Your subject: How to write either a good business plan, or proposal. Review this chapter to decide on your content, the points that you believe are most important to make. Then either using a simple storyboard or the two-column script approach shown, plan the audio and visual segments, in tandem. Pretend you have a substantial budget and brainstorm at each step about what visuals can be created or drawn upon to explain, illustrate and engage (for example, still photos, documents, original footage.) Aim for a strong lead and close, and try to minimize the words.

Chapter 10

WRITING FOR WEBSITES AND THE WIRED WORLD

LEARN HOW TO . . .

➤ Understand the difference between print and online writing
➤ Plan a website based on "goal," "audience" and the right "tone"
➤ Create copy that works for websites and online media
➤ Brainstorm content ideas
➤ Plan and build your home page

> *I write my own website and I've taken a really long time doing it. . . . I want to make it just as clear and intuitive as I can. I'm absolutely convinced that clear writing makes my business succeed.*
>
> —Jason Fried, founder/president of the software firm 37 signals; coauthor of the best-selling book, *Rework.*

WEBSITE WRITING: WHAT'S DIFFERENT, WHAT'S NOT

Is writing for online media different from writing for print?

Yes and no: In some ways it's very different, but basically it involves new ways to apply the same principles.

This book's basic premise is that contemporary business writing works best when it's conversational—as opposed to the stilted, formal language that used to be the norm. If you've absorbed this idea, you have a virtual head start.

Like all practical writing, online material needs to be accessible, clear, friendly and audience oriented, but even more so.

> *I'm seeing more smart long-form content on the web. People used to go to their web site developer with copy that was like a place holder—but people are consuming news, they're reading articles, so there's more and more demand for smart comment.*
>
> —Dan Gerstein, President/Founder of Gotham Gostwriters and political consultant, analyst and commentator

For online media, you must be especially concise. As you can confirm from your own experience, people generally resist reading long, dense material on a computer, let alone a tiny, handheld device. And for both physical and psychological reasons, we read electronic material more slowly.

Graphics matter online—headlines, sub-heads, sidebars, a readable typeface. But surprisingly, research (by the Nielsen Norman Group) finds that even the website, which we think of as a visual medium, is basically text driven. People focus first on headlines, not photographs, and generally are uninterested in images that don't relate directly to content.

Online media definitely demand "correctness": good grammar (though web writing can take big liberties) and definitely good spelling. Correctness is critical because anyone reading a website, blog or online article is looking for clues to credibility, consciously or not. Since the virtual world enables anyone to be an author, critic or expert, the unspoken question is always, "Why should I trust you? Why should I accept this site as authoritative or even honest?"

Good writing, which requires good editing and proofing, is one sign that you're credible and can be taken seriously.

Some Special Characteristics of Websites

Here's a big difference between writing for print and online media: *When it comes to online media, writing is not just about writing anymore. It has*

1. **More dimensions.** A website, blog or social media posting can incorporate not only design and images, but can integrate or link to video, blogs, podcasts, articles and other sites. All these possibilities should be considered in planning content.

2. **Interactive thinking.** Traditional print media have a one-way direction—"here's the word from the author." (Although nowadays, newspapers and magazines encourage reader comment.) A lot of online media aim to connect with readers directly and foster dialogue. They operate more along the lines, "Here's what I think, what do you think?"

3. **Nonlinear nature.** Print documents are conceived as linear information flows with a beginning, middle and end. We assume, rightly or wrongly, that people will start at A and finish at Z. This is definitely not a useful assumption

with websites. A large percentage of viewers will never look at your home page and may only read a single page that contains the information they want. Even on that page, their eyes typically jump around and focus on various spots rather than proceeding from A to Z. So it's necessary to repeat information in different places, make each page self-explanatory, supply easy connections to other parts of the site and clearly indicate the reader's next step on every page.

4. "Information packaging" outlook. Because the virtual world furnishes so much competing material and it's hard to keep people engaged, information must be delivered in different ways. Techniques like "chunking" material into short digestible lumps, finding alternate ways to attract attention and using interpretive visuals are essential. Older media like newspapers and magazines are also adopting these approaches.

5. Scannability. We're not writing for readers any more—we're writing for scanners and divers and robots. Observe how you use the Internet yourself. You're usually looking for something specific, whether it's a product to solve a leaking pipe, a plumber, advice from people who solved a similar problem or a discussion about dealing with plumbers. So you Google what you need, scan a few of the first sites listed to see if they're what you want, and perhaps do some comparison shopping. To suit this search habit, successful sites use short blocks of copy with short words and scan-friendly sentences, clear subheads and appropriate key words to help people and search engine robots find them.

6. Delivery speed. A traditional document can take a long time to prepare, get off press and deliver. Once printed, it can't readily be changed. Producing a good virtual document still requires a lot of prep time, but it's totally mutable and can be delivered anytime, anywhere, with a click. Speed breeds speed, too. We expect instant responses or answers and are very impatient when we don't get them.

These factors hold a lot of implications not only for writing, but also for basic ideas about communication. For most of recorded history, one-way communication was the norm: Those with authority delivered their opinions and orders. Talking back took enormous resources or pressure from masses of people.

How Websites Open the Playing Field

Today, there is no barrier to entering the forum beyond possessing the minimal technology. Anyone can be a player—expressing ideas, gaining a following, disagreeing. Social critics call it democratization: a growing trend that enables anyone to be an authority and weigh in equally with trained journalists, academics and professionals.

Is this altogether good? Who's to say? Either way, people haven't yet caught up with the impact of a virtual world and since communication media keep evolving, we won't anytime soon.

So here's the bad news: There are no definitive guidelines to follow for using virtual media well. And the good news: The fundamental ideas about writing that you're practicing remain as useful as ever, plus there's plenty of room to experiment with what works for your purposes.

More good news/bad news: Such a tsunami of written material vies for our online attention (including 400 million English-language blogs last time I checked) that if you're writing for anyone beyond your mother or best buddy, what you write must be good.

Websites and You

More people in recent years have gained at least some website responsibility because

1. Websites are so critical to nearly every business today

2. Websites can be incredibly time-intensive to create, maintain and update

Factor #2 is in many cases tempered by the blurring line between a website and a blog. Large organizations are unlikely to give up their "formal" websites soon, though many are adding blogs. And there's growing recognition that for many reasons a website should be "social," promoting interaction and conversation, rather than just serving as a static online brochure.

So you may find yourself developing content for a company or department site, building and maintaining a site for your own business or consultancy or developing a site in your own name, perhaps as part of a job-hunting strategy.

Let's give a minute to the fact that websites haven't always been around. They've revolutionized communication and marketing so much since the mid 1990s that it's hard to realize how new they are. Before then, organizations depended on advertising and public relations to broadcast their messages to millions of people so that those in the market for a new car, or toothpaste, would be enticed to buy their products. The bigger the company, the bigger the marketing budget could be.

Websites are the great leveler. An individual or small company can have a strategically planned, well-presented, searchable website that people will come to when they need a product or service. Unlike employees, the website operates every day, all day and night, without complaint. Millions of businesses are now strictly virtual: no buildings, no offices, maybe no staff or inventory. They thrive according to their ability to serve a need, be found by customers, pitch effectively online and deliver as promised.

FAQS: HOW PEOPLE READ WEBSITES

Researchers study how people look at websites by tracking their eye movements across a page. They've found a common pattern that's roughly shaped like an "F": Eyes fixate first in the page's upper left area then move right, and eventually down. Material toward the bottom gets the least viewer attention. Many professional designers take this into account when planning a home page, and place the most important element in the upper left corner.

More findings:

- Text is usually the reader's entry point, not photographs. Strong headlines draw the eye most effectively, especially when placed upper left.
- Headlines grab attention for less than a second—so the first few words are important. The same is true with sentences.
- People prefer straightforward headlines and single-column text.
- Short paragraphs (one to three sentences) draw twice the attention as long ones.
- Readers don't like generic stock images and images not related to content—they do like bigger images and those with people looking directly at them, but "real" people, not professional models.
- We read up to 25% more slowly on the web than on the printed page.

The research is most notably conducted by the Nielsen Norman Group (nngroup .com) and the Poynter Institute (poynter.org); check their sites for a wealth of information and updates.

HOW TO PLAN A WEBSITE

Whether you're developing your own website or participating in a team effort, remember that words play a major role in the planning and writing stages. Many website developers move too quickly to the technical stage—design and functionality.

Ideally, the process is a push–pull enterprise with other specialists, whatever the size of your team.

If you're starting a brand new site, you need to think through what the site will contain and determine its overall "architecture"—the sequence of pages, basically, and how each page will lead to the next and connect in other ways, through hyperlinks. Many planners think of this structure as a tree, with roots branching out and down in various directions.

It's best to think about how you envision the site "now" and also down the line in the future, whether a month, six months or a year or more. That enables you to build a framework that easily accommodates growth and development.

You'll probably want a "stable" section of the site that remains basically unchanged, and other pages that are designed from the beginning for easy updating—for example, blogs, commentary, news, announcements and any interactive elements where you engage directly with your audience, such as Q&As or contests.

At the top of your tree—or the top of your piece of real or virtual paper—stands your home page, your site's face. This should represent and lead to the rest of the content, even though many viewers may not see it at all. If they're seeking something specific they will land on the page that describes that. (If you sell a variety of handbags, for example, someone might Google "men's messenger bags" and be directed to that specific page.)

Does using a blog format (officially an "online web log") lessen the importance of this kind of planning? Individuals and small businesses can *somewhat* bypass the need for heavy investment by going the blog route. That is, the blog format and online service sites (such as Wordpress, Blogger and Blogspot) can be used to create a more ad hoc kind of website, geared to interaction and easy updating.

Especially if you don't have tech and design team backup, this can be a good approach. But just because a blog site may be easier to get online doesn't mean you can skip planning.

Probably more often than developing an original site, you may be involved in site revamps. Here, the existing architecture is a big factor. You may only be able to make changes within the established structure. It's like a building—once the overall footprint and infrastructure are in place, you can fill each room however you want, but it may be hard to add more rooms or move the walls.

Major changes become simpler to incorporate as the technology gets easier to use. But to update or renovate an established site, you'll have to work closely with the tech people.

Applying the "Goal" and "Audience" Concepts

Think About Goals

Defining what you want a site to accomplish is essential. Nevertheless, many people skip this step. Here's a list of possible goals.

- Sell a product or service or introduce a new one
- Develop new business
- Establish credibility
- Provide customer support
- Build brand awareness and "image"
- Market an individual as an expert, a speaker, a personality and so on.
- Find collaborators

- Find and encourage investors
- Interact with and learn from customers
- Give the organization a personality
- Raise the corporate profile as a socially committed enterprise
- Attract and interest new employees
- Facilitate interaction with vendors
- Communicate with government agencies or regulators
- Educate the public about a subject
- Inform the press and public about the company's position on issues
- Achieve media coverage
- Unite staff scattered in many locations
- Give a unified face to a complex multi-division, multi-location firm

Nonprofit organizations typically share many of these goals and also have their own—for example, to attract donations and volunteers, recognize these groups, support grant applications and humanize the organization.

You or your firm may have other goals than those listed. ***Whatever they are, write them down and break them into specifics.*** For example, if you want to achieve media coverage, do you want it from the trade press, your local newspaper, the *Wall Street Journal* or the *Huffington Post?* If you want to attract and impress donors or investors, do you mean people under 35 or elderly millionaires?

Prioritize your set of goals and make it your touchstone for decision making through every stage of development. When sites represent a group or organization rather than one person, agreement on goals is crucial.

Ideally, goals should be measurable so you can evaluate how well you're achieving them. Websites offer many more chances to quantify results than print media, because data on number of visitors, length of visit, where viewers spend time, inquiries, direct purchases and much more can be easily tracked and analyzed.

ACTION TIME: "READING" WEBSITES

Pick a leading organization in the field you want to pursue. Review the organization's website closely and based on what you see, draw up a list of what goals the site seeks to accomplish, and what specific audiences it's designed to reach. What are the clues to the organization's rationale? How well does it achieve its goals?

Think About Audience

As with all media, you must think about your audience along with goals. Here's why you simply can't produce a good website without careful audience analysis: Online media work in ways radically different from "legacy media." It's like fishing. A print ad casts a wide net to catch all the fish within reach, so you can filter out the particular fish you want, let's say, mackerel. A website, on the other hand, empowers you to specifically attract mackerel and draw them neatly to your net. But this only works if you lure them with the right food—or in the case of websites, the right information.

A good website is not created as an isolated communication product. It should completely integrate with all the organization's other marketing efforts both in what it says and how it looks. Consistency is key to branding. This applies to individuals as well as companies and nonprofits. Whatever marketing vehicles you use, whether websites, print materials, blogs or résumés, they must have a consistent graphic look and style. All should describe you, or the organization, in similar ways.

Developing a website is such an intensive process that it often ends up reframing a company's messaging in all other media.

ACTION TIME: PREPLAN A WEBSITE

Decide on a website you want to produce for yourself, a company or a group. List its goals. Then identify and prioritize the target audiences. Characterize them in as much detail as you can, referring to the audience criteria covered in Chapter 2 plus additional factors you think relevant to your goal. Also consider whether you want to reach a geographically focused audience, or a regional, national or international one. Write a synopsis of your goals and an audience profile.

Choosing Your Tone

As with all media, defining your goal and audience enables you to choose the appropriate tone of voice. Note that if you ask colleagues to identify the websites they like best, they will often mention idiosyncratic sites that stand out because of their humor, spontaneous feel and edginess (two examples of this: woot.com and saddlebackleather.com). Such sites achieve an individualistic style that at best, effectively embodies the business's nature. But this approach is unlikely to work for an insurance company.

Another caveat to planning an entertaining site: It's hard. It takes talent and usually enormous work over an extended period of time. Be cautious about creating a funny or witty site; it's smart to try it out on members of your intended audience and ask for their honest opinion.

Fortunately, a solid, effective site can be built with a straightforward tone. Aim for simplicity and you won't go wrong. Avoid a formal, stilted, abstract spirit. A site should be friendly, highly accessible, lively and concrete.

Look at everything through the viewer's eyes and write in terms of "you" as much as possible. Don't say, "Customers will save hours of time in their account keeping"; better to say, "You'll save hours of accounting time." Framing in the first person rather than the abstract third person will help you more easily achieve the personal, warm tone you want, and will lead you to use wording that's more friendly and direct.

VIEW FROM THE FIELD: WHAT'S TOUGH ABOUT WEBSITE WRITING

How do you make web copy good? Get a spontaneous notion on paper, take a deep breath and go back and do the crafting. Spontaneity is hard to achieve. We've edited some of our website copy 15 or 20 times, and have been polishing some of it for 20 years. In an age of e-mail and messaging, the idea of stopping to rewrite tends to disappear.

Web writing is not to be taken lightly: You're writing for two audiences simultaneously, a human one and a robot audience. You can't ignore either one and have to combine the different information needs of both. It's tricky, because you're rewarded for originality but punished for doing the unexpected—because people have expectations about how to find information and get to links. This diminishes the opportunity to be wildly entertaining and creative with a capital K.

—Bob Killian, branding strategist, Killian Branding

HOW TO WRITE COPY THAT WORKS ONLINE

Translating Print Content and Style to Virtual Media

As a general rule, never take a piece of print copy and plaster it on your website. The tone will be wrong and so will the writing style. Print pieces are typically much more diffuse and formal than good online writing, which must distill the subject and feel informal.

For example, here is some writing drawn from material a business consultant has used in print media.

Executive On Call: Business Counseling When You Need It

Since 1999, Executive on Call has served a distinct niche in the Tanner Region, consulting to the CEOs of small and mid-sized businesses that need knowledgeable advice, a resource of best practices, and a sounding board to advance to the next level. Founder/CEO Ellen Black, who has successfully founded and operated three enterprises, draws on her own extensive experience and works with a team of specialists to help owners develop and align their business mission with strategic vision and goals.

Ellen helps clients reassess the constantly shifting marketplace, reevaluate their working approaches so they don't miss good opportunities, and recognize and strengthen their own resources so they can better focus on the future. Typically, results include a steady 10% annual growth rate.

In a print medium, this copy would come across as reasonably clear and down-to-earth. But online, it would feel empty and rhetorical. Someone looking for a consultant will probably not make it past the first sentence or two. The reasons:

1. There's no instant engagement, an essential of online copy via the headline and/or lead.

2. It fails the speed test. Long, complex sentences, formal wording and a rambling, almost literary tone s-l-o-w it all down.

3. The writing is abstract and altogether lacks a "you" perspective.

4. The copy is dense and uninviting visually—it looks like reading it would be work.

5. The case for the company is not compelling. This is much more obvious on the web, which may be the best comparison-shopping tool ever devised. In former times, a client in search of a service would need to identify suitable resources, request material from each and screen suppliers' qualifications. Now, limitless sources are a click away.

How might this material be recast? Here's one way a home page could be written.

Do you need business counseling?

Here are three ways to know.

- ✓ You're missing chances to grow your business
- ✓ It feels like the marketplace is shifting under your feet
- ✓ You can't find time to focus on reaching the future

If you're a Tanner Region entrepreneur and this strikes a chord, talk to us at Executive on Call. We'll show you how to realign your business with the marketplace and **achieve a steady 10% growth rate.**

If you look at your firm's competitors, you'll find that many of them treated copy as an adjunct to site development. Often the technical side—design, coding and production—takes center stage. Pieces of copy are picked up from old material to fill the space left for it or hastily written words are plugged in at the last minute. This guarantees a second-rate site no matter how much effort goes into it.

As writers of course believe, and the research bears out, it's the words that matter most. Moreover, all the thinking behind the plan must be done with words. So words should come first, but throughout the process must be adapted to design and behind-the-scenes needs.

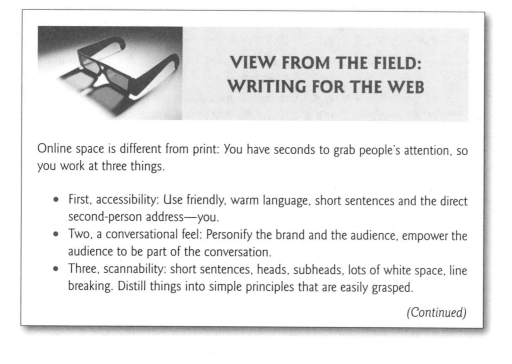

VIEW FROM THE FIELD: WRITING FOR THE WEB

Online space is different from print: You have seconds to grab people's attention, so you work at three things.

- First, accessibility: Use friendly, warm language, short sentences and the direct second-person address—you.
- Two, a conversational feel: Personify the brand and the audience, empower the audience to be part of the conversation.
- Three, scannability: short sentences, heads, subheads, lots of white space, line breaking. Distill things into simple principles that are easily grasped.

(Continued)

(Continued)

Don't throw around all those superlatives. It's much more important to demonstrate why something is true. Web copy should also be actionable—don't just tell readers something, give them the next step and lead them somewhere.

But fundamentally good writing hasn't changed. Web writing is like storytelling and that's not much different from the caveman days—it needs clear sentences, coherence, a structure, a point of view, resonance. Spontaneous-engaging-fun is hard to do but important to strive for. Whatever the subject, if you can clearly say something or even say it with a sense of wit, it's a breath of fresh air.

—Amanda McCormick, founder of Jellybeanboom.com;
social media consultant/web communications specialist

Guidelines for Online Writing

These general guidelines apply to most writing for the virtual world.

Stay short.

- Use simple one- and two-syllable words.
- Write simple, clear sentences without a lot of clauses, averaging 8 to 16 words long. Work in an occasional one-word sentence.
- Keep paragraphs between one to three sentences long, and make a point of keeping some paragraphs to one sentence.
- Keep pages short enough to read with minimal scrolling. People often don't scroll down past what's on the original screen and may miss most of your message.

Stay positive. Keep the tone light and bright and upbeat, unless common sense dictates otherwise (if the company is a funeral home, for example).

Use "inverted pyramid style." Like journalists, put the most important information at the beginning because you'll lose readers steadily as they're asked to move down the page. And, to accommodate scanners, keep the most important words of each headline and sentence on the left. This may mean not using an anecdote to open, unless you're writing a personal blog or the story is very magnetic.

Stay in a "you" framework. Focus on how what you're writing about will help the reader, not an anonymous third person, and use the word "you." "We" works too.

Create information "chunks." Small chunks are easily absorbed and remembered. Cognitive psychology research claims that the brain can only remember seven or eight pieces of information at a time, whether words, numbers, sentences—or bullet points. Unless you're writing for people who like a lot of long, dense information, break material down into short pieces.

Be specific and concrete. If your company focuses on telecommunications or recruitment, say so, rather than referring to "management services." If your filtration systems are designed for water in hot climates, say so. If you only serve customers in Delaware, say so.

Stick with action verbs. Don't water things down with "will be," "can be," "should be" and a passive style. Use strong verbs and nouns to carry the ideas, not adjectives and adverbs that make meaningless claims ("most experienced," "amazingly efficient," "revolutionary," "groundbreaking," etc.)

Keep writing "say-able." A conversational style is especially best for online writing, so test it out by reading it aloud. Be ready to take liberties with conventional English. You don't need formal "literate" statements. Fragments are fine if meaning is clear. You needn't (and shouldn't) say,

> If you're interested in finding out how we at GBH can customize our consulting services to increase your company's telecommunications efficiency, please call us at xxx-xxx-xxxx during business hours.

Better:

> Want more efficient phone service? Let's talk. Right now. xxx-xxx-xxxx.

Remember the scanners and divers. Include your selected search terms in copy and headlines and consciously think about what you want viewers to notice. Think about graphic devices to help attract and focus attention strategically—size and color of type, white space, images, headlines, subheads. Put the most important information at the beginning of headlines and sentences.

Q&A: WHY KEEP PAGES SHORT AND WORDS TIGHT?

Jakob Nielsen, the leading expert on web "usability," calculates that when a web page contains 111 words or less, the average visitor will read half the information.

(Continued)

(Continued)

When the page contains 593 words (the average in his sample), users may read 28%, but are much more likely to read only 20%.

Brevity is most important if you're addressing a mass audience. If you're consciously targeting a sophisticated readership, you may want to assume that longer, in-depth material is valued.

Another useful research clue: People are very annoyed and impatient with splash screens (an image that appears while the site is loading) and intro pages, especially if there's no obvious way to bypass them.

For details on this study: http://www.useit.com/alertbox/percent-text-read.html

Much more Nielsen research at www.useit.com

Spend time on your headlines. A book can be written about headline writing—in fact, some have been. Try for clear, compelling and accurate—that is, don't promise anything in your headline that the copy doesn't deliver. Think what's-in-it-for-me from the audience perspective: what is your desired viewer looking for? What will impress him about what you offer? Think of the headline as waving a sign.

Create good subheads. They are important for both graphic and chunking reasons. Each subhead is a new chance to attract and engage the scanner. They also keep you organized. A number of writers create the subheads first, as a progressive series of statements. This method forces you to decide what's most important to cover and how to sequence it. Then you fill the copy in, via short, manageable chunks. This method helps pull readers through, too, especially if their first language is not English.

Edit, edit, edit. Trim all the fat in both wording and information. Tighten the copy as much as you possibly can; pretend it's a sign you're holding up to a passing train. But don't just condense so you lose the detail, example, or phrase that brings the copy alive. It's better to say less and enable what's there to breathe.

Lots of "calls to action." For websites, many specialists recommend including a next step or call to action on every page, such as "Buy today!" "Call us now at xxx-xxx-xxxx" or "To learn more about this service . . ." Remember that visitors are not viewing your pages sequentially; don't leave them wondering where to go if they want to follow through—lead them. You can also refer them to other parts of your site—for example, "Check out more products you may like" or "Read what our clients say about us." Or lead them to your blog, offer them a newsletter, entice them to take a quiz and so on.

Cut the hype, give them proof. Skip the jargon and hype. Inflationary words and descriptors work against you in the web world. Adopt the writer's axiom, "Show don't tell." Don't make claims—cite evidence.

What if what you can say is radically limited?

Here's some business management copy that annoyed *New York Times* columnist Thomas Frank in a column called "Spies (All Too Much) Like Us." The web copy describes consulting services:

> The mission is to inspire clients "by leveraging our global senior-management experience to ensure optimal, yet realistic and practical solutions."

And, on a related site,

> A firm that specialized in "enabling leaders to build proactive, future-oriented decision cultures."

The columnist was writing about a successful consultant accused of being a long-term undercover Russian spy. The problem, he observed, was that such language is just like that of mainstream American business culture—which should teach us that "much of what we regard as economic genius is nothing but pretense, a matter of posture and assertion, a grand confidence game with awful consequences."

Naturally, you don't want to go there. But how can you avoid writing such overblown, empty statements if in fact your work is similar to your competitors and differentiating yourself is hard?

Go for transparent simplicity. For example, the first statement might say,

> As senior managers who've led global enterprises, we work with you on practical solutions to the problems facing today's CEO.

That may not say much but suggests a way to amplify the idea—the copy might go on to specify the kinds of problems the group helps with.

How to simplify the second statement? You can try but it doesn't really have enough meaning to work with. Sometimes you cut the hype and buzzwords and find that you're left with . . . nothing. Then, either figure out what you mean to say in simple, clear language, or find something else to talk about.

WE'RE ALL SCREENWRITERS: BUT HOW SMALL CAN THOSE SCREENS GET?

Remember that more and more often, your online writing will be viewed in miniature or abbreviated form on a smart phone or other handheld device. Further, search engines sometimes offer viewers "instant previews" of sites in tiny format to help searchers decide which are worth their time. So the basic guidelines for an effective site are more important than ever.

- Keep design simple: no clutter, lots of white space, few colors, few typefaces
- Don't use visuals that distract or interfere: skip the flash, splash and intro pages, and most animation unless it's important to your story
- Work to attract and guide the eye: big headlines, clear subheads
- Build clear navigation: crystal-clear pathways to your content
- Tighten copy: edit your story down to the core and then distill it

---

BRAINSTORMING CONTENT IDEAS

Delivering Your Best

How do you attract "the right people" to your site or blog, keep them there to fulfill their needs (and yours) and bring them back?

There is remarkable agreement among Internet experts on what you need: compelling content. But there is no single answer to what that should be. You have to figure it out based on your goals and audience. With your written priority lists in hand, think about what each of your important audiences wants to know, will find interesting and will value—*in context of your own goals and information you can share.* There's no point in establishing expertise in motorcycle repair if you're selling cosmetics (at least, not as a central theme; it could make great blog material or help you humanize someone in a profile).

Commit to delivering your best possible ideas, information and advice to the readers you hope to capture. The Internet is an almost unimaginable source of free information. Don't stockpile your expertise—find ways to give it away generously. That's how to succeed on the web and the Internet as a whole.

Build on your strengths or your company's. Realistically, many industries limit what can be used in a public forum. Attorneys and management consultants, for example, may not be able to showcase client case studies or demonstrate unique capabilities. Insurance brokers are limited by strict government regulation.

A nonprofit that helps abused women can't highlight individuals. Schools avoid showing actual students on the Internet.

So it's not always easy to use what might speak for you best.

Build Content On Strengths

As this chapter has stressed, a good website means good content. Design and functionality should support content—they are not ends in themselves, though a great many websites behave as if they are. So, thoughtful planning is critical to shaping (or reshaping) your site. And because it's important to keep the site fresh and updated, the plan must be sustainable. That means pinpointing as early as possible which areas can be further developed, and what you can comfortably add over time.

The following checklist outlines some of your content choices. Use it as a planning aid if you're working on a new site or revamping one, and to identify good opportunities for ongoing development. Beyond these ideas, mine your own industry in depth to come up with ways to attract, engage, intrigue, sell and help your audience. You want them not just to come, but to come back.

Strength	Content
Successful track record	Show in • Statistics or data • Video • Images • Charts and graphs • Client testimonials (video or written) • Case studies about how clients were helped or problems solved • Announcements of company awards
Good visuals	If you have them and they're relevant, use them BIG.
Staff credentials and achievements	Cite in profiles and news items: awards, honors, publications, speaking engagements, impressive appointments
Staff expertise	Show in • Videos of speaker presentations • Podcasts • Articles and white papers

(Continued)

(Continued)

Strength	Content
Third-party recognition	Case histories about the company written by other sources, client testimonials
Media coverage	Of the organization, leaders and employees, including local and industry coverage, product reviews
Thought leadership	In-depth papers contributing to the industry, such as • Research • Advice and insights • Trend forecasts
A continuous flow of news	About products, people, recognition, community involvement and so on
Community and good-cause engagement	Increasingly important for companies to demonstrate: Do good things and report on them, and recount individual employee contributions to the common good. Communicate about donations of money and time, and leadership positions in charitable organizations.
Valuable or interesting blogs	Essential today in most industries. Find one or more people to write them regularly.
Potential for fun and entertaining features	Figure out ways to offer contests, quizzes, games
Interactive possibilities	Look for chances to include Q&A, discussions, collaborative projects.
"Great man" or "great woman"	If the CEO or other staff member is a well-known or interesting person, make the most of it.
Giveaways	Such as • Items, including small, "fun" ones • Newsletter subscriptions • White papers • E-books • Free sample services or products
People	Know the members of your staff and scout the larger organization for good storytellers—potential bloggers who can write about things that are directly and perhaps indirectly related to your service, or have a talent for framing what the organization does in an out-of-the-box way.

THE HOME PAGE: HOW TO PLAN IT

Here's a useful way to plan a home page.

Suppose you're selling handmade crocheted hats. The first imperative is to be findable; the second is to reassure a visitor that she's come to the right place.

For both purposes, it helps if your business title and website address reflect the product. Putting the generic product first can be a plus—for example, Hats by Max. But even if you're entrenched in a less explicit business name, like Max's Head Cases, you can use a tagline. Catchy is good. But straightforward is okay too and often better. For example:

Catchy:

> HATS BY MAX
> From my hand to your head

Plain vanilla:

> HATS BY MAX
> Hand-crocheted hats with a high-fashion look

Since your product is visual, using one or more images of hats is a natural. Together with your business name and tagline it helps make what the site offers unmistakable. If the customer is looking for your product, she's a good prospect, providing she likes the price and styles and the site delivers a good customer experience.

Of course, it's harder to telegraph the nature of many services and products that are more abstract than hats. Even if you devise a visual that is relevant, the words become more important. You need them to clearly identify what your organization is and does. It sounds obvious, but a great many websites fail to do this.

Even a good tagline may not explain your service well enough. A positioning statement is almost always essential if you're not a household name. Even if you are, viewers may be unaware of your organization's size and scope, and you need to set them up to view you in a positive way. For example, here's General Electric's home page statement:

> GE IS IMAGINATION AT WORK. From jet engines to power generation, financial services to water processing, and medical imaging to media content, GE people worldwide are dedicated to turning imaginative ideas into leading products and services that help solve some of the world's toughest problems.

The positioning statement on a website has the same function as an in-person "elevator speech": to instantly identify the individual or organization as clearly and advantageously as possible. Aim for a statement that says

1. What you do (e.g., "J&L is . . .")

2. Who you help ("We help small businesses . . .") and the geographic area you serve if relevant

3. Your main competitive advantage or differentiator

For example:

> J&L is a consulting firm that helps small New England businesses solve their training problems. Our psychologists and talent specialists create custom programs that bring key hires up to speed quickly.

Or, once you have your ideas in place, you can play with the ideas and language:

> Does your small New England firm struggle to train new staff, costing you time and money? Our psychologists and talent managers team with you on custom training programs. We'll bring your key hires up to speed—fast.

A good positioning statement can be a sentence or a paragraph long, or provide most of the home page copy. Try to say your most important words at the beginning.

Keep It Simple

Navigation and Menu Tabs

Make it as easy as you possibly can for people to find their way around your site. Avoid subtle directions that are clever or attractive, but might confuse someone who didn't speak the language well, can't read tiny type or might misinterpret a graphic symbol.

The menu tabs must reflect the overall site content. They should be short and snappy but most of all, crystal clear.

While creativity is always a plus, it's best not to fool too much with audience expectations. "Services," for example, should usually say "Services," unless there's a reason not to. If you're linking to an "About Us" page, viewers will know what you mean if you use "About" or "Us," or "Who we are," but it may not pay to go farther afield. A solo entrepreneur, however, might use "Meet Jane," or something of the sort.

Visuals

Remember that your home page is increasingly apt to be viewed on a smart phone or other tiny screen. Don't load it up with copy and unrelated visuals.

And avoid totally anything that makes the site slow to come up, or delays the viewer's diving and scanning. For most sites this includes

- Splash and intro pages
- Flash animation
- Any sound including theme music

If you want to demonstrate creativity beyond good design and writing, do so "inside" the site so your viewer has a choice about whether or not to go there.

Links

Use hyperlinks to cross-reference between sections and pages on your site so viewers have alternative paths to the information. Link to other resources you offer—and material on other sites—to provide a deeper experience to those who want it. But use judgment; don't overload your own material with leads off-site. Often, visitors will not return, and reading anything with underlined links every few lines is distracting visually.

GOING DEEPER: GRAPHIC GUIDELINES FOR WEBSITES

Legibility is King: This applies to all online media as well as websites. The most common mistakes: too many fonts, too many colors, too busy.

Clean, simple and well-organized home pages make it easy for users to get where they need to go, quickly. Understand that you cannot overwhelm or bully someone into reading every word on your website. In our attention-deficit world, effective headlines, meaningful graphics, and bite-size chunks of information go a long way.

Use bite-size pieces of information with links to the long-form version of the content. This quickly defines the nature of the content and acts as a trigger to pull a user into your website. (For two brilliant examples, see http://www.newyorker.com/ and http://www .good.is/.)

(Continued)

(Continued)

Color: Don't use too many colors. We recommend a limited palette of two or three colors—a handful can do a lot to set a mood or tone. Typographer Robert Bringhurst once wrote, *typography exists to honor content.* This statement rings true especially for web design. The trick is to be objective and honest with yourself. Does bright red type on a camouflage background make it *easier* or *harder* for someone to read the content? Obviously, this is an extreme example, but the point is important. We have found light color, heavy type on a dark background works best for short ideas like headlines, while darker text on a lighter background works best for long passages.

A great resource is http://colorexplorer.com/.

Typefaces: The more sophisticated and elegant websites use only one or two fonts, and use them well. Remember that what's legible on your 30-inch high-definition monitor might not be on a 14-inch laptop or mobile device. If in doubt, make the size of the body text bigger.

We generally try to match a client's brand style but favor legibility and try to find the closest match based on standardized web-safe font sets that work universally across Mac, PC and mobile devices. A terrific resource for testing font legibility is http://www.typetester.org/.

These font families provide adequate cross-browser compatibility.

Sans-serif Family: Arial, Verdana, Geneva, Helvetica

Serif Family: Georgia, Times New Roman, Times

Monospace Family: Courier, Courier New

Never, ever use Comic Sans.

Images: Choose images that are relevant to the site's content. Don't steal them! If it's not in the public domain, or a photo you took yourself, or one that you purchased or have the photographer's express consent to use, it is not yours to use.

Scrolling: Avoiding the need to scroll on the home page used to be the rule, but many developers are abandoning simplicity for higher search engine ranking opportunities. Finding a good balance is very subjective.

Professional Design Goal: Our overarching goal with design is to communicate and build the client's brand in a simple and effective way. This is subjective based on a client's goals and initiatives.

—Christopher Sanna, partner/creative director,
Atomic Wash Design Studio (http://www.atomicwash.com)

Examples: Two Home Pages, Two Purposes

The Glover Park Group (GPG) is a Washington, D.C.–based strategic communications firm. Its home page demonstrates a well-thought-out simplicity both in language and visually. The copy says exactly what GPG does concisely and without unnecessary hype. The visuals produce a "friendly" feeling and use white space generously and to good effect. The tagline, *"Your point. Well made"* is strong. The overall impression is very professional, but welcoming rather than intimidating. The page successfully shows off skills the firm is marketing.

NDI is the National Democratic Institute, a nongovernmental organization that seeks to foster democracy in countries around the world. This home page is inviting and colorful and maintains a feeling of simplicity. Focus is on the organization's activities and world events related to its cause. The copy is straightforward and journalistic. The page feels current and lively, encouraging return visits. Like many home pages, this one requires scrolling; this means more information is provided, but the risk of losing readers is high.

SOME STRATEGIES FOR CREATING SUCCESSFUL WEBSITES

Take Account of SEO

Because people typically find websites or blogs through search engines, pitching to Google and their competitors has become a high art and a major rationale for search engine optimization (SEO) services that can be very expensive. An optimized site is one that ranks high on search engine rankings so that it comes up when you're looking for that category of product or service.

Visibility is a big factor for Internet success: a route by which small companies can gain big business, and a way for large ones to outmaneuver the competition. Unless you're HTML proficient and understand SEO, you'll likely need help with "front end" and "back end" development to write the coding. But most aspects of making your site highly visible are not technical in nature.

Search engines use very complex formulas to rate the value of sites, but—just like people—they value "original content" that makes a real informational contribution rather than a self-serving sales pitch. Useful information can include articles, research, FAQs, Q&A, white papers, insight sharing, conference reports and advice related to your subject. In considering your own subject, interpret what might interest the readers you want to attract.

The crocheted hat website might, for example, run material on the history of headwear; how a hat should fit; how these particular hats are made; where the yarn comes from and how that's made; how new styles are developed; an interview with the designer; how to buy a hat for someone else; how to match hats to different outfits; hats around the world and so on.

An accountant's site could include a wide range of material on how to choose an accountant and work with one, keep records, interpret tax forms and so forth. A firm serving large corporations can feature more complex advice on investments, changes in tax regulations and so on.

> *My rule of thumb is build a site for a user not a spider.*
>
> —Dave Naylor, DavidNaylor.co.uk

Brainstorm the possibilities to come up with content ideas—and don't forget you need to produce the material.

Search engines also value and reward change: new information, ideas and other content. This is where many businesses fall short. Unless a static brochure-style site serves your purposes, relentless development is important. It not only attracts the search engine robots, but engages your customers and keeps them coming back. Try to become your audience's best resource.

This is time-consuming. Both individuals and organizations can review existing resources—what is already available in their files—and adapt it for online use. A business can also canvass staff and find out what members can contribute. It may help to provide incentives for people to write. Content development also helps achieve another SEO priority, "inbound links"—legitimate leads to your site from other sites.

To many people, the most confusing SEO criterion is the key word, AKA the search word, search term and metatag. Most simply, these are the terms people type into search engines when they're looking for something. The work here is to figure out how people think about your product or service.

Key words need to be placed in your title tags, page descriptions, key word "metatags," headlines and body copy. Here, I'll just note how the key word factor affects writing. But there's ample help online according to your level of technical know-how, and good free help in selecting the best key words for your business.

Google Adwords and Word Tracker, for example, let you input a set of key words and find out how many people are using each and the level of competition. Aim to identify words or phrases that are popular for your category, but narrow it down in some way—for example, according to the type of service, geographic location, key product ingredient or other factor.

Most advice suggests aiming for 5 to 10 key words and using them in your headlines and body copy. Some website production houses use formulas, such as, "place eight key words per page." However, search engines have grown suspicious of such formulas and you want to avoid irritating readers. But make sure the search terms are there. In articles, it's a good idea to use them in the first sentence to identify what your content is about, and bold them where they appear throughout.

SEO is one of the subjects most frequently blogged about so it's easy to explore in-depth—but the viewpoints and explanations can be very confusing. Remember that many who write about SEO are selling their services.

Treat Company Websites as Cooperative Ventures

Because an organization's website is its most public and universally accessible face, it's typically where every function and operation meet—and often clash. So websites are inherently political. They are prone to whatever pressures various interests can bring to bear. Moreover, to maintain and develop the site, broad buy-in is needed.

So, every element of the organization should be involved in planning and setting guidelines. It's effective to draw a steering committee from this larger group so the process is less unwieldy.

Despite the trouble, team thinking and buy-in is essential to both developing and maintaining a site. These principles apply to Intranet sites as well, of course—as do all the ideas in this chapter.

VIEW FROM THE FIELD: WEBSITES AND LARGE ORGANIZATIONS

A well-designed architecture, state-of-the-art technology and easy navigation are critical elements when developing a new website. However, one requirement on which true success is built, and which is too often overlooked, is the website team's positive relationships with their colleagues throughout the organization. If the team is viewed as an ally and as a group that delivers genuine value, it can more easily achieve key website milestones such as obtaining the most relevant and insightful content, securing necessary approvals, and winning employee buy-in and long-term support—all major factors in the site's ultimate success.

Other important strategies include keeping the site's tone and messaging consistent, writing crisp and succinct copy, using descriptive and eye-catching section headings, and understanding that the launch is only the beginning of the process. The new site's features, functionality and content need to be reviewed regularly, with improvements and updates made as needed to keep the site relevant and vibrant. A website is a living portrait of an organization and one of its most valuable communication resources, so the investment made in its creation and maintenance will yield big benefits for years to come.

—Mark Murray, communications consultant and former
global communications director of Burson-Marsteller and Weber Shandwick

Think Global: Websites Go Everywhere

The Internet becomes more global every year, as millions in India, China, Latin America, the Arab world and elsewhere expand their access to it. At the same time, opportunities to buy from sites in their own languages are increasing, and it's natural for people to prefer doing so. Thus, if you want to reach an international audience through a website—or think you could benefit from doing so—consider non-native English speakers in the early planning stage.

Graphics, navigation and writing are all big factors to consider when you're targeting an audience whose main language is not English, or want to include such audiences. This is true even as online translation capabilities improve or translation services are used. In both cases, writing must be crafted to translate easily.

To launch you on the right track, here are some basics. They should reinforce your commitment to simplicity.

Keep graphics simple and uncluttered. Make navigation as clear and straightforward as you possibly can. Make all your headers unambiguous and don't get too clever; be sure the viewer knows how to get from point to point—skip subtle graphic devices. Build in plenty of white space.

Keep wording especially simple and direct. That means no slang, no idioms, no clichés and minimal colloquial expressions. Use short words, one or two syllables as much as you can. Try to avoid abstract words and words that can be misinterpreted. Contractions can confuse so opt for "we have" rather than "we've," "is not" rather than "isn't." Avoid even commonplace abbreviations like ASAP—spell it out.

Keep language structure especially simple. Use short sentences averaging 12 to 18 words. Avoid complicated sentence structure with many clauses, and "there is" and "that is" constructions. Also cut wordy phrasing as much as you can like those with prepositions—for example, "in a position to" (better: "able"); "in order to" (better: "to"); "give a justification for" (better: "justify"). Keep paragraphs short, one to three sentences; use space between paragraphs and substantial margins.

Try to be aware of cultural differences. You should be able to find out some of the basic differences among cultures, in how they cite dates, times, numbers and other formal basics. But you must know another culture and its language really well to understand its idioms, attitudes, sensitivities and inside jokes. Even then, you may not always "get it." Advertising and politics are prone to translation gaffes even today. One famous case in point: President John F. Kennedy once addressed an audience in Germany's capital by saying, in German, "I am a Berliner." In fact, what the audience heard was, "I am a donut."

If you're aiming to reach a particular language-speaking group, it's wise to have someone from inside the culture review your copy. Remember that a widely used language such as Spanish has many cultures, and there are real differences between a Spanish, Cuban and Argentine audience, for example.

When it's important for the message to reach a global audience effectively, you may want to consult with specialists and use good translation services.

Note that if you're writing for a global institution with facilities in other parts of the world, you're automatically writing for a multiple-language workforce and need to consider cross-cultural guidelines.

Moreover, writing to be understood by non-native English speakers is similar to writing for the diverse audience that characterizes many U.S. workplaces and the country as a whole.

In general: Drill down to the core of your content. Know exactly what message you want to deliver. Eliminate all overinflated hype, unsubstantiated claims and vague ideas not directly related to your message. People with basic English skills are an especially impatient audience and will not invest time in finding your important points, so don't bury them in material that doesn't matter or is there just to be clever.

Does writing for international readers mean you'll have to strip the color and make the message duller? Yes, that may be the case. Again, that's why you must really know your goals and priorities. A website aimed at a world audience is necessarily a balancing act.

Here are two resources to use if writing for international audiences and for translation are important to you. Both address print media as well as online.

Edmond H. Weiss, *The Elements of International English Style: A Guide to Writing Correspondence, Reports, Technical Documents, and Internet Pages for a Global Audience* (2005)

John R. Kohl, *The Global English Style Guide: Writing Clear, Translatable Documentation for a Global Market* (2008)

As the problem becomes more widely acknowledged, a range of material is appearing on the Internet; Google "writing international English," "international websites" or something similar to find useful advice.

You now have a foundation for understanding what people expect from online writing and guidelines for accomplishing it. Let's move on to what can be the fun side: writing for social media, blogs and other online purposes.

PRACTICE OPPORTUNITIES

I. Group Project: Build a Website for a Good Cause

Plan a website for the charitable cause you invented for Chapter 9's Practice Opportunities II. Collaborate on draft copy for the home page, including all necessary tabs and heads. Share the result with another group and evaluate its website plan; provide a helpful written critique to the other group.

II. Group Project: Evaluate and Compare

As a small group, select three firms in any field of interest and, in detail, compare/evaluate their websites. Look critically at overall site plan, content, writing, design and visuals, navigation, the home page. Are the site's overall goals clear? Can you define the targeted audiences? Do you see any missed opportunities? Use your evaluations to come up with a list of criteria for websites in general that the whole group agrees with.

Discuss: Each group should share its criteria list with the rest of the class. How are the lists the same? Different? Assemble one full list that the class agrees upon.

III. Evaluate Foreign-Language Sites

Do online research to identify websites of overseas organizations that use the language you studied in school or gained a basic knowledge of for some other reason. Pick three websites in that language. How easy are they to understand and use? What presents the biggest barriers? Which work better for you and why? Compile a written list, and share it with the class or in small groups; together, assemble a list of "do's" and "don'ts" for international websites that validates and extends the guidelines given here (or disagrees with them).

IV. Build Your Own

Write a home page for your own website. See it as an element of your next job search, or for a business you'd like to operate. First, articulate (in writing) your goal, audience, selected tone and proposed content. Create a basic plan for the words, graphics and architecture of the site.

Chapter 11

BUSINESS MEETS THE INTERACTIVE WORLD

BLOGGING, SOCIAL MEDIA AND MICROMEDIA

LEARN HOW TO . . .

➢ Understand how business sees social media
➢ Use social media to achieve business and professional goals
➢ Plan and write blogs and comments
➢ Create online profiles that work for you
➢ Use micromedia in a business framework

Have something to say, and say it as clearly as you can. That is the only secret.

—Matthew Arnold

To offer advice about social media is a lot like standing on the beach and watching the sand shift under your feet. Popular sites recede and new ones ride in on the tide. Technology advances and new vistas, not previously imagined, open up. So what can be usefully communicated about writing for this world?

Quite a lot, actually. There are three reasons.

First, as the most sophisticated social media (SM) users will tell you, the new media are basically different ways to distribute information and move people to thought or action. Only the speed is different. The tools may be new to the communication arsenal but the same principles must frame their use.

Second, even though you may be a "native" user of SM and find it as natural as talking, you may not have thought about using it for strategic business or career purposes. This requires a different mind-set than using sites purely for social networking.

And third, if you do want to use SM channels to promote your career in any way, whether as a job seeker, employee, consultant or business owner, you'll find that the arena is amazingly crowded and competitive. So much good stuff is given away for free that it isn't easy to engage audiences with your message. It takes your best thinking and writing skills. And standards for thinking and writing have essentially not changed and will not change.

Because of those shifting sands, however, use the guidelines in this chapter with extra imagination. A particular channel may have been outdated by a newbie when you read this, but the ideas will show you how to handle whatever may come.

HOW BUSINESS SEES SOCIAL MEDIA

Asked back in the 1930s why he robbed banks, Willie Sutton famously said, "Because that's where the money is." Today's smart businesses might say that they invest in online communication because that's where the people are.

If social media are a natural part of your life, step back for a minute to view this revolution in a broader context. Never before has there been a way to instantly connect with so many people at once, find a community or create a following. The possibilities are turning corporate communications and marketing upside down, not to mention politics, government and information industries. But for many people in power positions, entrenched in traditional media, accepting the power of SM has been a struggle.

Today, online communication is creating a culture in which trusted opinions come not from professional reviewers, critics and other authority figures, but from peers and credible strangers.

Businesses see the Internet as a chance to raise awareness of what they offer and build good "image," and also to listen to customers and engage in dialogues that help them improve their marketing and products. They use blogs and social media to announce new services and events and even build communities around their product. Nonprofits, too, have added social media to the mix for communication, fund-raising and volunteer recruitment efforts.

Organizations (and governments) have also learned that displeased consumers or ordinary citizens can now generate not just a complaint, but a mass protest or boycott—without spending a penny.

Corporate communicators used to talk about generating good media relations so when a crisis arose, the company had a solid base with which to manage public opinion. Today, companies find that a sturdy social media network must be in place not only to proactively influence the public, but as a defense mechanism so they are ready to respond to problems.

Beyond all this, the big draw of digital tools for savvy organizations is their popularity. People of all ages are embracing SM in their everyday work and personal life. And businesspeople know that SM channels are key to how people in their 20s and below relate to the world. Social media represent current or future customers, potential recruits, an increasingly influential public, new donors, and much more. Even business leaders who dislike social media are finding that they must go there, because that's where the people are.

So the virtual world is transforming business communications. But what's not changing is your basic communication tool kit. Writing remains the most important ingredient of success.

When you're competing with the whole world, your best strategies are good planning and good writing. All the skills you build for traditional media and even e-mail will work for you here, with some adaptation.

GENERAL PRINCIPLES FOR USING SOCIAL MEDIA WELL

Principle 1. Don't forget you're telling the world

Never post anything that could humiliate you should it end up on your boss's desk, the front page of your daily newspaper or the screens of 10 million Facebook users.

Every time you apply for a job, assume that the prospective employer will check out everything online that he can find about you, and by you. Which includes everything you've ever posted. The recruitment firm, hiring manager, human resources department and/or the information technology people will find it all. Accept that you cannot protect your privacy when you post blogs, text, pictures, video, tweets—anything at all—online.

And that principle remains true forever. When you run for office or compete for a top position in 10 or 20 years, you don't want to be capsized by your younger self. So think before you share. Remember that the Internet is a public forum. Don't count on features that restrict access to "just friends." You must also police what other people are saying about you or posting. Try to avoid situations such as embarrassing party pictures.

In short, start your reputation management now.

A corollary: Never use online channels to badmouth an individual or group. You can disagree with a position or statement or piece of information, or critique a product or company, but never personalize it. You'll create enemies *and* undermine your own credibility.

And never, never use the power or presumed anonymity of SM to embarrass or poke fun at anyone. Cyber-bullying is for people who don't understand the idea of consequences.

Principle 2. Build in the interaction

Social media by definition are the opposite of traditional one-way communication. Aim not to give lectures or perform in a vacuum. Expect, feed and encourage audience participation. Don't just ask for reader opinions—work at presenting ideas or information in ways that entice a response. Ask thoughtfully created questions, request opinions and input, share an idea that's a bit edgy or controversial. And follow up with responses so the conversation doesn't fade away sooner than it might.

Principle 3. It's about relationships

For both individuals and organizations, social media are about building relationships. And just like in the face-to-face world, this takes time. Don't expect to post a comment or blog and become an overnight sensation. The online world is already very heavily populated, and a lot of what's there is very good.

In fact, you may want to take hints from the way we make new friends or join a social circle. Notice how children do it: they'll watch a group from the sidelines for a while, feeling things out by observing the interaction and rules of the game. Then they'll "kibbitz" a little—make comments about the action. Eventually, they feel comfortable asking to join the play.

It makes sense to dig into your communities of interest. So once you've identified what they are, do the research on the relevant blogs, groups and content communities. See what people are talking about and what concerns them. Contribute thoughtful comments. Ask questions. Start conversations, follow what others say and continue to contribute. Write guest blogs. As you do this you'll absorb the culture and start to see what it values, and what you might contribute.

Principle 4. Start with a plan

Some SM gurus maintain that new media have no real rules yet, and that it's best to just plunge in and find out what works. This approach might suit you but trial and error can be expensive. Defining your goal and audience goes a long way toward telling you what to talk about, and where to do the talking.

Assuming you want to build relationships, why? With whom? Do you want to expand your social or professional circles? Find people with similar interests, or potential customers? Interest prospective employers?

You might want to establish your credibility, or your organization's; share information; learn something; sell something; gain a reputation as a leading blogger or tweeter; find a job; maybe all of the above, at different times.

You may see your blogs or Facebook posts as purely personal, in which case you could define the goal as, "to keep up with friends." That's fine, provided you keep the public nature of the Internet in mind, and know that a good case can be made for clear communication even among friends.

Or you may see blogging and SM as ways to cast your best thinking into the wide universe of knowledge, or a narrower sphere of professional or personal interests. That is also OK—in fact, it's good. The Internet is fueled by generosity. Writing about something you're passionate about without expecting a return on the investment is in that spirit. Again, a well-written contribution works better.

But if you view your online life professionally—in terms of business and career—define what you want to achieve and the audience you want to reach. It will lead you to choose what you write about and where you post it strategically, rather than randomly. Especially because online media can be intensely time-consuming, knowing how to invest your energy matters a lot.

For practical purposes, we can see networking sites as three basic categories: social networking (like Facebook, MySpace), professional networking sites (like LinkedIn, the European XING and a host of focused sites for industries and specialists); and microblog sites such as Twitter. The lines are of course increasingly blurry since Facebook added "fan pages" for businesses to its mix, and because Facebook, Second Life and many other "social" sites encourage business applications such as virtual meetings and information sharing.

Once you know your goals, you can identify sites in line with those goals in various ways. You might scout for sites and discussion groups of like-minded people. You can also look for competitors' sites to see what they're saying and doing. And you can identify sites your target market frequents.

If you're a graphic designer who wants to share ideas and problems, for example, you could join an online community of design professionals, assess your competition and

SUCCESS TIP: CHOOSING YOUR SOCIAL MEDIA WORDS

Think twice before you speak once—that's incredibly important. Does it fit with your message, your image? Try to keep the message consistent and stay in context of your online persona.

Your writing must be clear and concise so people don't misconstrue what you say—they'll read into it and interpret, a big problem online. So write unambiguously. Keep away from sarcasm, many people don't get it. Never write when you're angry or impassioned. No vulgarity: it damages your credibility completely.

Use terminology that promotes your expertise and makes your message searchable by interjecting key words like for SEO [search engine optimization]. I keep a list of the top words I want to include handy. Also you can check out what you write with a word cloud [e.g., via www.wordle.net] so you can look at a visual of your message and see what words you used the most.

—Bill Corbett, president, Corbett Public Relations

learn from it and/or build a presence among potential buyers—business owners, communicators or editors.

Creating a clear strategy enables you to decide on the best sites, communities and discussion groups to achieve what you want. It also lets you incorporate social media tools into a larger marketing mix that includes print media and websites. Knowing how all the potential pieces fit together, and using them to cross-promote the others, lets you use each more effectively and build your personal brand so that one plus one adds up to more than two.

Principle 5. Provide solid substance

Substance is the lifeblood of the online world. Offer something genuinely useful to somebody and that person is far more likely to find you and tell everyone he knows. Where does substance come from? You. Canvass your own resources. What do you know that's worth sharing?

If you can write a how-to piece about anything at all, you probably have a great blog or article subject or source of tweets. If you've identified a problem that bedevils many of your clients, customers or colleagues and can offer even a partial solution, go for it. If something piques your interest and you want to know more, do some research, report on it and invite reader input. If you have a story to tell that will make people laugh, or feel good or think, write about it.

People particularly look for leads to valuable material they don't run across themselves. With so much out there, it takes many eyes to find the gems. So sharing discoveries is an excellent way to build your own virtual presence, whether you're blogging or tweeting. Give people direct links when you can.

VIEW FROM THE FIELD: HOW TO LAUNCH A STRATEGIC SM CAMPAIGN

People start at the wrong end, with the tools—it's like asking how do I use this hammer or screwdriver? They jump on the tools instead of what they're trying to accomplish. Before leaping into social media, conduct an SM marketing audit. Know your objective and who you want to connect with. Then ask, where do these people participate? First listen—people don't listen enough.

Start there, learn what this community you're building or joining is looking for. Next think about what you want to share and how and whether the content is in sharable form so you can go viral. If you can identify information gaps and fill those you'll quickly and naturally gain a standing in that community and a following. It's good to work to a theme, chunk your content down. If your resources are limited, limit your scope so you can make a solid effort—it's hard to boil the ocean.

—Arthur Germain, principal and chief brandteller,
Communication Strategy Group

Principle 6. Softsoap the commercial

When your purpose is to promote a product or service, or yourself, never make it blatant. Suppose you're an accountant blogging about an unusual tax loophole. Devoting a big chunk of content to your firm and its greatness would turn off most readers—and what's more, it isn't necessary.

Your material should establish your expertise and authority. All you need beyond that is a clear tagline identifying who you are, how to reach you, and perhaps, the kind of clients your business serves and/or its range of services.

There are also times when your new product, or a solution to a problem, is what you're writing about. This is fine as long as it's audience relevant, but don't let empty hype creep in. Give content with value. With so much to choose from, online readers steer clear of everything that seems self-serving.

Principle 7. Remember the wider audience

The plus side of managing your online reputation is that more and more employers are reading blogs and looking at LinkedIn, Twitter and other sites for hiring purposes. Write well consistently, comment thoughtfully on your subject, and you may find yourself being scouted.

SUCCESS TIP: THE SOCIAL MEDIA ADVANTAGE

Don't overlook the importance of social media know-how in the job market. Many people aren't comfortable using SM and look for that facility in job candidates. Some add it to the "old" job responsibilities in many job categories. Others hire a new kind of specialist. So consider putting your SM skills up front in your résumé and for interviews. Perhaps give some thought to how the organization is currently using social media—and what you would recommend if you are asked; don't take the initiative on this.

SIDELIGHT: USING SOCIAL MEDIA FOR SOCIAL ENTERPRISE

We use social media to share interesting and inspiring news and content with our supporters, both about Acumen Fund and the world around them. We use it to establish thought leadership, to have a dialogue with our supporters, to drive them to action, and to help them feel smarter, more interconnected, more grateful, and more generous along the way.

Most importantly, we use social media to show them that we are human and immensely appreciative of their support.

Compared with Twitter, it's a little more difficult to carry on a two-way conversation with individual supporters on Facebook. But, we're able to ask questions that can dig a little deeper to get at who they are. For example, we occasionally ask questions on Facebook like: Who's a social entrepreneur who's inspired you? Where did you first hear about the Acumen Fund? What does dignity—a core concept for Acumen—mean to you? We're always shocked at the quantity and quality of answers we get.

It's important to remember that while social media are incredibly effective for distribution and engagement, it's just another tool in your marketing and communications tool bag. I get excited about new technologies because the possibilities for engaging supporters increase exponentially. But what always matters most is having a powerful story that you can share in an authentic way. This is something that's been true since the beginning of civilization. Understand your brand story and your purpose—these elements are paramount and will always serve at the core of why you do what you do, and why your supporters choose to support you through thick and thin.

—James Wu, senior associate, Business Development, Acumen Fund

TO BLOG OR NOT TO BLOG . . .

In the olden days, to reach a substantial audience with information and ideas you'd write an article. The process could take a year—to research, pitch, interact with an editor, draft, revise and so on.

While some publishing still works that way, notably newsstand magazines and many professional journals, today anyone can be a published author. There's no gatekeeping editor to block your voice, or demand that you meet her standards.

In 10 minutes, you can write and post a blog on someone else's site or a discussion forum. If you want your own blog site, blogging sites make it very easy to set up at little or no cost. Then you become your own publisher as well.

There's a catch: To succeed you must perform most of the editorial functions yourself—choose a good topic; angle it right for the audience; write, edit and proofread. That's a lot of responsibility!

And it takes real time, considering that you typically need to blog at least once every week to keep people steadily engaged. If you're working for a larger entity, scout for resources beyond your own to multiply what you can handle. If you're blogging for yourself, consider how much time you're able to commit.

There are many ways to go about blogging. For example, you can

1. Present yourself as a person with a unique viewpoint, whose ideas, opinions and response to experience are worth reading about because they're interesting, insightful, inspiring, entertaining and so on.

2. Offer valuable information and insights about a specific subject or field based on your own knowledge or access.

3. Write about something that provokes your curiosity and start a conversation.

4. Relay someone else's ideas or information and add your own commentary.

The most popular bloggers typically do all this and more. But creating an online personality can take talent plus trial-and-error experience. The best starting point and one you can count on is to provide useful information.

Take an accountant, for example. She could break her expertise down into a great many absorbable pieces, such as how to prepare for an audit, organize records, choose an accountant, work with an accountant, take advantage of tax loopholes, the pros and cons of online tax software, revamping a financial system and so on.

She could also blog about

- How a movie presented an outdated view of the profession
- How she solved a problem for a client, a problem that readers might share
- A conference that covered the impact of new tax laws
- A problem the profession is facing
- Something interesting about tax law that someone else wrote
- A professional view of a relevant court case, or issue in the news
- Common mistakes people make on their tax returns
- How to evaluate your accountant's service

And/or, if she chooses, she can write about a passionate hobby, an interesting experience, an inspiring book. In fact, many bloggers-for-business deliberately choose to concentrate on a hobby or pastime, rather than the work itself, because of the relationship-building factor.

If a company seeks to cultivate clients in its local area, for example, it can benefit by showcasing employees' off-hour activities rather than sticking to business. This offers a point of connection on a person-to-person level. At the other extreme, some large multinationals encourage employees to blog about personal passions because this provides a wide range of humanizing connections.

So, choice of subject matter relates to your goals and the nature of the business you want to promote.

Notice that the theoretical list made up for the accountant suggests ideas that translate to many professions. If you're a business student right now and define that as your profession, you can come up with a similar list of knowledge areas and viewpoints worth sharing. For example, the impact of a brand new tax law that you learned about, an interesting celebrity lecture, an observation on effective teaching methods and so on.

In your work as a student, you may look at cutting-edge research, interesting statistics, trends, big-picture thinking and insights on current problems or legislation that will affect businesspeople. Or you may engage in debates or conversations about ethical issues. People in the workforce rarely have time to keep up with such subjects and might like to read about them.

And, of course, you can choose to blog about your passionate hobby, fitness program, travel, experience living on $50 per week, whatever. Never think your own present world is not a potential gold mine for sharing and conversation with people even beyond your peers. It just takes some thinking.

VIEW FROM THE FIELD: HOW A PUBLIC RELATIONS PROFESSIONAL BLOGS

When I write a blog, I write it as if I'm talking to somebody. I want readers to open up, trust me, feel they can have a conversation with me. Unlike an article, a blog is not structured and analytical, it's looser and more conversational. I'd say you should blog the way you speak. But make sure the blog represents you in a positive way. Try to avoid using slang. Also, make sure there are no grammatical or spelling errors.

I write about what I'm involved in, like running . . . business situations . . . things I find funny, an unusual experience. I make it personal. You're trying to build a relationship with the people in your community, really get to know them, and hope it leads to business. Eventually it does.

—Hilary JM Topper, president/CEO, HJMT Communications; author of *Everything You Ever Wanted to Know About Social Media But Were Afraid to Ask*

Whatever you write about, try to come across as the person you are. You can't build relationships by sounding like a research journal. Some excellent bloggers even aim to come across as the person they'd like to be, or invent another persona, because they find this frees them psychologically to be more original or forceful.

And as with websites, you need to decide for whom you're writing. Your readers are infinite in theory—but in practice, you must choose your targets and then offer them the right material.

If you're blogging for professional purposes, remember the advantage of consistency. People like knowing what they'll find if they return to a site repeatedly. It may be ineffective to present as a motorcycle repair expert one week and an insurance salesman the next, because you're bound to disappoint one audience or the other.

The challenge is to figure out how to keep mining your general subject so you have something fresh to say regularly.

Q&A: HOW LONG SHOULD A BLOG POST BE?

That depends. Goal, audience and subject matter are all determining factors: Are you aiming to establish expertise? Share complex information with an audience that values it? Writing for an educated, intelligent segment of the population? Then longer pieces will succeed. But in many instances, a short, to-the-point piece is called for. One solid idea can work. Check out author Seth Godin, who many people see as a master blogger.

As with all writing, give the subject what it's worth. And it's perfectly OK to veer between a paragraph and a solid article length at different times.

ACTION TIME: INVENTORY YOUR OWN BLOGGING CAPITAL

Think through the subject matter you might blog about right now. Consider what you're currently engaged in (including school), past working experiences, hobbies, pastimes, enthusiasms, skills, background and so on.

Pick three possible subjects and for each, list as many specific blogs ideas as you can think of. Which looks most promising? What would such a blog accomplish for you? How much time do you estimate would be needed to blog once a week?

WRITING TIPS FOR BLOGGING

If you're writing a "me" blog—meaning your real subject is your opinions, ideas, experience and/or reactions to life around you—you're into a creative realm. It's hard to offer guidelines on how to be an interesting person. Your natural writing style might flow beautifully for this medium. If so, have fun.

The tips in this chapter are geared more to informational blogging—posts that share concrete advice on a subject of choice—because this is a more practical kind of writing for most people. It's also a good career-building strategy that helps establish professional authority.

But whichever way you go, remember the old question: If a tree falls in the forest and nobody hears it, is there a sound? The corollary—if you can't articulate an idea in a way that other people understand, does the idea really exist?

The point: Many of the tips also apply to personal-expression-type blogs and can help your writing work better. They also apply to writing articles for both print and online media, meaning more formal, carefully structured pieces in the tradition of journalism.

Start with strong headlines. Think carefully about how to engage your target audience. You need a strong descriptive headline that tells viewers instantly what's in it for them. Here are a few I saw and liked recently.

What to Do When You're Shtickless: How To Add Humor To Presentations.

> Blogger Rejects Apology. But Why?
>
> Where do ideas come from?
>
> What can communicators learn from Cosmo? A lot
>
> Tips to Topple Procrastination
>
> Why a Bad Memory's Not Such a Bad Thing
>
> What's Your Social IQ? Some Notes from the Field of Social Analytics

Notice that you may or may not be drawn to read the piece. But if you have any interest at all in the subject, the headline is, well, a head start. For the writer, creating a headline that targets the reader is often a very good way to frame and organize content.

Numbers are especially effective for blog headlines (and articles), and give you an almost automatic way to organize what follows. For example:

> Five reasons your surveys are generating low response
>
> 8 Incredibly Simple Ways to Get More People to Read Your Content

> Six ways to change people's minds—and make them like it
>
> 10 Easy Tips to Save You 100 minutes per day
>
> Five ways to increase your web site traffic 20%—instantly

Focusing on people's "pain"—what they fear or worry about—is a great technique for online writing, such as

> 9 simple methods to foil "shrinkage"
>
> How to turn workplace obstacles into miraculous wins
>
> Three ways to turn a monster boss into a booster
>
> How to say "no" to a contractor and keep the door open
>
> Secrets of an IRS insider: How to prevent an audit

Notice that many of these sample headlines tend toward a bit of drama or exaggeration and are heavy on the adjectives. This tone works better on the web than understatement. Questions are good. Suggesting that you will share "secrets," insider information, or something new or surprising are attractive tactics.

But don't shortchange your readers: Give them what you promise—practical advice they can put to work or ideas to stimulate their thinking.

By the way, to see how some of the best-paid professionals in publishing think about headlines and apply these ideas and more, scan a magazine rack. A few I noticed the last time I looked:

> 653 Fashion & Beauty Secrets *(Seventeen)*
>
> Eat Up & Lose Weight: 4 Women Did It. Next, Your Turn *(Self)*
>
> 22 Trips of a Lifetime *(Travel & Leisure)*
>
> New supermarket finds for quick & easy dinners *(Bon Appétit)*

Craft an engaging lead. Once you've hooked your readers with the headline, keep them with you by starting strong. You can start with a question. Or connect the reader directly to the problem you're more or less solving for them. As an example, a lead for the piece on "Three ways to turn a critical boss into a booster" might read,

> Nothing makes life more miserable than a critical, carping boss who's always waiting to pounce on your mistakes. If this is your workday experience, do you assume that grin and bear it is your only option? Not necessarily so. Here are three approaches that can turn the situation around overnight.

Another good tack is to use an anecdote, your own or someone else's, to make an instant connection. For example, "How to say no to a contractor—and keep the door open" could lead,

> Have you ever had the experience of saying "no" to a supplier or contractor, and then found out you made a mistake because the guy you did hire screwed up?
>
> It happened to me last week. The job seemed simple enough . . .

Write clearly and to the point. Once you've pulled readers in, keep them with you by crafting well-written material that makes sense, sticks to the point and moves quickly. If you've promised six tips, move through them and label them that way.

Use the short, basic, unpretentious words as much as you can and try for lively verbs. Keep your average sentence short, though length can be closer to that of print material than websites, namely, 12 to 22 words.

Keep paragraphs short: generally one to three sentences. It helps to use some single-sentence paragraphs.

Use simple sentence structures and avoid complicated ones that make the meaning indirect, such as those that require words ending in -*ing* and a lot of "is" and "are" phrases, as well as those that include "to" and "of." You need to pull readers in and retain them with fast-reading material.

Build in subheads both for your own sake and readers'. Writing a set of sequential subheads first is an approach that works very well for blogs. Bullets and numbered lists can help you speed through some material.

Work hard at your transitions between sentences and paragraphs. Making it absolutely clear how one sentence or paragraph connects to the next is critical in a medium that is read quickly, and on screen to boot. It makes you more convincing, too.

Consider graphic effect. Short paragraphs give you some helpful white space, and build in more so that the eye is not challenged by a formidable mass of copy. Avoid formats based on single columns that stretch across most of the screen width. Very wide columns don't work in print media because reading them takes more effort. They have an even worse effect on screen. Where you can use relevant or entertaining graphics to liven things up, do so. Use boldface judiciously.

Edit, edit, edit. Cut every unnecessary idea and word. Say things as tightly and simply as you can. Skip the empty hype, jargon and buzzwords. Look for repetition;

weak, boring verbs; awkward constructions, and make fixes. Use the say-it-aloud test. In other words, apply all the techniques described in Chapters 4 and 5.

Proof, proof, proof. Observe the blogs you like best and chances are excellent that you'll find virtually no grammatical or spelling errors. If you want to get respect, be correct. But that doesn't mean a stiff, formal style.

Sound spontaneous. This probably seems contradictory given the foregoing guidelines, but a warm, friendly, easy-flowing style suits the medium. But just as with websites, spontaneity can take work.

To get the right tone, practice the tools of informality. Sentence fragments are fine as long as meaning is clear. Starting sentences with "and" and "but" works well; forget the elementary school grammar lessons. Contractions are better than formal versions—such as "can't" for "cannot." Try for a conversational tone. Unless you're writing in a personal vein where "I" is appropriate, try for a "you"-focused orientation. For example:

IS BLOGGING FOR YOU?

ANSWER THREE SIMPLE QUESTIONS AND FIND OUT

Wondering whether to make blogging part of your life?

Here's how to decide. First ask yourself, **"What's in it for me?"** What will you gain professionally, or how can your business benefit? Be specific. Strategic blogging has accomplished miracles for many people, and maybe it would for you too.

Your second question: **"What's in it for them?"**—meaning the readers you want to write for. Figure out what you know that's worth sharing—it's probably a lot more than you think. Try writing a list of subject ideas and see if that inspires you.

And third, think about **"How much time can I give it?"** No question, it takes time to produce blogs that are useful, interesting and well written. So besides answering the practical questions, think about whether blogging would be fun, or satisfying. Whether it could lead you in new directions and help you build new relationships.

If you do want to plunge ahead, **here's a starting point** I know has worked for others. . . .

Link, link, link. Enrich what you offer by linking to other online material, yours or other people's, that offers more dimensions on a particular aspect or proves your point. It makes you more credible by demonstrating that you know what's out there besides your own viewpoint, too. But don't weigh your post down with links on every other line, they're distracting for most readers even when they don't click through.

Involve your readers. Ask direct questions. It's a great way to end a blog post. The blog about handling critical bosses might, for example, end with,

> What about you? Have you worked for a critical boss and tried a technique for improving the relationship? Did it make things better? Or worse? Share your experience!

Here's how one blog I read recently, titled "Be Intimate With Your Blog Readers," chose to end: "What are some of the ways that you've used your blog to get intimate with your customers?"

And here's what journalist Nicholas Kristof, a very popular blogger, asked his readers:

> I need advice. I'd like to make my Facebook fan page more useful, and I had a great conversation today with FB's Nick Grudin about that. (I'm installing a secret widget that will lead FB fans to lose 10 pounds, enjoy better sex and double their income: tell your friends!) What else do you suggest? Should I post more of . . .

To see how three widely admired bloggers go about it (and to get some good advice in general) check out

> Seth Godin
>
> http://sethgodin.typepad.com
>
> Guy Kawasaki
>
> http://blog.guykawasaki.com
>
> Chris Brogan
>
> http://www.chrisbrogan.com

As you dig into social media and connect with the communities you relate to, add bloggers you like to your personal list and check them out regularly. And review their posts analytically: What works well? What can you learn? Most professional writers have a shortlist (or a long list) of other writers they admire, not because they want to imitate them, but because they find it inspiring to read their work. You'll find it inspiring, too.

SIDELIGHT: A JOURNALIST'S TAKE ON MULTIDIMENSIONAL COMMUNICATING

The written word doesn't always tell the complete story. We surround it with other information—photos, videos, tweets—so we communicate with people in any way they're comfortable with, not just as one-way journalism.

Business can be tightlipped. Don't be afraid to have a conversation with your audience—"Hey, this is what we're up to, what do you think and how can we make this product better?" Business can and should create messages that are multidimensional—and so should individuals.

—Carl Corry, online editor, *Newsday*

Posting Comments

As I mentioned earlier, posting good comments on the blogs you read can be a good way to introduce yourself to a community. And it's a strategy that, more and more, can work to attract the interest of employers. How to do it well?

Essentially, have something real to contribute or don't do it at all. Begin by connecting immediately with what you're responding to and preferably say something positive, then move into what you want to add to the conversation. For example:

> I appreciate your suggestions on how to avoid an audit—you've created a great checklist for entrepreneurs to use when preparing their taxes. I'd like to add one more idea, which came to me the hard way, in the course of being audited.

If actually you disagree with all or some of the blogger's post, still begin politely; it will make you more credible.

> I appreciate your suggestions on how to avoid an audit. It's a useful checklist for entrepreneurs and I agree with most of the points. However, I've learned something the hard way—through being audited—that gives me a better way to avoid questions on paperwork.

Then present your experience, idea or comment concisely—a paragraph is often enough. Between 100 and 300 words is "average." But again, know your audience and the medium. If you're contributing to a political blog that boasts a well-informed readership, and comments run 1,500 words, then write on—provided you have the substance.

There's a big plus factor to commenting on what other people in your field write: It links you directly to your business competitors, who are part of the community you want to join. Here too the Internet is shifting how we look at relationships. Smart people in every profession benefit by sharing far more information than used to be the norm. And, surprisingly often, they create collaborations and refer work to each other.

Posting good comments can open many doors for you.

SIDELIGHT: HOW TO GENERATE AN ONLINE CONVERSATION

Search by key words for people who are interested in what you're interested in, read them, see what they think, go in with a how-can-I-help-you attitude. A community is about a purpose, a shared passion, maybe a vision of a better future or something everyone can believe in and get on board with. Once you see what the culture is like, add value. Start conversations. Ask curiosity-based questions, which are often better conversation starters than statements. A question can relate to the topic or culture of the group, it can pique people's interest and beg for a response. It can help promote your interests, too.

For example, I asked on LinkedIn, "What comes up when you Google your name or brand?" A few people responded in ways that made it clear they were open to help that I was able to give without selling. I've asked, "What impact has SEO had on your business?" This is a much-misunderstood subject and the question opened up revealing dialogues. I've also asked, "What is the worst or funniest experience you've had on a website?" I heard from angry, frustrated people and it helped my own knowledge base—and ability to deal with clients.

—Jerry Allocca, founder of CORE Interactive; author of *Connected Culture*

As with all Internet communication, be careful not to come across as self-interested or grinding a personal ax of any kind. If you're commenting on the "avoid an audit" example and you're a CPA, identify yourself as such in the signature, or in the body of the post say at most something like, "As a CPA of seven years' experience, I'd like to point out . . ."

If your comment looks like a self-promoting commercial, people will probably never read it at all.

YOU ARE WHAT YOU WRITE: THE ONLINE PROFILE

Presenting your credentials well online can make a big difference in how you're perceived by employers, clients, prospects, collaborators and everyone else. This is a relatively new challenge so there are no set guidelines for writing a good virtual profile. If you scan self-descriptions even of well-known individuals, you'll find a very wide range in content, style and level of detail. Many are minimalist. Why should you take the trouble to do this task well?

If you stand to gain by making professional connections, then online profiles for sites like LinkedIn are worth a lot. For one thing, almost universally, employers will check out your profile and take it seriously as part of your job application (so beware of contradicting your "official résumé").

Employers and other site users also expect to find more insight into your personality and way of looking at things than your official résumé affords. Use the "Summary" to deliver this and get across who you are, what you believe and what you've accomplished. It should be in line with your overall social media strategy. And it should tilt toward the future—where you want to go—using your past as the platform.

As always when communicating, know your goal: to support your general networking? Job hunting? Prospecting for clients, customers or people to work with? Will you use the profile to back up your in-person contacts or e-mail approaches? Online profiles give you a chance to reverse the marketing equation: Instead of hunting for promising contacts, you may succeed in leading them to you.

Where to start? Your own background gives you the best clues. Explore what energizes you, motivates you, gives you the biggest rewards, makes you happiest.

SIDELIGHT: PUT YOUR PROFILE TO WORK

My core message to clients is that an Internet presence gives small businesses and individuals the same tools that once would have been the playground of very large companies.

One important way to use the power behind it is to flesh out your online profile: The more you can keep it pointing at your expertise and intelligence and can get recognized as an expert at what you do, someone who is a knowledgeable information resource, the better. So make a concerted effort to update your status. Link to blogs you've written, note if you're giving a speech or win an award, or tweet— everything counts.

—Adrian Miller, CEO, Adrian Miller Sales Training; founder of Adrian's Network

Here are some concrete ideas to draw on.

1. Use an "I" framework. It helps you share who you are with more genuine feeling and warmth, and feels more authentic than talking about yourself in the third person. Some people, however, believe it's more professional to use the third person for LinkedIn and other business networking sites. Scout the site that interests you to see what most people use and which style you like better.

Even if you think you need a statement written in the third person, consider writing it in first person anyway, then translate it into "he" or "she." It will pick up more life that way.

2. Write with a clear sense of where you want to go. Your profile should take account of not just your immediate goals—like to generate new connections—but the longer range. Maybe you hope to connect with a future employer, forge alliances, find people to brainstorm with, whatever. The clearer your goals, the more your content, focus and style will help you achieve them. Read other people's profiles and you'll find that the best are very clear on where the person is now and what she or he wants.

3. Make it easy for people to grasp who you are with a strong opening statement that positions you immediately. One way is to go beyond résumé-speak and say something about why you chose your work or what you like about it. Here's one example:

> As a customer service trainer, I love showing managers how to improve customers' experience and turn them into raving fans. Drawing on all my work experience as . . .

And a third-person introduction:

> In just two years, Ellen has created a revolutionary new women's business community. Foxy Network's mission is to provide ongoing support for women as they work their way through life . . .

Here's how some people who are quoted in this book and a few who are popular bloggers introduce themselves online:

> I've got roles in a few companies right now. (Chris Brogan)
>
> My personal mantra is "empower entrepreneurs." When all is said and done, I'm a marketing guy. (Guy Kawasaki)

I help people write, publish, distribute and extend information assets. (Ivan Walsh)

Socially engaged, technology savvy web communications specialist with excellent writing, web development and video production skills. (Amanda McCormick)

I work with executives at technology, professional services and media firms to develop and deliver brand stories that can be remembered, repeated and rewarded. (Arthur Germain)

4. Show your passion, or at least enthusiasm, for your work (or the work you plan to do). As in all written and spoken communication, these feelings are contagious. You don't necessarily have to say "I love what I do," but you can build in a bit of *why* you love it. If that isn't comfortable, try statements that start out with the words "I help . . ."

People respond to passion in other people. Given a choice, we'll always opt for the enthusiastic, dedicated individual. They're more rewarding to deal with and we want them on our side.

This is a good tack to take if you're not yet embarked on the career you're studying for. You can focus on your attitude or personal orientation, as in

A marketing career found me when I was in college—even though I'd begun as a chemistry major.

I've always been the person people come to when they can't settle an argument.

5. Find the achievement in what you do—the things you're most proud of. Get past the jargon and vague generalizations we all find so easy to write and convey a sense of what you've actually done, what it means, and what your capabilities are. (For ideas on how to do this see the résumé section of Chapter 12.)

If your brainstorming suggests some particular evidence of why you're good at your work, like an anecdote about an achievement or a glamorous credential, work it in.

6. Keep the overall profile simple and focused. But it's fine to add more personal elements. If you're a Big Brother or Big Sister, for example, or an enthusiastic member of an amateur theater troupe, or raise money for the local arts council, readers can be expected to relate. But be cautious about including any that might prove a turnoff to some people, like a specific religious or political affiliation.

GOING DEEPER: FOR ADVICE ON SOCIAL MEDIA AND THE INTERNET

What's possible is changing so fast that the only way to keep up with the virtual world is online. Here are some resources to know about.

Website/Blog	Address	Description
Mashable	http://mashable.com	Daily portal to a wide mix of social media news and information
Bnet: CBS Interactive Business Network	http://www.bnet.com	Wide range of material on business and entrepreneurship
Copyblogger	http://www.copyblogger.com	Online copywriting and content marketing strategies
Bplans	http://www.Bplans.com	Downloadable business plan templates and advice
Hubspot	http://blog.hubspot.com	"Inbound Internet Marketing Blog"
Magneto Communications	http://www.magneto.net.au	Advice from an Australian communications firm
Psyblog	http://www.spring.org.uk	"Understand your mind" creativity ideas
Psychotactics	http://www.psychotactics.com/blog	New Zealand site on the psychology of buying (Sean D'Souza)
Media Bistro	http://www.mediabistro.com	Media news, blogs, job listings
Investment Writing	http://investmentwriting.com/blog	Susan B. Weiner, advice on financial writing
Blogging Bookshelf	http://www.bloggingbookshelf.com	Blogging tips from Tristan and a directory of blogs to check out
Nerd Alert	http://erinflis.com	A blog by Erin Flis; good ideas and news-sharing reports on conferences, presentations
Klariti	http://www.Klariti.com	Ivan Walsh, with advice on business documents
Before&After	http://www.bamagazine.com	An amazing resource for professional designers that will sharpen your eye

MICRO MAGIC: USING TWITTER POWER

When you're only working with 140 characters, it's hard to believe that you're using a highly effective business communication tool, let alone one that fosters political revolutions—but, of course, you are. But refrain from telling people what you're eating for lunch and give them something useful or genuinely interesting. (Unless you're a famous chef; then your lunch choice might rivet your followers.)

Of course you can tweet to solve problems, get help with something, let people know where you are and much more. One way to look at it is that you're throwing information out into the world and just might get surprising unexpected results. We all know stories like that: a reporter who won a plum assignment because an editor noticed he's vacationing in a hot spot; a company that fixed a problem because they saw a complaint tweet; somebody who lands a dream job because of an intelligent Twitter exchange that an executive noticed.

Rather than using Twitter in a random way, you can make it part of your strategic campaign to promote your own goals. It's a very effective way to establish yourself as a subject expert, and an extraordinary chance to connect with people you'd ordinarily have no hope of accessing. It's also a great way to bring attention to more substantial social media efforts, like your blog or website.

All you have to do is be relevant, useful and interesting! This involves thinking about good content and crafting your tweets. The fact is that audiences expect from micromedia very much the same things as they want from other media: substance and relevance to their interests.

Asked to explain his goal in tweeting, widely respected social media commenter Steve Rubel said, "To share my passion with the community and solicit ideas all with the intent of moving me toward my long-term goal of revolutionizing marketing communications through technology."

Your own goal may be a lot more modest than that, but articulating it empowers you to identify good subjects to help you accomplish it. As with all social media, first listen—tune in to conversations, especially among groups that share your interests. Find discussions that excite you. Think about what you can contribute.

You can be a firsthand source of information or ideas if you're positioned to provide that. Or like many people, you can successfully mine your universe for interesting things other people are saying or doing and link to, or retweet, that information.

Ask questions. Initiate conversations. Share.

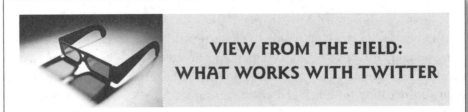

VIEW FROM THE FIELD: WHAT WORKS WITH TWITTER

It's no secret that the click-through rate on Twitter is notoriously low, like 1%; so if you've included a link to something you want people to click through to, like a blog or a post, the name of the game is to get retweeted as many times as possible, which makes you think really hard about those 140 characters.

What compels someone to retweet? Stuff that is proactive, potentially controversial, emotive. People will retweet things that make them appear smart, funny or interesting. So you have to make sure what you're posting delivers social value. People also like retweeting finite lists: 25 beautiful photos, 10 most popular posts of the year—numbers tend to inspire retweets.

We often tweet to find volunteers with specific skill sets, and sometimes we use our Twitter followers as a quick focus group—inviting them to comment on a new idea, concept or design for example.

—James Wu, senior associate, Business Development, Acumen Fund

And as always, write well. Provided you do, Twitter gives you a formidable way to keep in contact with employers after an interview, build your acquaintance with someone you met at a meeting, introduce yourself to someone you want to know and keep your presence alive in the minds of clients or prospects. Assuming, of course, they actively use the medium.

Some Twitter Writing Tips

- Use less than the allotted 140 characters—130 at most—to facilitate retweeting.
- Abbreviations are fine *if you're sure your audience will understand them.* If you aim to connect with human resources managers, for example, don't assume they will understand texting shortcuts. Find a different, tighter way to say what you mean.
- Go for an active tone. Use simple direct sentences—avoid *-ing, -ize* and similar kinds of words as well as cluttered constructions that need "is" and "are." Good active verbs go a long way.

- Use short, basic words and only those that are essential to the message. Cut every unnecessary word and phrase.
- Stick to one topic. Make sure the finished message doesn't get so telegraphic that it's hard to understand.
- Check online sources (like Twitter itself) for up-to-date guidance on using the medium's particular conventions, like hashtags.
- Don't send first drafts—review your message and work on simplicity, clarity and wording. All the editing guidelines in Chapters 4 and 5 apply.

Notice that every element of writing tweets is the same as for effective letters, e-mails and proposals. This super-condensed format is a good test of your editing skills.

And the guidelines for media not yet imagined will also, essentially, remain the same. Practice the principles and you'll be equipped for everything that comes your way.

Remember to integrate your social media channels with each other, and with whatever traditional print media you use. Add your Twitter and Facebook accounts to your e-mail signature, and/or others that are important to you. Use e-mail and Twitter and social sites to call attention to your blog. Use sites that aggregate your social media output so when you do something new it is widely distributed. Tools to do this are getting better, and they will help you maximize your time.

The idea of branding used to belong to big organizations that could hugely invest in making themselves household names. Today, this too has become democratized. The online world gives the small organization every opportunity to brand itself—to become known and to showcase what it offers—and reach a specific audience rather than a mass market. This is equally true for individuals.

You have the power to brand yourself. Why do this? Because you can determine what you want to be known for and how you want to be seen. Then you can use all the tools of virtual and legacy media to present a consistent, thoughtful, strategic "you." A "you" that can make the most of opportunities and accomplish what you want.

Of course, this is a lifetime enterprise. Your goals will change and so will the tools of communication. Plan to stay flexible and learn to use new channels and vehicles as they appear.

But if you follow the concepts of this book, and keep practicing your skills, you'll be equipped with the most important constant—good writing.

In the next chapter, learn how to put your best foot forward in written form with résumés and cover letters that enable you to stand out from the crowd.

PRACTICE OPPORTUNITIES

I. Create and Post a Comment

Identify at least three bloggers who write about a subject that interests you. Read at least five posts for each one. Write a paragraph or more saying what you think works, being specific, and also what doesn't work for you as a reader. Then choose a post suggesting an idea and write a comment. Exchange the draft with a partner, make changes based on the input according to your judgment—and post your comment.

II. Plan and Write a Blog

This series of activities can be done in pairs so each student receives sustained feedback.

1. Find a subject that relates to your current expertise or interest, and that will contribute in some way to your professional image or career.

2. In writing, plan a blog by considering your goal and audience. Also do online research to locate bloggers in your area of interest and review those that would compete with you.

3. Brainstorm content ideas and make a list of at least 10 topics for suitable blogs.

4. Write the first blog explaining your purpose, who you are, what you'll be writing about as you think appropriate—or just plunge right in and focus on a relevant subject.

5. Plan a program, in writing, to promote your blog and find readers you want.

6. Based on the plan, write promotional messages enticing people to subscribe to your blog suitable for e-mail, Twitter and so on.

III. Group Discussion: An Ethical Issue

Is it appropriate to have other people blog in someone else's name? Tweet? Create an online avatar or persona? Should authorship be explicit? Is it legitimate for companies to use staff members or outside public relations people to blog in the CEO's name? To tweet? Discuss in groups and share the results. Come up with written guidelines that the whole class can agree on.

IV. Tweet Practice

In a series of 10 tweets (max 140 characters each) distill the most useful information in this chapter as if you're sharing it with friends.

V. Build an Online Profile

If you have a LinkedIn profile, review and update it, taking into account the writing principles in this book. If you don't have one, create it now. Start by writing down your goals, and describing the characteristics, interests and needs of your intended audiences.

VI. Q&A Practice

Identify an affinity group new to you on LinkedIn or another site and review the Q&A. What self-interest can you identify for various contributors? What questions provoked discussion, which did not? Can you draw useful generalizations from this?

Can you offer answers to any of the questions? Do so.

Then think of five good questions to ask that would stir a conversation and give you something helpful—an idea, information, solution to a problem, a connection and so on.

VII. Plan a Social Media Program

In the same groups, look at the website you created for a charitable cause in Chapter 9. Plot out a comprehensive social media strategy for that charity. In context of goals and audience, what tools would you use, and how? How would you integrate with traditional marketing strategies (e.g., brochures, newsletters, marketing materials, mass-media campaigns, press releases) and cross-promote?

Chapter 12

PRESENTING YOURSELF

RÉSUMÉS AND ELEVATOR SPEECHES

➢ Plan a résumé that showcases your individual skills
➢ Tailor format and content to your goals and experience
➢ Use good writing to outshine the competition
➢ Introduce yourself with an elevator speech

> *There is nothing to writing. All you do is sit down at a typewriter and bleed.*

—Ernest Hemingway

KNOW THYSELF: HARD, BUT IMPORTANT

Writing résumés was never much fun, and faced with the need, you may empathize with the Hemingway quote above.

Let's be honest: Because almost every industry is more competitive than ever before, your résumé must be really good, better than those presented by other candidates for the job. This is true of "junior" positions for people just out of school, and also those with advanced credentials like an MBA and solid experience.

Current predictions say that you'll probably hold 10 or 12 jobs during your career. That means you'll probably need at least that many résumés. So crafting a strong résumé and keeping it alive will be part of your life.

For good or bad, the substance of writing good résumés has changed little, in the opinion of those who know best—the recruiters. The means of delivery may shift; most résumés are delivered digitally today rather than as pieces of paper. But the writing principles remain pretty much the same. You need to know what those principles are, and how to apply them.

Why So Hard?

Typically, you need a new résumé when you're at a crossroads. Various directions beckon but to pick the best one, you have to truly understand where you've been, what you're ready for and how to prove it. This demands that you think analytically about your life thus far and generalize about your experiences.

Everything is relevant: work, education, specific training, part-time jobs, internships, sport and hobby interests, accomplishments, volunteer work, personal qualities, what you did on your summer vacations and also, the kind of people you relate to. The work atmosphere you prefer. The assignments that make you happiest, and the ones that make you miserable. (Why put all that effort into getting an opportunity you'll hate?)

Consider all the elements of your personal history that have made you who you are.

Equally helpful: have an idea of where you want to be next year, and in five years, even though your direction may change radically.

None of this means that you can't toss off an OK résumé over the course of a few days and score some hits. But there's a big bonus to crafting an outstanding résumé: The process sharpens your career planning, helps you recognize good opportunities, and convinces you that you're equipped for the job—which prepares you to ace the interviews.

CAREER TIP: IN-PERSON NETWORKING WORKS

Find associations within your profession and network yourself at the local chapters. The associations all run websites and you can post your résumé on them, sometimes for a small fee. Also, go to the meetings and introduce yourself, you'll connect with key influencers as well as stay current with trends. If people like the way you present yourself you might easily get a job lead. Many young people don't see the value of showing up at industry events, so if you're in this age group, try it. Interacting with established professionals can give you real opportunities.

—Doug Silverman, general manager of human resources,
Nikon Inc.; president, Society of Human Resource Managers/Long Island

---

HOW TO PLAN YOUR RÉSUMÉ

Just as with every other writing format, plan your document based on the twin concepts of goal and audience.

Consider your goal: Do you think it's to win you a job? Actually not—the goal is more modest: to win you an interview so you can make your case in person. That may not change the content of your résumé, but it may mean giving it a different slant. It needs to work as a self-contained document and position you as worth interviewing, so you survive the initial filtering process.

Seeing those who will view your résumé as **your audience** reminds you that

- You should bring to bear everything you know or can ferret out about the organization, because the more you understand the recipient, the better you can gauge your message
- Your application, if successful, will be read by a series of reviewers on different levels, so your message of qualification must be clear to all
- The typical reader sees the review assignment as tedious and probably overwhelming; he or she will happily trash your effort on the least provocation—typos, poor writing, poor appearance, content not on target, maybe even because it's boring.

Always assume your target organization is deluged with applications. Yours must be better in every respect. *You may get less than 30 seconds of a reader's time to make the cut.*

What Do You Mean, Traditional?

When an employer requests a résumé, whether e-mailed, snail-mailed or delivered in person, assume a traditional format is in order. That means presenting your skills, experience, education and related background in a standard order on a piece of paper—real or virtual—using a reverse chronology (most recent first).

The ground rule applies even if you're trying for a creative position. Someone hiring a staff art director, for example, wants to see a portfolio, but still wants to know about a candidate's experience, track record, education, reliability and so on. The trick for creative people is to demonstrate their originality within the restrictive standard format: a writer, for example, through terrific writing, and a designer by making the document look great.

The biggest exception to this rule of thumb is the social media résumé, which exploits online capabilities to deliver a multidimensional impression of a person. This usually involves creating a website and using video, podcasts and social media links to showcase multiple aspects of your abilities and personality. When is this a good idea? It depends on your social media skills, the type of job involved, the company, who will review your qualifications and many other factors.

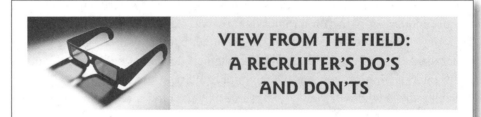

VIEW FROM THE FIELD: A RECRUITER'S DO'S AND DON'TS

A great résumé has flow, a presence. It captures the targeted industry. Its purpose is not to get the job but the interview, giving you the opportunity to sell yourself. So see it as a teaser and keep it down to one to two pages. Aim to speak about yourself with subtle confidence.

Based on my own peeves and what I hear from colleagues and employers, my advice is

1. Don't change the standard format: Keep it simple and chronological.

2. Put it in an easy-to-e-mail format like Word.

3. No typos! That's the biggest complaint we get from employers, and it amazes me.

4. Don't clutter the layout, change fonts, vary the type size—keep it clean and easy for that 30-second capture, which is the most time you have to make an impression.

5. Use the industry's key words throughout but omit words that aren't searchable, like abbreviations.

If you have time gaps, definitely mention and address them—otherwise it's a red flag. And everything is so easy to check on now by Googling someone's name. Remember that the Internet is also your résumé and an employer can immediately find out if you're part of any dark side of the world. Use the Internet to your benefit, and build a sub-résumé on sites like LinkedIn or Spoke.com, which people look at when hiring.

—Tina Ruark, senior vice president of strategic staffing, Access Staffing

Even with traditional résumés, you can take some liberties. The point is to present you at your best, so look for ways to adapt the format to what works. For example:

- To soften your job chronology if you jumped around a lot in a short period of time, or there are many gaps in your work history, put the dates of employment at the end of job descriptions rather than more prominently in a column on the left.
- Group brief jobs and generalize about them so they don't clutter up your landscape and make you look scattershot. Part-time or summer jobs, for example, can be grouped as such with a clear heading rather than listed separately:

Retail Sales Experience, Summers of 2010, 2011 and 2012

Salesperson for Macy's, Ben & Jerry Ice Cream, March Gift Shop.

Intensive customer interaction and problem-solving experiences. On-the-job training in customer relations, inventory management, large and small store operations.

- If a personal interest or pastime is relevant to the job and helps you stand out, find a way to cover it early on.
- If you're jumping careers or don't have a relevant job history for any reason, focus on "Skills" up front and make it clear why you can transfer them from whatever experience you do have.

PRESENTATION: FORMATTING AND CATEGORIES

Your goal is to present your information in a way that looks simple, accessible and easy to absorb. Creativity is usually not called for, but use fonts, layout and white space to produce an inviting document. Usually it's best to use a standard format, such as the one shown on the next page, and adapt it to what shows you off best.

This is also true with choosing the categories to include.

The usual essentials after your masthead/contact information and overview are experience, education, professional organizations and awards. "Skills" is another useful category. If you're at an early career stage, you may want to lead with this section. If you're experienced, you may want to put "Skills" at the bottom if not already covered—factors such as technical capabilities, software expertise, public speaking, foreign languages and so on.

But exercise some imagination to incorporate sections that let you include your strong points. Here are some to consider.

- Awards and recognition
- Strengths
- Social networks
- Technical training
- Clubs and associations
- Certifications
- Pro bono work
- Community service (better than volunteer activities)
- A catchall category such as Additional Data, Related Experience, Special Qualifications or Career Highlights

Sample Format

Name

Address

Telephone, e-mail, website if you have one

Summary of Qualifications

Employment
Dates, job title, name of company, location
Big-picture overview of your role and capsule description of the company
Bullet points representing accomplishments, up to six

For previous jobs, most recent first:
Same format as current one but less detail (unless the earlier job shows especially relevant experience)

Career Highlights
Community service, special training, capabilities not covered by job descriptions, publications, speaking

Education
Starting with most recent:
Degree, name of school, location
For graduate work and college, brief summary of what you studied and any honors
Include dates (unless you don't want to indicate age)

Distinctions
All awards, honors, recognition—including any given for character or time given to a good cause as well as academic achievement (if not covered under Education)

Skills
Technical, language, social media, certifications

Interests
Hobbies, community service (if not already covered), activities

Vary the sample format based on your career status and industry. If you will be entering the job market with an MBA and a few years or more of work experience, then put the experience first because it will be of more interest to employers. If you're a business school student looking for a first or second job, or an internship, list education first.

The narrative "summary of experience" is in my opinion valuable but whether you need it "depends." You might prefer to include an overview of who you are and what you can do in your cover letter. But if the employer doesn't want a cover letter, the résumé should carry the summary.

Also, industries vary in their expectations. If you apply for a communications job, the summary is mandatory, but this is not true in the case of many business jobs. Where does a marketing job fall? Use your judgment.

Definitely provide a summary of experience if you are changing careers or need to explain a break from the workforce.

Opinions on whether to include activities and incorporate narrative statements in the body of the résumé vary, as you'll see in "View from the Field: Make It Easy." Take into account also that a professional recruiter's viewpoint can differ from that of a human resources specialist or department head. Consider all the advice and apply what works best for you—always remembering goal and audience.

VIEW FROM THE FIELD: MAKE IT EASY

Despite all the electronic changes, the basic foundation of the résumé and interviewing has not changed. Stay away from anything cutesy, just zero in on what the recruiter is looking for. Make it easy for the reader to find out who you are and why you should be getting the job.

We won't spend much time on a résumé or even print it out unless you catch our attention in a businesslike way. So start with the skills you offer, a brief overview with three to six bullets, such as "Expertise in integrating social media into marketing campaigns." Then present your work experience—company, job title, length of time, description of what you did. Do not include your picture, references, or activities— save that for the second or third interview. Avoid even a single typo.

Everything you put in the résumé must add value to your profession.

—Rich Young, senior recruiter, Chaloner Associates

WRITING GUIDELINES TO OUTSTRIP THE COMPETITION

A résumé must be crystal clear, concise, instantly understood and fast to read. It should be concrete, built on short words and sentences, and scrupulously edited. In other words, follow all the guidelines I've already set down for business writing in general. Don't shortchange the proofing process; borrow another set of eyes to double-check because one bad typo, and poof! There goes your credibility. No matter what kind of job you're applying for.

Do you need full sentences? Not necessarily—you don't have room for that. Résumé real estate is at a premium. You can reduce some of the "I's" and "a's" and "the's," for example. But don't distill statements to fragments that may mislead, or make you look illiterate.

For example, you needn't say,

> I completed all the requirements for my Executive MBA in three years.

Nor should you say,

> Exec. MBA, completed three years

Better:

> Completed Executive MBA requirements in three years

Do you need key words? Yes. Many recruiters scan job applications (visually or via computer) and discard those that appear not to have the right qualifications. So build in the terms that characterize the industry and that denote required skills. Almost always you can glean these from the job posting and some online research.

Do you need action verbs? Absolutely. Good résumés hinge on action verbs. If you want to come across as an active rather than passive person, someone who is outstanding rather than just capable and brings initiative and spark, make every verb zing. This is also how to take credit for your accomplishments. To find hundreds of great possibilities just Google "action verbs" and scout out those that will work for you. (You might find this a good way to jump-start your résumé-think.)

For example, here are some strong verbs for describing management capabilities.

- Authorized
- Consolidated
- Generated
- Chaired
- Secured
- Reorganized
- Steered
- Streamlined
- Strengthened
- Originated
- Launched
- Oversaw
- Instituted
- Rejuvenated
- Shepherded
- Mobilized
- Navigated
- Recreated
- Redirected
- Designed

You are entitled to use such words to convey a big-picture view of your work product. For example, don't say "I entered information into the database." Better to say, "I managed the customer database and upgrade system."

Do you need bullets? Yes, bullets are an excellent way to list skills or achievements in a short amount of space. But depending on bullets totally may not serve you well. Good narrative statements make sense of what otherwise come across as laundry lists, a disconnected collection of statements. This kind of disjointed rundown violates a fundamental principle I talked about earlier—that the writer take responsibility for interpreting the message, rather than allowing readers to draw their own conclusions.

If you choose to go the all-bullet route, be sure you compose strong statements and make them easily absorbed and uniform in style.

Do you need to state a job objective? No—even if you're relatively new to the job market. Employers don't care about what you want; they care about what you can do for them.

Do you need to customize your résumé for every job application? Yes.

Writing successful cover letters is separately covered in Chapter 7. Review that section for more ideas on presenting yourself in writing.

Writing the Summary of Experience

It's very helpful to write a summary of experience even if you don't use it on your résumé, because it forces you to articulate who you are and what you're ready for.

You can begin with a clear definition of who you are professionally. At an early career stage, you have less to work with—so keep it simple. For example, if you're a recent graduate applying to a leadership training program at a multinational organization:

> Business Honor Society graduate with BS focused on marketing and leadership. Related internship experiences with three global organizations. Four years part-time work in retail sales with progressive responsibility, culminating in position of Team Leader. Excellent written and in-person communication skills, proven analytic abilities, fluent in Spanish.

This statement puts the writer's assets right up front and establishes a set of competitive advantages. Scour your own background: If your degree is from a prestigious school, work that in. If you edited the newspaper, graduated in the top 10%, were honored as a volunteer, helped a professor with an impressive project, won three scholarships, earned your way through college, created a business while still in school, lived part of your life in another country—all such factors set you apart.

A Business Communications Example

In her original résumé draft, this writer began with an objective:

> To obtain a challenging position in internal corporate communications that utilizes my prior experience in employee communications, internal web writing/editing and executive communications/correspondence.

Persuaded to begin with a summary of experience instead, she developed the following:

Employee Communications Specialist: Strong track record originating and directing programs to engage employees, build morale and generate a positive work environment. Four years multinational Fortune 500 experience producing publications, video features, online material and executive speeches. Adept in balancing, print, online and social media channels to achieve company goals. Excellent written and oral communication skills enhanced by advanced training.

ACTION TIME: KNOW WHAT WORKS

Which statement does a better job of selling the candidate—the objective or the summary of experience? Why? How does she come across in each? Look at each from an employer's perspective. Can you improve the second statement?

Notice that with more experience to work with, this writer is able to follow up the "who I am" first statement with a very broad view of what her work achieves: NOT her specific job responsibilities. Then she moves to her major credentials and some specific work products and ends up referencing some differentiating skills. This is a useful pattern to try, but shape your summary so it shows off *your* best selling points.

Here's an alternative format you may prefer. It combines a short opening overview statement with a bulleted list of skills.

Profile

Hands-on, collaborative communications leader. Strategic thinker with a passion for helping organizations shape customer and employee perception to grow a healthy business. Recognized for

- Exceptional Communications Skills
  Can effectively simplify the complex to deliver clear, concise and compelling communications.
- Trusted Communications Counsel to Executives
  Have helped CEOs effectively develop and deliver their messages to multiple audiences.

- Equally Strong Left Brain/Right Brain
  Ability to think creatively and execute effectively. Strong project management and analytical skills.
- Developing High-Performance Teams
  Track record of execution through teams, driven by a genuine desire to help others succeed.

Your goal with the summary profile is to bridge between what you have done in the past and what you can do for a new employer. To simply list responsibilities qualifies you for the job you already have, and what's the point of that? *In the summary statement, and the rest of the résumé too, try to avoid the words, "responsible for." Think about proven capabilities instead.*

When you produce an opening profile, you have a writing advantage: You know what content to focus on in the rest of the résumé. It should back up your claims with convincing detail.

Presenting Your Work Experience

Start with your most recent job and follow with the rest in reverse chronological order. Logically, a current job merits the most description—but what if it's a diversion from your career path or you've only held it briefly? Then say as much as it's worth, and use fuller descriptions for one or more of your earlier jobs.

Try for a short narrative paragraph generalizing about the position and/or employer. For example:

2009–Present JFL Inc., Seattle, WA

Increasingly responsible marketing roles for Fortune 1000 firm, second-largest distributor of home repair supplies on West Coast, employing 7,000 people. Skills range from market research to program planning, project management, presentation writing and design, and customer relations.

The reason for explaining the company is that either the reader (1) won't readily know what it is, or (2) may recognize the firm's name, but probably won't know its scope. In both cases, positioning the company—especially as significant in some way in size or standing—makes your experience look all the better.

Following up in the same pattern, name each position in reverse chronological order with a short narrative and three to six bullet points for each.

VIEW FROM THE FIELD: WHAT A HUMAN RESOURCES MANAGER WANTS

When I hire for a position like marketing, I get easily seven or eight hundred résumés. Realistically, you have 5 or 10 seconds. So don't tell me—sell me.

You don't have to include everything you've done, but put it in a way that makes sense. For example, one résumé I reviewed said, "Managed a variety of integrated marketing programs." I asked her to explain and she redefined it to, "Launched 1.5 million person direct mail piece with a response rate exceeding 20%." Similarly, a line that read "Managed creative and production processes to ensure budget delivery" is better as, "Created new internal budgeting process that kept more than $700,000 worth of production under budget."

So write less, be more accurate and to the point. Try using the STAR approach: situation-task-action-result—to make a sentence or brief paragraph.

—Doug Silverman, general manager of human resources,
Nikon Inc.; president, Society of Human Resource Managers/Long Island

Here are some strategies that can give you the edge.

To Stand Out From the Crowd

Accomplishments, not responsibilities. A list of responsibilities you've carried out is a lot less interesting than evidence that you performed this work in an outstanding way. Employers want to know how you made a difference to the organization.

To understand how to do this, note the contrast between A and B in each of the following.

Statement A

Manage, write and budget enterprise-wide employee contest for two company intranet sites.

Statement B

Invent ideas for employee pop culture contests to engage a diverse workforce, regularly drawing 2,000 to 3,000 entries per month and contributing to a positive culture aligned with the entertainment industry.

Statement A
Responsible for managing and improving inventory process and supplying regular reports to team leaders.

Statement B
Revamped company's inventory process and introduced new controls that reduced shrinkage 17% and saved 24% in staff costs, earning a department commendation.

Statement A
Redesigned a warehouse.

Statement B
Transformed a disorganized warehouse into an efficient operation by totally redesigning the layout, saving an estimated $50,000 annually in recovered stock.

Notice in particular that the "B" statements

1. Use the industries' power words and action verbs to frame the work and energize the writing.

2. Relate *either* to major ongoing aspects of the position, or to a project. Because project work has a beginning and end, think through projects you've handled to identify accomplishments worth citing.

3. Quantify accomplishments in terms of time or money saved, efficiency achieved, or other contribution to company goals—all music to every prospective employer's ears.

Numbers are magical and talk the bottom line language of all business, so quantify everything you possibly can. This is challenging but well worth the effort. When you can't quantify, think about how to suggest a positive outcome in other terms. For example:

Launched knowledge management processes to promote better use of resources companywide, introducing new tools such as orientation tool kits and e-newsletters.

Created new process to streamline online purchasing, now being adopted organizationwide.

VIEW FROM THE FIELD: AN EXAMPLE OF QUANTIFIED ACCOMPLISHMENTS

Here's how a recruitment manager describes her work for one employer. Note the active verbs and tight writing as well as the way she brings in numbers to show success.

Interim National Professional Recruitment Manager

- Designed innovative talent sourcing strategies to meet a 185% increase in hiring targets.

Professional Recruitment Manager

- Led 25-person hiring team; managed staff of 3; interviewed 150+ candidates annually.
- Controlled $2.2M budget, managed monthly variances and projections.

National Shareholder Recruitment Coordinator

- Re-engineered shareholder agreement reporting to enable 100% contract compliance.

Professional Recruitment Coordinator

- Initiated internship training series resulting in a 25% increase in partner participation.

Another good technique for bringing your résumé alive is to look past the glib-type generalizations we tend to include and find the concrete facts behind them—what we do can be much more interesting than the generalizations. For example, I recently questioned a young woman whose résumé contained lines like

> I monitor executive e-mail shadowboxes and manage the executive correspondence processes.

What did she mean? That on a weekly basis, she scans about 300 e-mails in the company's general in-box, assesses their importance, responds according to her judgment and prepares a trend report.

This might be phrased something like

> Monitor public input: Review hundreds of e-mails weekly, evaluate their importance, frame answers and report on trends to top management.

Promotions. Does your work history overall, or with a major job, demonstrate a steady advance in title or responsibility? Or fast progress? Make the most of it up front in your overview profile and in the way you detail the job. Recruiters will assume that impressing one employer means you're a good bet for their firms.

Personal attributes. Your "soft skills" can be very important to an employer: for example, leadership or facilitation abilities, good teaming, fast learning, consistent willingness to go above and beyond, ability to inspire others and so on. Are you unflappable under pressure? Good at training new staff members or mentoring? Able to handle multiple projects and deliver on tight deadlines? Play your strong suits.

Endorsements. Let others say it for you. This can be terrific if you're switching careers or are relatively new to the job market. Have a former boss or even coworker state how valuable you were to the team, how hard you worked and took initiative, how reliable you were. Endorsements need not come from employers. Your mother's word might not hold much weight, but a colleague's might, or the head of an organization for which you've done volunteer work.

When including an endorsement, use quotation marks, italics, and a full attribution—the person's name, title and affiliation. Put it at the top of your résumé, or better, the bottom.

Pro bono work. Especially in tough times, people on every level find themselves out of work and choose to give time on a nonpaid basis to a worthy cause, or organization they can learn from. Don't shrink from saying so—it demonstrates a mind-set that many recruiters will appreciate.

Teaching and presenting. If you've taught anything that's career related, even remotely, use it. If you've given lectures, mentored others, coached a team or taught a course even at your local high school, say so. Being able to teach shows mastery of the subject or at the least, a great sharing attitude. Presentation skills are highly valued in most fields.

Your own business? Even if you didn't succeed with it, starting and running a business testifies to your initiative, courage, and big-picture thinking. Include it and say what you learned from the experience. But be prepared to convince the recruiter that you're not looking for an opportunity to go back to entrepreneurial life anytime soon.

When your job title is inaccurate, vague or unimpressive. Take the liberty of titling your job generically, but keep it lowercase to be honest. For example, if you are officially Third Assistant Manager for Procurement Support, use a more descriptive title to set the stage—such as procurement specialist for recycled metals.

Play the social media card. Here's where the generation gap can be employed to your advantage. Many, many older people—meaning those above their early 30s—are not natural users of social media. However, in more and more industries, the people in charge recognize that social media is critical to their marketing, customer relations and employee communications. If you are adept with social media, be sure your résumé spells it out. Usually, this is worth including in a cover letter as well.

Other skills and talents? If you've raised championship bulldogs, grew up on a farm, lived in another country, win dance contests or chess tournaments, play in the community orchestra, captained the college soccer team—whatever: It may or may not be worth mentioning in your résumé. A growing number of employers value social consciousness, so evidence of your commitment to something bigger than yourself may give you a plus. You must judge the value according to the job you're targeting. Always be aware of other people's sensibilities: Mentioning that you work for a particular political party or collect guns will probably not help your cause in some circles.

Make it look great. Take trouble with your layout; enlist the help of an artistic friend if you need to. Stick to one typeface—Times Roman is usually best for readability—and make it at least 11 point. Resist the temptation to make margins narrower than one inch. Make judicious use of bold, capitals and italics. Build in enough white space, even if this means cutting a bullet or two.

Use good paper. Don't depend on color for appearance or emphasis; the document will probably be printed out in stark black on white. And don't rely on special effects. One recruiter told me that when he prints out some résumés, graphic techniques like a shadowed font may not print at all—and if it's used for the heading, there goes your name.

GOING DEEPER: Q&A WITH A RÉSUMÉ CONSULTANT

What are the most common mistakes you see in business résumés?

Three things come up in any industry, no matter how senior the people are.

1. Listing responsibilities rather than impact. You need both: You managed a budget, but what did you do with it? Manage it within a 2% variance?

(Continued)

(Continued)

Saved money? Use the situation-action-result method: State what you were responsible for, the problem, the result. For example, I increased x by 23%.

2. Including laundry lists of everything you've done instead of everything that's relevant to the job you're looking for. Just use related things or interesting ones, to build a focus.

3. Too much jargon. MBA graduates and career changers especially tend to be saturated with jargon from their old world that people in the new world might not understand. If you're applying for a marketing job, discount the real estate jargon. If you're changing careers, you need to translate so readers will understand—you can't expect them to on their own.

Which should you present first, experience or education?

If you've been in the workforce for years, place education at the bottom. But if by chance you're applying for jobs using your business school network, or for a posting you found on the alumni job board, you might want to keep it at the top because that is the point of connection you're leveraging.

Should you include personal information?

Yes, but it has to be interesting. Use something that's a hook with an interviewer, something you're passionate about, but it should be specific. For example, don't just say "traveling," but "travel in Mongolia." Think about what conversation could lead from it: "I love games" isn't as good as "I love Scrabble." It's something to talk about and puts the interviewer at ease, too.

How long should a résumé be?

Keep it to one page unless you have 10 to 15 years' experience that's related to the job. If you have that much experience but it's not related to the role you're applying for, it's best to be concise and not include detail. For a two-page résumé, be sure to include your name in the header or footer on page 2, because the pages can easily get separated.

—Stephanie Shambroom Boms, consultant for strategy,
leadership development and recruitment; MBA, Yale School of Management

See the Alexandra Lyon résumé example next and note Boms' comments, demonstrating how even a well-done résumé can be improved.

ALEXANDRA LYON

37 Trumbull Street, Apt. #1D ⊠ Cincinnati, Ohio
Tel. 213-940-4921⊠ E-mail: Alyon@uc.com

EDUCATION

SCHOOL OF BUSINESS, UNIVERSITY OF CINCINNATI	**Cincinnati, OH**
Candidate for Master of Business Administration (MBA)	**2011**

- Founding member of Career Development Office's First-Year Strategic Initiatives Group
- ~~Manager of Central Cafe,~~ a student-run socially responsible business ~~benefitting~~benefiting student internship ~~the School's Internship f~~Funds
- ~~); M~~member of Net Impact; member of Consulting Club
- Recipient, Dean's Merit Scholarship;
- GMAT: 790 / 800 (99th percentile)

NORTHWESTERN UNIVERSITY	**Evanston, IL**
Master of Science (MS), Mechanical Engineering	**2005**

- Founding member of International Office Advisory Board liaising between international student community and International Office staff & University administration
- Founding Secretary & Webmaster of Mechanical Engineering Graduate Student Society, representing graduate student voice at several departmental and school-wide faculty & administration meetings
- GRE: 2370 / 2400 (99th percentile); GPA: 3.94 / 4.00

BIRLA INSTITUTE OF TECHNOLOGY & SCIENCE	**Pilani, India**
Bachelor of Engineering (BE), Mechanical Engineering	**2000**

- Core member and leader of the Audio/Visual Department, providing audio expertise and equipment to over 30 diverse campus events annually, including theater productions, music concerts, and dance recitals
- GPA: 8.91 / 10.00

PROFESSIONAL EXPERIENCE

ACE CONSULTING	**Chicago, IL**
Associate	**2007-2009**

- Created and implemented North America-wide corporate compliance program across 13 locations and 11 functional areas for the Chief Compliance Officer of a Top 3 automotive manufacturer
- Developed manufacturing footprint consolidation strategy yielding over $12M in ongoing annual savings for a large North American consumer packaging manufacturer
- Designed optimal transaction processing model for Human Resources organization of a major insurance services provider reducing regulatory risk and processing times, and increasing customer satisfaction
- Served as Class Manager for Northwestern University undergraduate recruiting, responsible for coordinating overall strategy, managing eight-member team and $7,500 budget, and screening 200+ candidates each year

Senior Business Analyst   2005-2007

- Carried out assessment of plant maintenance operations for Chief Operations Officer of large electric utility, identifying over $5M annual savings through easy-to-implement process & technology enhancements
- Conducted ~~medium-term~~ growth strategy assessment for a large Canadian telecommunications company
- Performed analysis of financial and operating performance for over 120 automotive manufacturers and Tier I suppliers for Ace 2006 Townsend Briefing on important trends in the automotive industry

ADDITIONAL INFORMATION

- Volunteered at Foster Park Elementary School in Chicago in partnership with Junior Achievement to introduce underprivileged middle school children to the business environment.
- AT&T Leadership Award 2000 recipient (one of 38 in Asia-Pacific region).
- Avid interest in wildlife conservation, traveling, hiking, cycling, tennis, and music.

Comment [FN1]: Excellent bullets here – they utilize the SAR framework well (Situation, action, result)

Comment [FN2]: I imagine that you had a lot of management experience during your time at Ace– whether managing a project plan, a team, a work stream, a budget, a client relationship – etc. If you did, you may want to add that and demonstrate the volume/level of your experience in this area. It'll be relevant for any future role.

Comment [FN3]: Can you quantify any of these impacts? E.g. reduced processing times by X amount?

Comment [FN4]: What happened to this strategy? Did you present to clients? Did you get buy-in from senior leadership to develop new programs or change courses? Showing where this went will enhance your description here.

Comment [FN5]: Can you quantify the size of the company? What was the result of your assessment? Did the client change their strategy? Realize savings? Increase revenue by initiating projects resulting from your work?

Comment [FN6]: What did you do with your analysis? Can you showcase other skills in addition to strong analytics? E.g. presentation skills?

WE'RE ALL SCREENWRITERS: IS A SOCIAL MEDIA RÉSUMÉ RIGHT FOR YOU?

An online social media résumé may be a great way to showcase who you are and what you can do. One advantage is that in theory at least, recruiters can find you, rather than the other way around. Also, it presents you as a multidimensional individual who can be seen and heard. But, to pull it off, you need the creative skills to create a website or blog (preferably with HTML know-how and some design talent), produce your own videos and/or podcasts and, preferably, blog regularly. And need I mention, this all takes good writing skills. As with all online media, you must be committed to constantly updating your material so it doesn't grow stale.

A social media résumé also can connect your audience with some or all of your online "lives," such as Facebook, LinkedIn, YouTube and so on. But be sure you want prospective employers to see these sites and that they show you to good advantage. Many a job application has been scuttled by words or images that recruiters find offensive or inappropriate. Understand and exercise your privacy options, but don't count on them to protect you. Assume that if you put it online—they will come.

THE "ELEVATOR SPEECH"

If you're not familiar with the term "elevator speech," also known as "elevator pitch," it means "what to say to someone you want to connect with when you're in the same elevator and you have about 15 to 20 seconds till he gets out."

It's also the statement you make at a meeting when asked to introduce yourself, or any event where you meet new people and exchange business cards. Professionals of every kind who are networking, job hunting or looking for new customers tend to obsess about their elevator speeches.

Like a speech or presentation, this brief pitch about yourself is, of course, spoken—but first it must be written. By the way, the assumption used to be that the building had 50 floors and you had 60 seconds. But elevators move much faster now, not to mention the world, and most advisers would say 20 seconds is pushing it.

Everything you've learned about writing in terms of goal and audience applies to crafting an elevator speech, and you can draw on this chapter's ideas. Getting your statement brief enough is tough. In some training situations, participants must deliver their mini-speeches while holding a lit match, and finish without burning their fingers.

So the challenge is to distill what makes you special, what differentiates you, in that sliver of time. Try to see things from the audience viewpoint— what about you or what you offer could be relevant or interesting enough to hold them for 15 to 20 seconds and make them want to know more?

It often works to start with your name and what you do, mentioning the company if you work for one. Then explain: how you help, what problems you solve, how what you do can benefit your listener. If you have an intriguing example—or a famous client—work that in.

If you followed the advice for an online profile, you have a head start on a good elevator speech. But practice it aloud many times and adapt your script until it sounds natural and conversational. It must be comfortable for you to say. This dictates that sentences be shorter yet.

Here's an example of an online profile cited earlier:

> I've been a consultant from the age of six, when I discovered how rewarding it is to help other people succeed. Of course then, we were playing Candyland. Today, I advise medical practitioners with million-dollar portfolios.

A spoken version would work better along these lines:

> Hi, I'm Alan Green. I show doctors how to invest. I started giving people advice when I was six and realized I really liked helping other kids win the game. Now I show my clients how to win big—even when the economy is in a tailspin, like now.

SUCCESS TIP : A SOCIAL MEDIA PRIVACY ALERT

If you're someone who resists "compartmentalizing" your life and believes it's all open for sharing on your favorite social media sites, give some thought to generation gaps (see Chapter 2). The vast majority of employers do not want to see your party pictures or eavesdrop on your exchanges with friends. If you put things up they find embarrassing, they won't hire you. In fact, it's smart to monitor what your friends post about you, too. Otherwise, should someone shoot video on a mobile phone that shows you in a compromising position, for example, the long-term career impact may not amuse you.

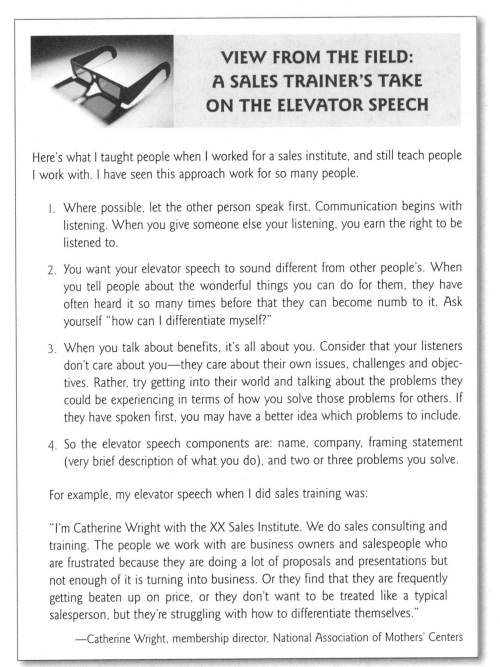

VIEW FROM THE FIELD: A SALES TRAINER'S TAKE ON THE ELEVATOR SPEECH

Here's what I taught people when I worked for a sales institute, and still teach people I work with. I have seen this approach work for so many people.

1. Where possible, let the other person speak first. Communication begins with listening. When you give someone else your listening, you earn the right to be listened to.

2. You want your elevator speech to sound different from other people's. When you tell people about the wonderful things you can do for them, they have often heard it so many times before that they can become numb to it. Ask yourself "how can I differentiate myself?"

3. When you talk about benefits, it's all about you. Consider that your listeners don't care about you—they care about their own issues, challenges and objectives. Rather, try getting into their world and talking about the problems they could be experiencing in terms of how you solve those problems for others. If they have spoken first, you may have a better idea which problems to include.

4. So the elevator speech components are: name, company, framing statement (very brief description of what you do), and two or three problems you solve.

For example, my elevator speech when I did sales training was:

"I'm Catherine Wright with the XX Sales Institute. We do sales consulting and training. The people we work with are business owners and salespeople who are frustrated because they are doing a lot of proposals and presentations but not enough of it is turning into business. Or they find that they are frequently getting beaten up on price, or they don't want to be treated like a typical salesperson, but they're struggling with how to differentiate themselves."

—Catherine Wright, membership director, National Association of Mothers' Centers

If You're a New Career Builder

If you're just starting out in your career field, or moving into a new one, should you feel shy about identifying yourself as a professional?

Absolutely not. Your serious intent entitles you to feel part of the profession. Just as writers are told to present themselves as writers even if they've not yet published anything, you're an accountant or consultant as soon as you have a few years of specialized training under your belt.

This is true if you're between jobs as well as when you're switching careers. If you're earning a living at something else until you complete a degree or get a career break, it's still legitimate to present yourself as what you want to be.

If this feels uncomfortable, identify yourself as a marketing specialist, or whatever, in training.

You can use your elevator speech and profile to advantage if you're at an interim or preliminary stage and the setting is hospitable. For example:

> Hi, I'm Margaret James. I'm working on my MBA and focusing on leadership development and organizational strategy. I expect to have my degree from White in May, and I'm ready for a good opportunity with a global company.
>
> Hi, I'm Jerry Jones. I'm a marketing specialist and I've worked at a Fortune 500 company that had to downsize, unfortunately. Right now I'm working as a retail sales manager, getting very hands on experience. I'm hoping to find the right opportunity to get back on track in marketing.

Now you can introduce yourself with confidence, whether in print, virtually or in person.

❖ ❖ ❖

And so, it's time to end this book and leave you on your own, feeling, I hope, more confident about your writing and better equipped to do it well. Most of all, I hope you're convinced that good writing matters and is worth your time and effort.

Take care with your writing—and your writing will take care of you. And when you secure an opportunity you've worked for, plan from the first day on to use your best writing skills. Draw on everything you learned from this book to create strategic, well-planned and well-crafted e-mails and letters targeted to your goal and audience, business documents that engage and persuade and online materials that accomplish your business (and personal) goals.

And, use the resources and ideas provided in these chapters to keep growing your awareness of successful writing and your own skills. I guarantee the rewards will come.

PRACTICE OPPORTUNITIES

I. Summer Job Planning

Will you be looking for an internship or summer associate position this year? If so,

1. Define—in writing—your set of goals, with detail. In addition to stating the job you'd like to have, specify what you want to gain from it.

2. Write the most complete profile you can of your audience—the people who'll review your application at the organization where you want to work.

3. In the framework of your answers to the first two tasks, brainstorm the content of your résumé. What should you include about your experience and personal qualifications?

II. Career Job Planning

Frame as closely as you can the job you'd like to have next. Then carry out the same three tasks as for Summer Job Planning.

III. Write a Posting for the Job You Want

Put yourself in your prospective employer's shoes and figure out how she would advertise your ideal job. Write a detailed posting that covers all relevant aspects. Then evaluate your qualifications against the posting. Are you well qualified? If so, does your résumé demonstrate that? Does this give you any ideas about how to improve your résumé?

IV. Question for Discussion

How would the content of a résumé for a summer job differ from one for your next career job? Compare notes with other class members. Keep track of ideas you hadn't thought of and consider how to use them in your next job search.

V. Write Your Summary

Draft the strongest profile/summary of experience as you can with a specific job goal in mind.

VI. Review Your Current Résumé

Evaluate how well it works in terms of what you've learned in this chapter, and the book as a whole, and decide how to improve it. Turn at least three of the responsibilities you describe into accomplishments and try to quantify them.

VII. Elevator Speech

Create a 20-second elevator speech to share with classmates; revise it based on their reaction and input. Assume it can take several rounds to get it "right."

Index

SAGE Research Methods Online

The essential tool for researchers

Sign up now at www.sagepub.com/srmo for more information.

An expert research tool

- An **expertly designed taxonomy** with more than 1,400 unique terms for social and behavioral science research methods
- **Visual and hierarchical search tools** to help you discover material and link to related methods

- Easy-to-use navigation tools
- Content organized by complexity
- Tools for citing, printing, and downloading content with ease
- Regularly updated content and features

A wealth of essential content

- The most comprehensive picture of quantitative, qualitative, and mixed methods available today
- More than **100,000 pages of SAGE book and reference material** on research methods as well as editorially selected material from SAGE journals
- More than **600 books** available in their entirety online

Launching 2011!

$SAGE research methods online